THE
NEPHILIM

and the
PYRAMID of the APOCALYPSE

www.nephilimapocalypse.com

THE NEPHILIM

and the
PYRAMID of the APOCALYPSE

Patrick Heron

xulon PRESS

The Nephilim and the Pyramid of the Apocalypse
by Patrick Heron

Printed in the United States of America

ISBN 1-594678-94-4

Library of Congress Control Number: 2004098507

A catalogue record for this book is available from the British Library.

Back cover and image (page 6) courtesy of www.egallery.ie
Artists impressions thanks to James Heron
Editor: John Butler

Scripture quotations taken from the Holy Bible, King James Version and New International Version. Copyright (c) 1973, 1978, 1984 by International Bible Society. Used by permission of Zondervan. All rights reserved. "NIV" is a regestered trademark of International Bible Society.

Previous books by Patrick Heron:
Apocalypse Soon (Bestseller in Ireland) (1997)
and *Apocalypse 2000* (1999)"

Cover design: Ashville Media Group

www.xulonpress.com

TABLE OF CONTENTS

Are the above images a mere figment of the artist's imagination or real beings?

INTRODUCTION

For almost 5,000 years, the pyramids have asked more questions than they have answered. Many books have been written which have propounded incredible facts concerning their construction and their astronomical qualities. We have learned that the Pyramids of Giza are aligned with certain star constellations.[1] It has likewise been discovered that other similar structures in Mexico and Cambodia also have astronomical significance.[2]

The Great Pyramid of Giza consists of circa 2.3 million stone blocks weighing about $2^1/_2$ tons each. Some of the blocks weigh up to 50 tons.[3] Yet, despite the vast numbers of blocks used, and the incredible weights involved, the mathematical accuracy of the layout of the structure is breathtaking. Other such puzzling buildings scattered around the world pose the same questions.

Who built them? How did their builders acquire such mathematical and astronomical knowledge? And what advanced technology was used in their construction?

To simply say that the Egyptians built them is not a satisfactory answer. For if man began at the stone age, progressed to the bronze and then to the iron age, we have the oldest pyramids popping up somewhere between the stone age and the bronze age.

This is akin to saying that at some point in time past man invented the wheel. Some time later, another made a cart. But in between the wheel and the cart we find a brand new Mercedes Benz! This is a realistic comparison when considering the construction of the pyramids.

Despite all the recent books written about them, the pyramids remain a conundrum wrapped in an enigma and surrounded by a paradox. Yes, these authors have discovered and charted their astronomical significance. They have unearthed their geometric alignments and mathematical properties. And the conclusion they have reached is that some lost civilisation or race of advanced people was responsible for these mammoth edifices.

But all these writers have one thing in common. They have failed to tell us who these people were and from whence they derived their knowledge and skills.

When one or two of these esteemed authors do hazard a guess as to who these mystery architects and builders may have been, their speculations amount to little more than sand castles built on the tidal reach of eternity.

It is my contention that the evidence advanced in this volume will provide satisfactory answers to all these questions.

Buried in ancient Hebrew texts, undiscovered and largely ignored by scholars, lies a wealth of information about a secret race of superhuman and supernatural people known as the *Nephilim.*[4]

In the first part of this volume I will provide a detailed study of this unknown race, showing:

- who they were
- where they came from
- where they acquired their mathematical and astronomical knowledge
- how they possessed the strength to construct these huge buildings
- why they chose the pyramid shape
- why the pyramids are aligned with celestial bodies
- where these people went

In the second part of this book I will show how these same age-old pyramids portend a future event. Analysing the ancient texts, I will provide an examination of the prophecies of the Book of Revelation and of the signs we are told would precede these imminent happenings. In doing so, we shall garner the necessary details and information whereby the reader will be able to audition the future.

Finally, having travelled back to an epoch dating to before our world began, and having journeyed forward to espy what lies ahead, this volume will culminate and climax in a phenomenon never before proposed or explored: *The Pyramid of The Apocalypse.*

We now invite you to participate in an excursion through time and space which could change your perceptions of life forever.

TIME WAS

Many people are aware of the phenomenal engineering feats involved in the construction of the Great Pyramid of Giza. For those who are not, I would like to give a brief and simple summary of some of these facts.

On the west bank of the River Nile, not too far from ancient Memphis and almost opposite present-day Cairo, stands the last one of the seven wonders of the ancient world: the Great Pyramid. This is the largest of all the pyramids and the first to have been built. It embodies in its construction a wealth of knowledge of mathematics and astronomy which indicates that its builders possessed amazing wisdom.

The original pyramid was built of granite and limestone rock and had a smooth exterior finish of white limestone which would have made it impossible to surmount.[5] Some legends say that its capstone was made of gold. In its original form, it must have been an awe-inspiring sight. But the passage of time and the wear and tear of countless storms have stripped away its limestone exterior and left us with what we have today. Now one can climb to the top, using the blocks as stairs, a feat which, in its initial form, would have been impossible. The esteemed architect and eschatologist Clarence Larkin made the following observations:[6]

- The base of the Great Pyramid covers about thirteen acres. It consists of approximately 2.3 million blocks of stone weighing around $2^1/_2$ tons each, some weighing up to 50 tons. Some huge granite blocks, weighing 100 tons, are situated within the pyramid structure at a height of 46 metres. The base of the pyramid is a square with right angles accurate to within one-twentieth of a degree. The sides are equilateral triangles and face exactly to the true north, south, east and west of the Earth.

- Taking the Hebrew cubit to be 25.025 inches (63.5 cm), the length of each side of the base is 365.2422 cubits, the exact number of days in the solar year (including the extra day for every four years).[7]

- The slope of the sides of the pyramid is of such an angle that they meet at the apex at the predetermined height of 232.52 cubits. If twice the length of a side at the base was to be be divided by the height of the pyramid, we would arrive at the figure 3.14159, which, when multiplied by the diameter of a circle, gives its circumference.

- The perimeter of the base of the pyramid (365.242 x 4 = 14609.68) is exactly equal to the circumference of a circle, whose diameter is twice the height of the pyramid (232.52 x 2 x 3.1416 = 14609.68). So here we have in these figures the solution to the problem of how to square a circle (see **Figure 1**).

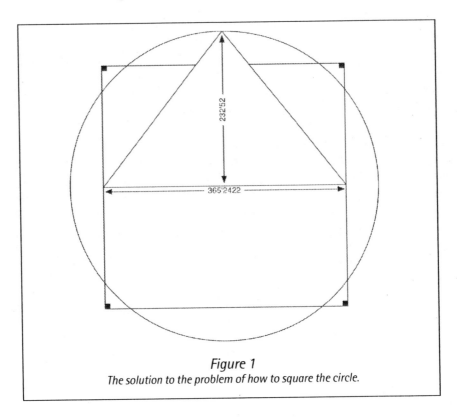

Figure 1
The solution to the problem of how to square the circle.

- The angle of slope of the sides is 10 to 9. That is, for every 10 feet you ascend, you rise in altitude by 9 feet. And if you multiply the altitude of the pyramid by 10 raised to the power of 9, you have 91,840,000, which, in miles, is the exact distance of the Sun from the Earth.[8]

- The year of the stars is called the "sidereal" year and the year of the seasons is called the "equinoctial." These differ by about 50 seconds per year. In other words, the stars in their rising and setting are retarded by about 50 seconds each year. For the "sidereal" and the "equinoctial" years to come around and coincide again it would take 25,827 years, which is known as a cycle. If we add together the diagonals of the pyramid's base in inches, we arrive at 25,827, or as many inches as the cycle has years.

The Great Pyramid stands at the exact centre of the world. It is midway between the west coast of Mexico and the east coast of China. Between the north cape of Norway and the Cape of Good Hope in South Africa. It stands at the intersection of the 30th parallel, both latitude and longitude.[9]

The Great Pyramid was the highest building in the world for thousands of years until modern man began building skyscrapers such as the World Trade Centre. If it were compared to a skyscraper, the Great Pyramid would be 42 storeys high. It contains enough stone to build a six foot high wall from New York to Los Angeles.[10]

Researchers Alan and Sally Lansburg provide the following statistics regarding this incredible edifice:

> *"Somehow the builders knew that the world was round but flattened at the poles, which caused a degree of latitude to lengthen at the top and bottom of the planet; that it rotated in one day on an axis tilted 23.5° to the ecliptic, causing night and day, and that this tilt caused the seasons; that earth circled the sun once in a year of 365 and a fraction days.*
>
> *The designers also must have known that earth's celestial north pole described a slow circle around the pole of the ecliptic, making the constellations appear to 'slip backward' (the precession of the equinoxes), and bring a new constellation of the Zodiac behind the sun at the equinox approximately every twenty-two hundred years in a grand cycle of about twenty-six thousand years. These facts, too, were part of the internal measurements of the pyramid".*[11]

We are asked to believe that primitive man, dressed in animal skins and roaming wild, constructed the Great Pyramid with all that it entails, yet these same builders had not yet invented the simple wheel!

From an astronomical point of view, we have learned some extraordinary facts.

There are four long narrow passageways or shafts built into the Great

Pyramid, two on the north face and two on the south. The two on the north point to two distinct stars: one at *Beta Ursa Minor* and one at *Alpha Draconis* in the constellation of Draco.

The star shafts on the south face point to *Sirius* and *Zeta Orionis*. In ancient Egyptian tradition, *Sirius* is associated with the goddess *Isis*. And *Zita Orionis*, which is the brightest star of three in *Orion's* belt, is identified with *Osiris*, the god of resurrection and rebirth in the remote epoch referred to as "*Zep Tepi*" or "*First Time*"[12] (see **Figure 2**).

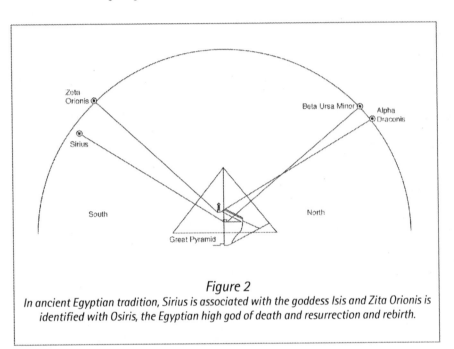

Figure 2
In ancient Egyptian tradition, Sirius is associated with the goddess Isis and Zita Orionis is identified with Osiris, the Egyptian high god of death and resurrection and rebirth.

Similarly, ancient monuments in Mexico and at Angkor Wat in Cambodia have celestial connections with Orion, Draco, Leo and Aquarius.[13]

At Nazca in Peru we find a huge combination of strange lines and drawings which only become discernible when viewed from the air. These lines cover a large area 60 kilometres (about 40 miles) square and could in no way be the work of mortal man. There are various sketches of the Nazca Monkey, Humming Bird, Whale, Spider, Dog and Condor, all etched into the rugged earth.[14] Scores of perfectly geometric lines and designs criss-cross the landscape. Some of the lines resemble runways which could be used for aircraft either landing or taking off. The longest of these lines measures almost 15 miles (23 kilometres). But what do they mean? Where did they come from and who made them? Again, the scholars and experts arrive at the same conclusion: they do not know. Speculation reigns.

There is an ancient temple at Baalbek in Lebanon known as the Temple of Jupiter. Incorporated in its foundations are three huge cut-stone blocks weighing 800 tons each. Not far away lies another gigantic stone block called the Stone of the South, weighing 1,000 tons. This is the combined weight of three 747 jumbo jets. How did the builders cut such large blocks and, more to the point, how did they move them into place?

Much has been chronicled regarding the building and astronomical parallels and mathematical properties of the many monuments which populate the globe. Scholars have mapped and measured these structures and charted their celestial counterparts with minute precision. Many books containing the finer details of their construction and stellar configuration are to be found in bookshops everywhere.

What message are these edifices relaying to us? Is there something we can learn from them which has so far eluded us? If the walls of these monuments could speak, what priceless information would they impart? Do they portend coming events? I believe that they do. And we shall now endeavour to unveil the riddle of the pyramids by identifying their likely architects.

THE MATRIX

Buried in the depths of the Pentateuch and other ancient Hebrew texts lies a wealth of information that has long been, by and large, invisible to most scholars. But how reliable are these age-old writings? Can we learn anything new from them or is our first instinct to dismiss any likely discoveries as mere fable? Before delving into these hidden scripts, I would like to put forth some interesting vignettes which may have previously been unknown to the reader.

In his best-selling book *The Bible Code*,[15] Michael Drosnin sets out his findings on a series of computer-based scientific tests carried out by himself and some eminent Jewish mathematicians. It was well known by Jewish scribes of old that a hidden code was encrypted in the Hebrew lettering of the Pentateuch, which is the name given to the first five books of the Old Testament.

These were written originally in Hebrew. If you take the first Hebrew letter in Genesis, skip 49 letters and take the next letter, and repeat the skip sequence, then every four letters spells **Torh** (the Hebrew word pronounced "Torah," meaning "The Law of God").

This holds all the way through the first two books of the Bible, *Genesis* and *Exodus*. When you get to the middle book of the five, *Leviticus*, it stops. However, when you apply the same skip sequence to *Deuteronomy* and the *Book of Numbers*, it spells **Hrot**, which is Torh backwards.

Go back now to the middle book of the five, *Leviticus*, use the skip sequence again, this time skipping every seven letters, and it spells **YHWH** (pronounced **YAWEH**). Which is the Hebrew name for God!

So we have every 49 letters in *Genesis* and *Exodus* spelling "The Law of God" and pointing to *Leviticus*, and every 49 letters of *Deuteronomy* and *Numbers* spelling "The Law of God" backwards and pointing to *Leviticus*. Every seven letters in this book spells YAWH: God himself.[16]

Genesis	Leviticus	Numbers
Torh -> Torh -> Torh ->	YHWH	<- Hrot <- Hrot <- Hrot
Exodus		Deuteronomy

Because Hebrew lettering is mathematical as well as literal, these scholars were able to put the whole of the Pentateuch into a computer programme.

Then they chose differing "skip" sequences and ran them through the programme. The results they found astounded them. Encoded throughout the texts they found messages concerning different aspects of life and history.

For instance, Drosnin himself, while running through a particular test one day, found the name Yitzhak Rabin encoded in the text. Written across this name was "Assassin That Will Assassinate." Perplexed and concerned by his findings, Drosnin wrote to Yitzhak Rabin (who was then Prime Minister of Israel), telling him of his findings.

Rabin wrote back and informed Drosnin that he was a humanist, a fatalist and unconcerned with these findings.

Some time later, while in a railway station in Canada, Drosnin was speaking on the telephone to a friend. His friend asked him if he had heard the latest news. "What news?" Drosnin asked. "Yitzhak Rabin has just been shot dead in Israel."

With that, Drosnin dropped the phone and began to shake. Before this, he had known in his mind that these codes were unique. But now he knew in his heart that these hidden codes were indeed real.

Michael Drosnin and the Jewish mathematicians who pioneered these studies have done thousands of these "skip" sequence tests. They have found all manner of information concerning events which have already happened and also some relating to the future. And the interesting thing is that there is no way they could have discovered these hidden codes without the use of computers. For the information is so vast, and the permutations are so great, that in no way could it be deciphered without the use of our modern-day computers.

After Yitzhak Rabin's assassin was arrested, Drosnin put this man's name into the programme and ran it through the same sequence he had used before. To his astonishment, right above the place where he had found the original message concerning Yitzhak Rabin, the assassin's name was encoded in the Hebrew text.

This is just a small snippet from Michael Drosnin's book. His findings, along with those of his Jewish colleagues, have been tested and scrutinised by many agencies such as the CIA and the US army, and none have been able to contradict or gainsay their conclusions.

This tells us that there is much we have yet to discover concerning these ancient texts, which have been largely ignored for so long.

Suppose you were asked to construct a genealogy of real people, but there are certain constraints. The number of words in this genealogy must:
- be evenly divisible by seven (with no remainders)
- the number of letters must be divisible by seven

- the number of vowels and consonants must be divisible by seven
- the number of words that begin with a vowel must be divisible by seven
- the number of words that begin with a consonant must be divisible by seven
- the number of words that occur more than once must be divisible by seven
- the number of words that occur in more than one form must be divisible by seven
- the number of words that occur only in one form must be divisible by seven
- the number of names in the genealogy must be divisible by seven
- the number of male names must be divisible by seven
- and the number of generations in the genealogy must be divisible by seven

Would it not be next to impossible to draw up such a genealogy? Yet this describes exactly the genealogy of the Messiah, as given in the Gospel of Matthew 1:2-17.[17]

From an academic and literary point of view, the Bible stands head and shoulders above any other book ever written, yet it has been largely ignored by academia. It has sold over eight billion copies in more than 2,000 languages. It was written by 40 different men over a period of 1,600 years, yet it remains uniform in its content. It has survived 40 centuries of history. It has more ancient manuscripts to authenticate it than any other ten pieces of ancient literature put together.

In fact, there are over 5,000 Greek manuscripts of the New Testament, over 10,000 in Latin and 9,300 in other languages, the oldest dating to around 68 AD. Compare this to only nine old copies of "Caesar's Gallic War," and the oldest of these dates to 900 years after Caesar's death. Yet nobody questions this (see **Figure 3**).

When copying was being carried out, the Hebrew scribes had enormous reverence for the text of the Bible. Copies were checked, double-checked and re-checked many times. If a small mistake was made, the whole page would be rewritten. When they came to the word "Yaweh," meaning God, they would burn the pen and change their clothes. Only photocopying is more accurate than the methods they followed to preserve the accuracy and integrity of the text.[18]

One would think that those who occupy the seats of higher learning would acknowledge the obvious literary merits of the Bible. It was, after all:

WORK	WHEN WRITTEN	EARLIEST COPY	TIME LAPSE	NO. OF COPIES
Herodotus	488-428 BC	AD 900	1,300 years	8
Thucydides	c.460-100 BC	c.AD 900	1,300 years	8
Tacitus	AD 100	AD 1100	1,000 years	20
Caesar's Gallic War	58-50 BC	AD 900	950 years	9-10
Livy's Roman History	59 BC-AD 17	AD 900	900 years	20
New Testament	AD 40-100	AD 130 (manuscripts AD 350)	30-310 years	5,000 + Greek 10,000 Latin 9,300 others

Figure 3
Source: The Alpha Course Manual, Alpha International, Holy Trinity Brompton, London

- The source of over 1,200 quotations used by William Shakespeare in his works.

- The inspiration for literary giants such as Milton, C.S. Lewis, Sir Walter Scott and Charles Dickens.

- The inspiration for Da Vinci's *Last Supper*, Michelangelo's *Pieta* and Handel's *Messiah*, which he wrote in 21 days, the entire text coming from the *Book of Isaiah*.

- The motivation for the work of Mother Teresa, Abraham Lincoln, Isaac Newton and Martin Luther King.[19]

Yet, despite its unrivalled position as an academic document, the Bible is ignored and withheld from students of literary works. It is sidelined and boycotted and scoffed at in favour of lesser works of men. You would think that even the humanist non-believer would pay tribute to the academic worth of this mighty tome and the effect it has had on the history of civilisation. But no, all are silent.

Let us now examine those same ancient texts and discover what they reveal concerning a mysterious race of whom the majority of people have never heard: the *Nephilim*.

THE NEPHILIM

Iwould now beg the reader to indulge me somewhat. For this study, I would ask that you put your mind in neutral. That is, put aside for the present your assumptions and prejudices concerning your opinion of the Old Testament scriptures. Allow, for the time being, that they may contain information that is useful and trustworthy and from which we can learn. Think of yourself as a juror awaiting the evidence. After all the facts are heard, you may then reach an informed verdict.

The year is 2348 BC, the year of the Noahic deluge. Genesis chapter six provides us with a startling revelation.

> And it came to pass, when men began to multiply on the face of the Earth, and daughters were born unto them,
> That the sons of God saw the daughters of men that they were fair; And they took them wives of all which they chose.
> There were giants (*Nephilim*) in the Earth in those days: and also after that, when the sons of God came in unto the daughters of men, and they bare children to them.
> The same became mighty men which were, of old, men of renown.
>
> *Genesis 6: 1,2,4*

We are informed that the "sons of God" saw the daughters of men and took them as wives. Who are these "sons of God" and from whence did they come? Our first task is to garner all information on these individuals and allow the material to define our conclusions.

The term "sons of God" is used eight times in the Old Testament. Let us examine some of these. The following is taken from a debate Yaweh (God) is having with Job:

> "Where wast thou when I laid the foundations of the Earth?
> "Who hath laid the measures thereof, if thou knowest?
> "Or who hath stretched the line upon it?
> "Whereupon are the foundations thereof fastened? Or who laid the cornerstone thereof?
> "When the morning stars sang together, and all the sons of God shouted for joy."
>
> *Job 38: 4-7*

In this discourse between Yaweh and Job there is an obvious reference to the time of the creation of the world. In this context the "Sons of God" refers to what we call angels, which are created spirit beings.[20] This is always the case where the expression "Sons of God" occurs in the Old Testament.[21]

> Who maketh His angels spirits,
> His ministers a flaming fire.
>
> *Psalm 104:4*

This also holds true for the New Testament:

> But to which of the angels said he: "Sit on my right hand ..." Are they not all ministering spirits ...
>
> *Hebrews 1: 13,14*

In the Book of Daniel, chapter 3, we are told of three men who were thrown into a blazing furnace by the king, Nebuchadnezzar, who then ...

> ... rose up in haste and said unto his counsellors: "Did we not cast three men into the midst of the fire? Lo, I see four men walking in the midst of the fire ... and the form of the fourth is like a son of God."

Nebuchadnezzar goes on to say:

> "Blessed be the God of Shadrach, Meshach and Abednego, who hath sent His angel and delivered His servants who trusted in him ..."
>
> *Daniel 3: 24,25,28*

It is clear from the above that the fourth being accompanying the three in the fire, who was referred to as a *son of God*, is in the following verse called an "angel."

In this next illustration from the Book of Job we observe a distant gathering of celestial bodies:

> Now there was a day when the sons of God (*angels*) came to present themselves before the Lord, and Satan came also among them.
>
> *Job 1:6*

In the Hebrew, the word *malak* is translated as *angel*. In the Greek it is *aggelos*. But a more accurate rendering of both these Hebrew and Greek words is *agent* or *messenger*. The word *angel* occurs over 300 times in both the Old and New Testaments. In all these places the word *agent* or *messenger* would, in my opinion, be a better translation, as our minds have been muddied and distorted by the word angel. For when this word is used we immediately conjure up an image of a naked infant cherubim with tiny wings and no genitalia floating around innocently and carrying a little bow and arrow. Or of a huge glorious being with enormous wings protruding from somewhere between his shoulder blades and illuminated from behind by a huge spotlight!

Nothing could be further from the truth. Later on in this study I shall present a more detailed evaluation of these messengers or agents. But lest we should stray from our present focus, suffice to say that these messengers always appear as men. They eat and drink and are mistaken for ordinary human beings. Some are referred to by name and are also called men. So they look like us. They eat and drink like us, they wear clothes and they can speak like us. But let us return to our original train of thought. In Genesis 6:2 it says:

> **The sons of God saw the daughters of men that they were fair; and they took them wives of all that they chose.**

Again it becomes clear from this passage that there is a distinction between the "*daughters of men,*" on the one hand, and the "*sons of God*" on the other.

What this verse is implying is that these "sons of God," who were created spirit beings, had intercourse with ordinary human women and produced children. But these were no ordinary offspring.

> **There were giants (*Nephilim*) in the Earth in those days: and also after that, when the sons of God came in unto the daughters of men, and they bare children to them.**
> **The same became mighty men which were, of old, men of renown.**
> *Genesis 6:4*

The Hebrew word for *giants* in the above verse is *Nephilim*, from the root word *naphal*, meaning *to fall*. So the offspring of these spirit beings with human women are called *giants* or *Nephilim*, meaning the *fallen ones*. The fallen spirit-men are themselves referred to as *Nephilim* also.[22] For they fell from grace, fell from Heaven and fell to Earth.

In the course of this book I shall examine why these spirit beings or messengers became "*fallen.*" But in order to maintain our focus on the riddle before us we shall continue with our study of the *Nephilim* and their impact on society at that time.

You will notice from the passages quoted that we are told these irruptions occurred on two occasions, i.e.

> "There were giants (*Nephilim*) in the Earth in <u>those days</u> and also <u>after that</u>."

"*In those days*" refers to the days of Noah. The expression "*and also after that*" tells us that these *Nephilim* were also on the Earth after the Flood of Noah.

So these two irruptions of fallen spirit beings with women occurred both before the Flood and then again some time later. For reasons which will become clearer as we progress with this thesis, I will firstly deal with the second, which occurred after the Flood. We are given much information about these giants when they inhabited the Earth in those days. After examining the evidence relating to them, we shall return to the earlier incursion of the *Nephilim* before the Flood and discuss the evidence as to how they left their mark on ancient civilisation at that time.

AFTER THE DELUGE

We now jump forward to 436 years after the Flood to find mention of these giants. Abraham enters the picture here. With his wife, Sarah, he returns from his sojourn in Egypt, and we are told that, by that time, several different tribes of these people are dwelling in the land of the Canaanites and have assumed differing names after their various forebears (see *Figure 4*). We read in Genesis 14:5:

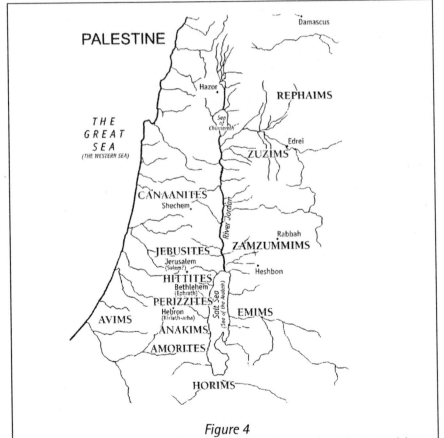

Figure 4

At the time Abraham journeyed through the Promised Land, and even in the much later period of Moses, several tribes of "giants", who were descended from the Nephilim, populated this entire area. The map above gives the principal tribes and their locations.

And in the fourteenth year came Chedorlaomer and the kings that were with him, and smote the Rephaims in Ashteroth Karnaim and the Zuzims in Ham and the Emims in Shaveh Kiriatheim.

The *Rephaims* spoken of here were the descendants of one *Rapha*. In the Hebrew, *Rapha* means *"fearful one; giant."* We note their mention in Deuteronomy chapter two along with another branch of these giants known as the *Anakims*.[23]

And when we passed by ... we turned and passed by the way of the wilderness of Moab.
The Emims dwelt there in times past.
A people great and many and tall as the Anakims.
Which also were accounted giants as the Anakims: but the Moabites call them Emmins.

Book of Deuteronomy 2:8,10,11

In the Hebrew, *Emmin* means *"terrible ones,"* and the *Anakims* were descended from one *Anak*, which translates as *"long-necked; giant."* *Anak* was the son of *Arba*, which in the Hebrew means *"strength of Baal."*

Arba was one of the *"sons of Heth"* who, seven years before the building of Zoan in Egypt (Genesis 23:2,3), built Hebron, which was hence called *Kirjath Arba*, meaning the city of Arba.

Anak, his son, had three distinguished descendants in the days of Moses and Joshua who were giants. Their names were Ahiman, Sheshai and Talmai, and they dwelt in Hebron circa 1490 BC.

At this point I would like to examine the story regarding Moses and Joshua. After the Exodus from Egypt, led by Moses, the children of Israel wandered in the wilderness for 40 years. Finally, they were ready to enter and possess the Promised Land which had been given to Abraham. Before invading, Moses sent 12 spies to check out the land and the people. We pick up the record in the Book of Numbers:

And Moses sent them to spy out the land of Canaan and said unto them:
"Get you up this way southward, and go up into the mountain.
And see the land what it is, and the people that dwell therein, whether they be strong or weak, few or many.
And what the land is, whether it be good or bad; and what cities that they dwell in; whether in tents or strongholds.
And be ye of good courage and bring of the fruit of the land."

Now the time was the time of the first ripe grapes.

So they went up and searched the land from the wilderness of Zin unto Rehob as men come to Hamath.

And they ascended from the south and came unto Hebron, where Ahiman, Sheshai and Talmai, the children of Anak, were. Now Hebron was built seven years before Zoan in Egypt.

And they came unto the brook of Eschol and cut down a branch with one cluster of grapes, and they bare it between two upon a staff; and they brought of the pomegranates and of the figs ...

And they returned from searching of the land after forty days.

And they came to Moses and to Aaron and to all the congregation of the children of Israel ... and showed them the fruit of all the land.

And they said: "We came unto the land whither thou sent us, and surely it flows with milk and honey, and this is the fruit of it.

Nevertheless, the people be strong that dwell in the land and the cities are walled and very great; and moreover we saw the children of Anak there."

And Caleb stilled the people before Moses and said: "Let us go up at once and possess it, for we are well able to overcome it."

But the men that went up with them said: "We be not able to go up against the people, for they are stronger than we."

And they brought up an evil report of the land which they had searched, saying: "The land which we have gone through to search is a land that eats up the inhabitants thereof, and all the people that we saw in it are men of great stature. And there we saw the giants (*Nephilim*), the sons of Anak, which come of the giants (*Nephilim*). And we were in our own sight as grasshoppers, and so we were in their sight."

Book of Numbers 13:17-33

Twelve spies were sent out. Ten out of the 12 reported that there was no way they could take this land, as it was filled with these giants, the descendants of Anak, and other huge people. Only two of the 12, Joshua and Caleb, believed that they could defeat this mighty people. But the children of Israel listened to the 10 others and, as a result, wanted to stone Moses and Aaron and Joshua and Caleb and return into bondage in Egypt. But later, under the leadership of Joshua, they did invade and defeat the giants who inhabited the land.

One interesting point from the above passage is the reference to the cluster of grapes they cut down and brought back to illustrate the richness of the land. It took two of the spies to carry just one cluster of grapes on a staff between them. That is one heavy cluster of grapes. Could it be that these giant people, who were the offspring of spirit-men *(sons of God; angels)* and human women, were practising genetic engineering or genetic modification? Because they were the offspring of these spirit-men, they would be superhuman and supernatural. They would possess powers and knowledge beyond mere natural men.

Big people need big food. If two strong, fit Israelite men had to bear just one cluster of grapes between them on a pole, over their shoulders, then it must have been extremely heavy.

Later on we will uncover more evidence which would suggest that these *Nephilim* did indeed practise genetic engineering.

Earlier in this chapter we noted the reference from the Book of Deuteronomy which mentioned various branches of these *Nephilim* known as *Emims* and *Anakims*. Further on in this same record we are informed of other tribes related to these monstrosities:

> And when thou comest nigh over against the children of Ammon, distress them not, nor meddle with them, for I will not give thee of the land of the children of Ammon any possession, because I have given it unto the children of Lot for a possession.
> That also was accounted a land of giants: giants dwelt therein in old time; and the Ammonites call them Zamzummims.
> A people great and many, and tall as the Anakims: but the Lord destroyed them ... As he destroyed the Horims from before them ... And the Avims which dwelt at Hazerim.
>
> *Deuteronomy 2:18-23*

The *Horims, Zamzummims* and *Avims* are all related to, and offspring of, the *Nephilim* and were destroyed and driven out by Joshua and the children of Israel when they went in to possess the land.

Horim in the Hebrew is *Troglodyte*, which means cavemen or those who dwelt in caves. They were the inhabitants of Mount Seir and were related to the *Emim* and *Rephaim*. Their excavated dwellings are still found in the sandstone cliffs and mountains of Edom, but especially at Petra.[24]

Zamzummim in Hebrew means *"powerful, vigorous;"* and these people were also related to the *Rephaim* dwelling in the region afterwards occupied by the Ammonites, who were also called *Zuzims,* which means *"prominent, strong, giant".*[25]

Lastly, the Israelites defeated Og, the king of Bashan.

> And we took all his cities at that time, three score cities, all the region of Argob, the kingdom of Og in Bashan.[26]
> All these cities were fenced with high walls, gates and bars: beside unwalled towns a great many ...
> For only Og, king of Bashan, remained of the remnant of giants; behold his bedstead was a bed of iron; nine cubits was the length thereof, and four cubits the breadth of it, after the cubit of a man.
>
> *Book of Deuteronomy 3:4,5,11*

So here we are told of the complete destruction of all these various tribes of related giants who had occupied this land for some time. In this last passage we are given further solid proof of the huge size of these people by reference to the measurements of King Og's bed, which is said to have been nine cubits in length and four cubits in width. Again taking the Hebrew cubit at 25.025 inches (63.5cm), we find that his bed was $18^3/_4$ feet long and $8^1/_3$ feet wide! This is further proof that these people were indeed giants in the land (see **Figure 5**).

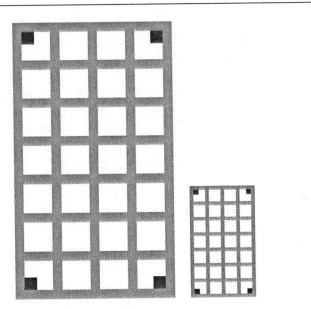

Figure 5
Joshua and his army defeated Og, king of Bashan, and captured sixty of the "giant cities" of Bashan. Deuteronomy 3:11 gives the size of Og's iron bedstead as nine cubits in length by four cubits in width (i.e. 18.75 feet long by 8.33 feet wide). The above figure compares Og's bed to a standard-size single bed.

Almost all these monstrous people were defeated by the Israelites, under the leadership of Joshua, at this time. But a remnant remained, as recorded in the Book of Joshua:

> And at that time came Joshua, and cut off the Anakims from the mountains, from Hebron, from Debir ...
> There was none of the Anakims left in the land of the children of Israel; only in Gath, Gaza and in Ashdod [they] there remained.
>
> *Book of Joshua 11:21:22*

We began this chapter showing that, at the time Abraham travelled through Canaan, these races of giants already inhabited the region. This was circa 1912 BC, about 436 years after the Flood of Noah. Because their number was already great, we may assume that they had begun to multiply sometime during these 400 years. So there was a second irruption of "fallen" spirit beings who had procreated with women during this period to produce these tribes of giants. By the time Moses and Joshua arrived on the scene and defeated these huge people, another 461 years had elapsed, taking us to 1451 BC. So these superhuman beings had all this time to multiply and grow in number.

We had the *Emim*, a race of gigantic stature dwelling to the east of the Salt Sea. In ancient times, the whole of the land of Canaan was held by this race of giants. The *Rephaim* inhabited the north. Next the *Zuzim*, then the *Emim*, with the *Horim* in the south. Afterwards, the kingdom of Bashan embraced the territories of the *Rephaim*; the Amonites that of the *Zuzim*; the Moabites that of the *Emim*; while Edom embraced the mountains of the *Horim*. The *Emim* were related to the *Anakim* and generally called by the same name, but the Moabites referred to them as the *"giants"* or *"terrible ones"*[27] (see **Figure 4**).

Now we come to the year 974 BC and a boy of 16 years named David. Another 477 years have elapsed since Joshua entered the Promised Land and destroyed all the giants. All, that is, except for a remnant at Gaza, Gath and Ashdod. We pick up the story in 1 Samuel 17:

> 2. And Saul and the men of Israel were gathered together, and pitched by the valley of Elah, and set the battle in array against the Philistines.
> 4. And there went out a champion out of the camp of the Philistines, named Goliath of Gath, whose height was six cubits and a span.
> 5. And he had a helmet of brass upon his head, and he was armed

with a coat of mail; and the weight of the coat was five thousand shekels of brass.

6. And he had greaves of brass upon his legs, and a target of brass between his shoulders.

7. And the staff of his spear was like a weaver's beam; and his spear's head weighed six hundred shekels of iron; and one bearing a shield went before him.

8. And he stood and cried unto the armies of Israel, and said unto them: "Why are ye come out to set your battle in array? Am not I a Philistine and ye servants to Saul? Choose you a man for you and let him come down to me. If he be able to fight with me, and to kill me, then will we be your servants. But if I prevail against him, and kill him, then shall ye be our servants, and serve us."

11. When Saul and all Israel heard those words of the Philistine, they were dismayed and greatly afraid.

12. Now David was the son of that Ephrathite of Bethlehem-Judah whose name was Jesse; and he had eight sons;

16. And the Philistine drew near morning and evening, and presented himself forty days.

26. And David spake to the men that stood by him, saying: "What shall be done to the man that killeth this Philistine, and taketh away the reproach from Israel? For who is this uncircumcised Philistine, that he should defy the armies of the living God?"

32. And David said to Saul: "Let no man's heart fail because of him. Thy servant will go and fight with this Philistine."

33. And Saul said to David: "Thou art not able to go against this Philistine to fight with him; for thou art but a youth, and he a man of war from his youth."

34. And David said unto Saul: "Thy servant kept his father's sheep, and there came a lion, and a bear, and took a lamb out of the flock. And I went out after him, and smote him, and delivered it out of his mouth, and when he arose against me, I caught him by his beard, and smote him, and slew him. Thy servant slew both the lion and the bear; and this uncircumcised Philistine shall be as one of them seeing that he hath defied the armies of the living God."

37. David said moreover: "The Lord that delivered me out of the paw of the lion, and out of the paw of the bear, He will deliver me out of the hand of this Philistine." And Saul said unto David: "Go, and the Lord be with thee."

40. And he took his staff in his hand, and chose him five smooth stones out of the brook and put them in a shepherd's bag which he

had, even in a scrip; and his sling was in his hand; and he drew near to the Philistine.

41. And the Philistine came on and drew near unto David; and the man that bare the shield went before him.

42. And when the Philistine looked about, and saw David, he disdained him; for he was but a youth, and ruddy, and of a fair countenance.

43. And the Philistine said unto David: "Am I a dog, that thou comest to me with staves?" And the Philistine cursed David by his gods.

44. And the Philistine said to David: "Come to me, and I will give thy flesh unto the fowls of the air, and to the beasts of the field."

45. Then said David to the Philistine: "Thou comest to me with a sword, and with a spear, and with a shield; and I come to thee in the name of the Lord of hosts, the God of the armies of Israel, Whom thou hast defied. This day will the Lord deliver thee into mine hand; and I will smite thee, and take thine head from thee; and I will give the carcases of the host of the Philistines this day unto the fowls of the air, and to the wild beasts of the Earth; that all the Earth may know that there is a God in Israel.

And all this assembly shall know that the Lord saveth not with sword and spear: for the battle is the Lord's and He will give you into our hands."

49. And David put his hand in his bag, and took thence a stone, and slang it, and smote the Philistine in his forehead, that the stone sunk into his forehead; and he fell upon his face to the earth.

50. So David prevailed over the Philistine with a sling and with a stone, and smote the Philistine, and slew him; but there was no sword in the hand of David.

51. Therefore David ran, and stood upon the Philistine, and took his sword, and drew it out of the sheath thereof, and slew him, and cut off his head therewith. And when the Philistines saw that their champion was dead, they fled.

The story of David versus Goliath has become an oft-used metaphor in our daily language. Let us now look a little closer at this record. Goliath was a champion of the Philistines (which are now the modern-day Palestinians). You will note that he hailed from Gath which, along with Gaza and Ashdod, was where a remnant of giants, who had not been defeated by the armies of Joshua 477 years earlier, escaped to. Goliath was descended from this remnant of giants.

This was a big man. His height is given as six cubits and a span. That would make him about 13 feet 6 inches tall at 25.025 inches to the Hebrew cubit. We are not given his weight, but it must have been in proportion to his height as his coat of mail weighed more than 11 stone. The head of his spear was over a stone in weight and the shaft was like a weaver's beam. He wore six pieces of armour in all, he was 6 cubits tall and his spearhead was 600 shekels in weight. Thus the number six is here stamped all over him like a hallmark. David, on the other hand, was between 16 and 17 years of age. He was so scrawny that, when they put the armour on him, he could not move. So he discarded this and went out to meet Goliath armed only with a shepherd's crook and a sling. He chose five stones, which is significant,[28] but only needed one to bring down the giant. When the stone sunk into Goliaths's forehead, he had not even bothered to draw his sword, such was his disdain for this unworthy whelp of an opponent. David subsequently drew out Goliath's sword and used it to chop off his head.

This victory by David was the beginning of his rise to the eventual kingship of Israel.

Now we go forward in time to note some more battles and obtain further evidence concerning the descendants of *Rapha*, who were of the *Nephilim*. First to the second book of Samuel:

> Moreover the Philistines had yet war with Israel; and David went down and his servants with him, and fought against the Philistines; and David waxed faint.
>
> And Ishbi-Benob, which was of the sons of the giant, the weight of whose spear was three hundred shekels of brass, he being girded with a new sword, said that he would slay David.
>
> But Abishai the son of Zeruiah succoured him and smote the Philistine and killed him.
>
> And it came to pass after this that there was again a battle with the Philistines at Gob; then Sibbechai the Hushathite slew Saph, which was of the son of the giant.
>
> And Elhanan the son of Jaare-Oregim, a Bethlehemite, slew Goliath the Gittite, the staff of whose spear was like a weaver's beam (*This giant was different from the Goliath David slew*).
>
> And there was yet a battle in Gath, where was a man of great stature that had on every hand six fingers, and on every foot six toes, four and twenty in number; and he also was born to the giant.
>
> And when he defied Israel, Jonathan the son of Shameah, the

brother of David, slew him.

These four were born to the giant in Gath and fell by the hand of David and by the hand of his servants.

2nd Book of Samuel 21:15-22

This record is corroborated in the first Book of Chronicles, which adds in some extra information:

And it came to pass after this there arose a war at Gezer with the Philistines at which time Sibbechai the Hushathite slew Sippai, that was of the children of the giant, and they were subdued.

And Elehanan the son of Jair slew Lahmi, the brother of Goliath the Gittite ...

And yet there was war at Gath, where was a man of great stature, whose fingers and toes were four and twenty, six on each hand, six on each foot, and he also was the son of the giant.

Jonathan the son of Shimea, David's brother, slew him.

These were born unto the giant in Gath and they fell by the hand of David and by the hand of his servants.

Ist Book of Chronicles 20:4-8

There are other passages not quoted which make mention of the *Rephaim*, which were another branch of the *Nephilim*. But I believe enough evidence is provided to give us a broad picture of the existence of this race of giants and the area they inhabited.[29]

In conclusion, let us briefly summarise the major points in this chapter.

We have seen that a group of spirit beings, called *sons of God*, took human women to wife and produced offspring. The record states that they chose "wives," which would suggest polygamy. The offspring they produced were superhuman in size and character and were monsters of iniquity.

The first irruption was before the Flood of Noah, which killed all living things on the Earth, according to Genesis. But we are told that there was a second irruption by the words "and also after that" – i.e. after the Flood.

So all the way down from the time of Abraham (1912 BC) to the entry into the Promised Land by Joshua (1451 BC) and to the time of David (974 BC; see App. 1), these giants were numerous in the land. This is a period of almost 1,000 years. But the land we have described here was called the land of Canaan. There is absolutely no reason to believe that these

Nephilim, and their related branches, did not travel and populate other areas of the then known world. In fact, later in this study I believe we shall prove that this was indeed the case.

We have seen that these giants were known by various names such as *Rephaim,* from one *Rapha,* a notable one among them. Also *Emim, Horim, Zamzummim* and *Avim,* as well as *Anakim.* The principal locality of the *Rephaim* was evidently "Ashtaroth Karnaim," while the *Emim* were in the plain of Kiriathaim (Genesis 14.5).

Ten out of the 12 spies sent in by Joshua were too afraid to invade the Promised Land. The cluster of grapes which two of them carried out on a pole was so heavy that it suggests genetic engineering. Also, one of the giants killed by David's men later on had six fingers and six toes on each hand and foot. Does this not also suggest genetic modification?

Goliath of Gath was 13 feet 6 inches tall. He may well have weighed in at around 40 to 45 stone (254-286 kg) or maybe more, given that his coat of mail was over 11 stone!

Let us not forget Og, king of Bashan, whose bed was $18^3/_4$ feet (5.7 metres) long and $8^1/_3$ feet (2.5 metres) wide. How would you like to wake up in the morning with this guy beside you? Og's strength and the strength of his people is seen in the 60 "giant cities of Bashan," the ruins of which still exist today. A detailed description of these cities is contained in a book written by Dr. Josias Leslie Porter entitled *Giant Cities of Bashan and Syria's Holy Places* (published in London, 1865).

The Flood occurred in the year 2348 BC. David defeated Goliath in 974 BC. So, for up to 1,374 years after the Flood, and up to the time of David, this race of superhuman giants was roaming the world. But what of those who existed before the Flood? How much do we know about them and what can we deduce about them from both history and the Hebrew texts?

SPACE ODYSSEY

Accentuating to the Book of Genesis (chapter 6), the sons of God had intercourse with the daughters of men and produced the Nephilim, the fallen ones who reigned on the Earth both before and after the Flood of Noah. Both the sons of God who impregnated the women and their offspring were exceedingly evil, for we are told in the ensuing verses:

> And God saw that the wickedness of man was great in the Earth, and that every thought of the imagination of his heart was only evil continually.
> And it repented the Lord that he had made man on the Earth, and it grieved him at his heart.
> The Earth also was corrupt before God and the Earth was filled with violence.
>
> *Genesis: 6: 5,6,11*

The Hebrew word for wickedness is the word "*zimmah*," which is defined as *meditated wickedness; plotted, planned* and *designed; wicked* or *lewd purpose*; especially the sins of unchastity.[30]

As a result of the marriage of these spirit beings with woman and the influence of their offspring, the whole population of the then known world, save for Noah and his family, had become corrupted beyond redemption. Violence and moral depravity filled the entire world.[31]

We shall return later to more specifics on these evil spirit beings and their likely unforgivable acts (for the one and only object of the Flood was to destroy all mankind). But first we will examine the background to these sons of God, who they were and where they came from.

Let us once again search out the texts of the Hebrew scriptures and allow the words to paint a picture of these spirit beings known to most as "angels." Is the image conjured up by this word the same as that portrayed in the words of the text of the scriptures?

One of the first appearances of these "men" occurs in a meeting between Abraham and three very important people in Genesis 18:

> And the Lord appeared unto him (Abraham) in the oaks of Mamre; and he sat in the tent door in the heat of the day.

And he lifted up his eyes and looked and, lo, three men stood by him.

And when he saw them, he ran to meet them from the tent door, and bowed himself towards the ground.

And he said: "My Lord, if I have now found favour in thy sight, pass not away, I pray thee, from thy servant.

"Let a little water, I pray thee, be fetched, and wash your feet, and rest yourselves under the tree.

"And I will fetch a morsel of bread and comfort ye your hearts; after that, ye shall pass on ..."

And they said: "So do as thou hast said."

And Abraham hastened into the tent unto Sarah and said: "Make ready quickly three measures of fine meal, knead it and make cakes upon the hearth."

And Abraham ran unto the herd and fetched a calf tender and good and gave it unto a young man; and he hastened to dress it.

And he took butter and milk and the calf which he had dressed, and set it before them; and he stood by them under the tree, and they did eat.

Genesis 18:1-8

Here we see Abraham displaying typical eastern hospitality. When he saw the three men he constrained them to wash their feet and take food and drink. Then, in keeping with the eastern culture, he served them and waited upon them but did not eat with them. But the most amazing aspect of this record is that the three men he spoke with and provided for were no less than the Lord (Jehovah) himself and two of his top aides.[32]

These three individuals are described as "men." Furthermore, they sat down in the shade, washed their feet, and then enjoyed a good meal of veal with bread and butter and washed the whole lot down with fresh milk! We can assume that these men wore clothes and appeared, more or less, as normal people.

The lesson from this is that Yaweh resembles a man. Or, looked at the other way around, men resemble Yaweh. Remember in Genesis 1:26 during the creation we read: "**Let us make man in our image: after our likeness.**" This informs us that our "image" and our "likeness" is fashioned after this person called Elohim, and more often referred to as Yahweh or Jehovah in the Hebrew tongue.[33] (See also Genesis 1:27; 5:1,3; 9:6; James 3:9).

Many believe that God, being a spirit, does not have form. But, just as the angels are referred to as "ministering spirits," they are always called "men" and appear as "men."

In this passage, the Hebrew word for Lord is Jehovah; and, in the course of the chapter, Jehovah (Lord) appears no less than 12 times. So one of the men Abraham entertained and then had a discussion with was no less than Jehovah himself.

After the three had finished their meal, they continued on their journey towards Sodom. Abraham had a rather feisty debate with the Lord and endeavoured to make a bargain with him. However, the other two men journeyed on alone. We learn more from the ensuing passage:

> And there came two angels (Hebrew: *malak; agents; sent ones; messengers*) to Sodom at evening; and Lot sat in the gate at Sodom; and Lot, seeing them, rose up to meet them; and he bowed himself with his face to the ground.
>
> And he said: "Behold now my Lords, turn in, I pray you, and tarry all night, and wash your feet, and ye shall rise up early, and go on your way." And they said: "Nay, we will abide in the street all night."
>
> And he pressed upon them greatly, and they turned in unto him and entered into his house, and he made them a feast, and did bake unleavened bread, and they did eat.
>
> But before they lay down, the men of the city, the men of Sodom, compassed the house around, both old and young, all the people from every quarter.
>
> And they called unto Lot: "Where are the men which came in unto thee this night? Bring them out unto us that we may know them."
>
> *Genesis 19:1-5*

Once again we see from this record that these two "messengers" were mistaken for ordinary men. Firstly, Lot sees them and offers his hospitality to them. They at first refuse before accepting his invitation to food and a bed. These men, although spirit beings who abide not on this Earth, obviously have good appetites, for they enjoyed a hearty meal for the second time that day.

The entrance of these men into Lot's house is not lost on the rest of the inhabitants of Sodom, for they all gather around Lot's abode and insist on meeting the two men so that they might "know" them. This tells us that these two angels, apart from appearing as men, must have been extremely attractive individuals in order to have caught the attention of virtually everyone in the town!

We are told in other places throughout the Old Testament that these "men" or "messengers" are created spirit beings. We are also informed that they existed far beyond the creation of this present world as we know it.

Concerning "angels" in Psalm 148:5, we read:

> Let them praise the name of the Lord.
> For He commanded, and they were created.

And in *Psalm 104:4* we are told:

> Who maketh his angels spirits;
> His ministers a flaming fire.

In Job, Yaweh is debating the creation of the world and says, concerning angels:

> When the morning stars sang together, and all the sons of God shouted for joy.
>
> *Book of Job 38:7*

As discussed previously, the "sons of God" are angels which are created spirit beings. But, as we have seen, they can appear as men and look and eat and drink and talk just like human beings. Also note from the above verse that these sons of God are referred to as the "*morning stars who sang together.*" This will become relevant later as we look at the astronomical significance of spiritual beings and at the alignment of certain buildings with star groupings and other Zodiacal considerations.

To emphasise that these spirit messengers, or agents, are men, I would like to present a few more brief records. From the Book of Daniel, the names of two of the leading entities in Yaweh's host are provided:

> Yea, while I was speaking in prayer <u>even the man Gabriel</u>, whom I had seen in the vision at the beginning, being caused to fly swiftly, touched me about the time of the evening oblation.
> And he informed me and talked with me and said: "O Daniel, I am now come forth to give thee skill and understanding."
>
> *Book of Daniel 9:21,22*

We learn from this passage that these agents have names and can fly, i.e. move very fast. Being spirit, they are not restricted to the laws of physics as we are. We see that this messenger's name is Gabriel. His main duty is to deliver messages, as he does in many places, especially in the New Testament. He is usually accompanied by another messenger whose name is Michael. His job seems to be the security aspect of the mission, as we see from this next extract:

And in the four and twentieth day of the first month, as I (Daniel) was by the side of the great river, which is Hiddekel:

Then I lifted up my eyes, and looked, and behold a <u>certain man</u> clothed in linen, whose loins were girded with fine gold of Uphaz; His body also was like the beryl, and his face as the appearance of lightning, and his eyes as lamps of fire, and his arms and his feet like in colour to polished brass, and the voice of his words like the voice of a multitude.

Then he said to me: "Fear not, Daniel, for from the first day that thou did set thine heart to understand, and to chasten thyself before thy God, thy words were heard ...

But the prince of the kingdom of Persia withstood me one and twenty days; but lo, Michael, one of the chief princes, came to help me; and remained there with the kings of Persia."

Book of Daniel 10:4-6; 11-13

This man, who is still Gabriel, appears here not quite in ordinary clothes but in some beautiful raiment. Again he reiterates that he has been "sent" to inform Daniel regarding events which are to take place in the latter days. But then something unusual occurs. He tells Daniel that, while *en route*, he was impeded in his journey by a "*prince of Persia,*" who held him up for 21 days. Apparently this *prince of Persia* is another spirit being, but an evil one. For Michael, the military aide, had to come to the assistance of Gabriel and remove this other evil agent so that Gabriel could accomplish his mission.

This provides some interesting insight into the realm of the spirit world. Again, Gabriel is a man sent on a mission to deliver information to another man, Daniel. He is ambushed by an obviously powerful evil angel named as the "*prince of Persia.*" Yet another celestial being, a military man by the name of Michael, comes to the rescue and clears the way for Gabriel to continue on and deliver his message.

All the personalities involved in this saga are men. Not human, flesh-and-blood men as we are. But spirit beings. Men of a different nature to us but men nevertheless. Because they are spirit beings they can travel faster than the speed of light and commute between Earth and wherever their celestial abode is.

Now we move forward to the time of the Gospels and briefly look at some of the appearances of these men in the days of the Messiah and afterwards.

In the first chapter of St. Luke's Gospel we are given the story of the birth of John the Baptist to his heretofore barren mother, Elizabeth, and her priest husband, Zacharias. While he carried out his priestly duties one day, an angel (Greek: *aggelos:* "*messenger*" or "*sent one*") appeared to him:

> And it came to pass that while he executed the priest's office before Yaweh in the order of his course.
> And there appeared unto him a messenger (*aggelos*) of Yaweh standing on the right side of the altar of incense.
> And the messenger (*aggelos*) said unto him: "I am Gabriel that stands in the presence of Yaweh, and I am sent to speak unto you and to show you these glad tidings."
>
> *Luke 1:8,11,19*

Later on in this chapter this same man, Gabriel, appears to Mary and informs her that she will shortly give birth to the Messiah. Mary was probably only a young girl between 14 and 18 years of age at the time. But what she saw and what Zacharias saw was a man who then proceeded to have a conversation with them just as he had done with Daniel in the earlier account.

We now move forward 33 years or so to the time of the death of the Messiah. Some of the women returned to the tomb where his body had been lain in order to embalm it.

> Now, upon the first day of the week, very early in the morning, they came into the sepulchre, bringing the spices which they had prepared, and certain others with them.
> And they found the stone rolled away from the sepulchre.
> And it came to pass, as they were much perplexed thereabout, behold <u>two men</u> stood by them in shining garments.
>
> *Luke 24:1,2,4*

These two beings entered into a discussion with this group who had come to embalm the body of the Messiah. In all of the other Gospels we find a similar account. People arrive at the tomb to find it empty, but meet two men in white clothing who divulge certain information to them. Again jumping ahead a few more years into the first century AD, to the account of the movements of the original followers of the Messiah, who were then labelled "Christians," there are numerous accounts of these spirit-men appearing to the disciples in order to give direction or help them out of difficult situations. Always these messengers are described as men.

Conclusion:

Throughout the entire text of both the Old and New Testaments there are almost 300 mentions of these celestial beings. Always they are described as men. Sometimes they were mistakenly treated as ordinary human beings. These men ate and drank upon occasion and usually were clothed in white shining raiment. Some of the time they appear in twos. Gabriel is the one who is sent to deliver messages and he is usually accompanied by another being who is named in some instances as Michael. It would appear that this latter gentleman is sent along as security for Gabriel. What we might today refer to as "muscle." We are also told that these entities existed long before the world, as we know it, came into being. They are created spirit-men as opposed to human beings.

So do the Scriptures describe another world wherein exists a different form of life, possibly superior in intelligence and power to that of our world? Yes indeed. These are men who look like us and their abode is a place called "Heaven," which seems to be some considerable distance from our planet. Are they benevolent towards mankind and interested in helping us in our times of trial? The answer is yes. So the leader of this celestial group is well-disposed towards mankind? Yes. His name is Yaweh, although sometimes he is called Elohim, and he definitely seems to want to help mankind. So there are no evil angels who want to hurt mankind and do us ill?

Well, yes there are, but so far we've only been talking about the good guys. So what's the story with these evil guys? That's coming up next.

> **Be not forgetful to entertain strangers: for thereby some have entertained angels unawares.**
>
> *Book of Hebrews 13:2*

The "*sons of God*" who married the "*daughters of men*" produced children, who were called the *Nephilim*. This means "*fallen ones.*" The reason they are named thus is because these "*sons of God*" were fallen angels. They were part of a band of malevolent spirit beings who, we are told, rebelled against Yaweh and tried to usurp his throne. A battle ensued, and these evil, fallen beings got the boot, so to speak, and were cast out of the presence of Yaweh.

The leader of this rebellion is given various names. But one of his original names was Lucifer, which means "shining one" or "morning star." We shall now look at the background to this particular spirit being and his host. Once we have done this, we will be better able to understand the situation which existed for several hundreds of years prior to the time of Noah.

41

CELESTIAL POTENTATE

Before time was, in a celestial kingdom ruled by Yaweh, there was an innumerable multitude of spirit beings known as "Sons of God." Lucifer was one of the brightest stars of this angelic congregation. Full of wisdom, knowledge and beauty, we are told something of his former glory in the Book of Ezekiel, chapter 28, where he is referred to as the "King of Tyre":

> Son of man, take up a lament against the King of Tyre and say to him:
> This is what the Sovereign Lord says:
> "You were the model of perfection, full of wisdom and perfect in beauty.
> You were in Eden, the Garden of God.
> Every precious stone adorned you: ruby, topaz and emerald, chrysolite, onyx and jasper, sapphire, turquoise and beryl. Your settings and mountings were made of gold; on the day you were created, they were prepared.
> You were anointed as a guardian cherub, for so I ordained you.
> You were on the holy mountain of God.
> You walked among the fiery stones.
> You were blameless in your ways from the day you were created till wickedness was found in you.
> Through your widespread trade you were filled with violence and you sinned.
> So I drove you in disgrace from the mountain of God, and I expelled you, O guardian cherub, from among the fiery stones.
> Your heart became proud on account of your beauty, and you corrupted your wisdom because of your splendour.
> So I threw you to the Earth."
>
> *Book of Ezekiel 28: 11-17*

Bear in mind that this person is a man, a son of God or angel, a spirit being who was once created by Yaweh and given a specific task. But because of hubris, he tripped up and fell, thus becoming a fallen angel. We are provided with some more background information on this entity in the Book of Isaiah.

> How you have fallen from Heaven, O Morning Star (*Hebrew:*
> *Lucifer*), son of the dawn.
> You have been cast down to the Earth, you who once laid low the
> nations.
> For you said in your heart: "I will ascend to Heaven.
> I will raise my throne above the stars of God.
> I will sit enthroned on the mount of assembly on the utmost
> heights of the sacred mountain.
> I will ascend above the tops of the clouds.
> I will make myself like the Most High."
>
> *Book of Isaiah 14: 12-14*

Please note that the name Lucifer translates as *the morning star*[34] and also that he said in his heart that he would raise his throne above the "stars of God." It is clear from this that the morning star, which is Venus, was named after Lucifer (or vice versa). It is also clear, and we shall examine other passages to clarify the point, that the angels of God are referred to as "stars" and apparently are named after certain stars and planets. This will become important as we consider the associations of the pyramids and other ancient monuments with the movements of certain stars and constellations.

The greatest trick the devil ever pulled was to convince the world that he does not exist. So said Kaiser Solsa in that great movie *The Usual Suspects*. In assimilating information concerning the leader of the fallen "sons of God," we find him first mentioned, in some detail, as early as the third chapter of the Book of Genesis. Nowhere as much as here has this elusive spirit-man covered his tracks and camouflaged his existence in a maze of fable and fairytale. For here we have the story of the Fall of Man. But here is no mention of an "apple" or of a "snake." There is, however, mention of a "serpent" and of the Tree of Knowledge of Good and Evil.

Having created Adam from the dust of the Earth, Yaweh laid down some ground rules.

> And the Lord God commanded the man, saying: "Of every tree of
> the garden thou mayest freely eat.
> But of the Tree of the Knowledge of Good and Evil, thou shalt not eat
> of it: for in the day that thou eatest thereof, thou shalt surely die."
>
> *Book of Genesis 2:16,17*

This would appear to be a very clear-cut and straightforward pronouncement. If you eat of this particular tree (no mention of apples here), you will surely die. Now enters for the first time the "serpent".

Now the serpent (Hebrew: *Nachash*) was more subtle (*crafty*) than any beast of the field which the Lord God had made. And he said unto the woman: "Did God really say you must not eat from any tree in the garden?"

The woman said to the serpent (*Nachash*):
"We may eat fruit from the trees in the garden, but God did say:
'You must not eat fruit from the tree that is in the middle of the garden,
or you must not touch it, or you will die'."

The serpent (*Nachash*) said to the woman:
"You will not surely die. For God knows that when you eat of it your eyes will be opened and you will be like God, knowing good and evil."

When the woman saw that the fruit of the tree was good for food and pleasing to the eye, and also desirable for gaining wisdom, she took some and ate it. She also gave some to her husband, and he ate it.

Then the eyes of them both were opened, and they realised that they were naked.

Genesis 3:1-7

The word serpent is the Hebrew word *nachash* and it requires closer scrutiny in order to provide us with a better understanding of its meaning. Figures of speech are used extensively throughout the text of the Old and New Testaments. A figure of speech is always used in order to bring attention to and intensify the *reality of the literal sense* and the veracity of the fact stated. So while the words used in the figure of speech may not be strictly true to the letter, they are all the more true to the truth conveyed by them. For instance, in the Scriptures, Herod is referred to as a "fox," Nero as a "lion" and Judah as a "lion's whelp." These are figures of speech. So when Satan is spoken of as a *serpent*, it no more means a snake than it does when Herod is called a "fox." When the word *serpent* is used, it is for the purpose of expressing the truth more impressively, and it is intended to be something much more real than the letter of the word.

Many times the Messiah is referred to as the "*Lamb of God*." But we all know this is a figure of speech and does not literally mean a four-legged woolly animal. The same applies when Satan is called "*the serpent*;" it does not mean a literal snake.

Thus the Hebrew word *nachash* means to *hiss, mutter, whisper* (as do enchanters). It also has the meaning *to be bright*. Sometimes the word *nachash* is translated as *fiery serpent*. In the earlier passage quoted, we saw that Lucifer was an exalted celestial being full of wisdom and beauty. *Nachash* is similarly used to imply a glorious spirit being.[35]

In the New Testament, we are informed that Eve was beguiled by a serpent who is spoken of as an **"angel (messenger) of light"** (II Corinthians 11:3). So we have in all this evidence the word *"serpent"* meaning a glorious spirit being of superior aspect, knowledge and wisdom, full of beauty and fascination, with the ability to enchant and charm. It was to this bright shining angel of light that Eve paid such great deference and with whom she held a conversation. Not with a mere snake.

It is worth noting here that, in describing the fall of Lucifer in Isaiah 14, the text refers to him as being a "man," just as Gabriel and Michael are referred to as "men".

> **Is this the man who shook the Earth and made kingdoms tremble? The man who made the world a desert ...?**
>
> *Book of Isaiah 14:16,17*

We are told that his heart was lifted up because of his beauty. Then he was told: **"Thou corrupted thy wisdom by reason of thy brightness."** As a result of this corruption, it was then said: **"I will cast thee to the ground. I will lay thee before kings that they may behold thee"** (*Ezekiel 28:17*).

We are also told that the serpent was **"more subtle than any beast of the field."** The word *subtle* means *wise* or *crafty*. The word *beast* is *chay* in Hebrew, which means *"living being."* So the serpent was wiser than any other living being created by Elohim.[36]

The idea of Eve holding a conversation with a snake is hard to fathom. But we can appreciate her being enchanted and fascinated by a spirit being who appeared as an angel of light, a glorious personage full of splendour and possessing supernatural knowledge and wisdom. This is the serpent of Genesis 3 and the figure of speech is used to emphasise the truth and reality of the situation. It is also remarkable that the word *nachash (serpent)* is often rendered to *enchant, fascinate, bewitch* in many other places throughout the Old Testament.

Many believe that the serpent of Genesis 3 is exactly that, a snake. But the author would like to refer to an in-depth study of this topic in Appendix 19 of *The Companion Bible* by E.W. Bullinger. Most Biblical scholars acknowledge Bullinger as one of the most esteemed and learned of all Biblical authors. He spoke fluent Greek, Hebrew, Aramaic, Latin and other languages and the breadth of work he did on scriptural writing is second to none. Bullinger asserts that the serpent is a figure of speech referring to Satan.

Returning to the core of the meeting between Lucifer and Eve, we note that the next verse, after they partake of the forbidden fruit, says that the eyes of Adam and Eve were opened and they knew that they were naked. This is known as the "Fall of Man."

Later, they made clothes of fig leaves to hide their nakedness. Then, when they heard the footsteps of Yaweh walking in the garden, they concealed themselves. Yaweh then confronts both Adam and Eve and Lucifer, and in His denunciation of their actions, He utters the first prophecy of the Messiah and that of the future doom of the serpent. In this one verse we have summarised the story of man's fall and redemption, spanning the whole of history from the first days in Genesis to the future demise and destruction of the old serpent in the latter parts of the Book of Revelation. This one verse also includes reference to the death of the future Messiah and outlines the astronomical patterns which would dominate the celestial story. It is verse 15 of Genesis chapter 3:

"And I will put enmity between you (Serpent: *Lucifer*) and the woman; and between your seed and her seed; it shall crush your head and you will bruise his heel."

Book of Genesis 3:15

This verse is the first great promise and prophecy and it is also a figure of speech. The seed of the woman here refers to the coming Messiah. Speaking to the serpent (*Lucifer*), Yaweh says "*you will bruise his heel*" – i.e. you will temporarily hurt the Messiah, the seed of the woman, referring to the Crucifixion. But ultimately the Messiah would "*crush your (Lucifer's) head,*" meaning that the final victory would be accomplished sometime in the future, when the serpent would be utterly destroyed by the seed of the woman. Thus the figure of speech refers to a rather minor bruising of a small part of the body (the heel) in a non-critical manner. But, in contrast, that same heel would crush the head of the serpent, the head being the most important part of the entity insofar as it contains the brain, the mind and the very control centre of the entire body. Thus, the figure of speech is once again emphasising the truth and reality of what is said.

We are not quite ready to pursue the astronomical implications of this and other passages at this point. But we may observe that the "seed of the woman" here refers to the virgin who would in the future bear the Messiah. Thus the virgin is in the Zodiacal sign of *Virgo*. Her seed, whose heel would be bruised by the serpent, is the promised Messiah, star sign *Leo (the lion)*. And the serpent who would bruise the heel of the Messiah, but who would have his head crushed in the final contest, is depicted in *Scorpio*.

But the story of Adam and Eve is only a fable, I hear you say. What about prehistoric man and the dinosaurs and fossils and the billions of years the Earth has existed? I can assure the reader that there is absolutely no contradiction between prehistoric man and prehistory and the opening chapters of the Book of Genesis, but that is a debate for another day. For now, let us continue with our exposition of this angelic spirit being so full of splendour and wisdom and knowledge – this most highly-exalted and mightiest supernatural being ever created by Yaweh, the Most High God. Never was the serpent's wisdom more craftily utilised than in securing universal acceptance of the traditional story of a *"snake"* and an *"apple,"* thus blinding us to the true identity of the nature of that wise and subtle serpent, Satan. The greatest trick the devil ever pulled was to convince the world that he does not exist.

STARGATE

The Great Pyramid of Giza, the temples of Egypt and the great monuments of Mexico, Peru and Cambodia all have one thing in common: they are aligned with the stars.

From whence did their builders receive this astronomical information? And why were their architects seemingly obsessed with the celestial bodies and their positions? It is widely held that the ancient Egyptians and other cultures possessed this knowledge and constructed these great monuments. But to suggest that the technology and mathematical knowledge plus the physical ability to construct these edifices came out of the heads of simple people living somewhere in a desert is beyond logic and probability. To give credence to such a notion is to believe that if you give a screwdriver to a chimpanzee he could construct a television set. Yet these ancient structures seem to have just popped up out of nowhere at a time when man was supposedly somewhere between the stone age and the iron age. Most experts state that the Great Pyramid was built by Khufu, known to the Greeks as Cheops. But if it was built in Khufus's reign, which spanned 23 years, and over two million blocks were used, one block would have had to be moved into place every five minutes to complete the work.[37]

We have briefly touched on the astronomical associations of the men referred to in the old Hebrew texts as "agents" or "messengers" and whom we call "angels." Let us now examine more closely many of the Scriptures relating to stars and their relationship with these spirit-men.

We have already seen that, in the King James Version, Isaiah 14:12 translates as:

How art thou fallen from heaven, O Lucifer, son of the morning.

But in the New International Version this same verse is rendered thus:

How you have fallen from heaven, O morning star, son of the dawn!

We see in this that a clear connection is drawn between this person spoken of (Lucifer), and the morning star, which is Venus. This is the bright star which can be seen in the east at dawn when the other stars have vanished from the sky. So this being is named after, and associated with, the morning star.

This distinction is again made in Job 38:4-7, where all the celestial beings are coupled with stars:

> "Where were you when I laid the Earth's foundations? Tell me, if you have understanding.
> Who marked off its dimension? Surely you know.
> Who stretched a measuring line across it?
> On what were its footings set, or who laid its cornerstone?
> When the morning stars sang together and all the sons of God shouted for joy."

In the New International Version this last phrase "sons of God" is rendered "all the angels shouted for joy." Again we see that these "sons of God" are the angels and are referred to as "stars." This is illustrated in many places throughout the entirety of the Scriptures. For instance, we are informed in the Book of Revelation that when Satan was cast out of Heaven he took one-third of the "stars" with him.

> And there appeared another wonder in Heaven; and behold, a great red dragon having seven heads and ten horns, and seven crowns upon his heads.
> And his tail drew a third part of the stars of Heaven, and did cast them to the Earth ...

Book of Revelation 12:3,4

As if we were in any doubt as to who the dragon and the stars are, we are told in verse seven:

> And there was war in Heaven:
> Michael and his angels fought against the dragon; and the dragon fought and his angels.
> And the great dragon was cast out, that old serpent called the devil and Satan, which deceives the whole world: he was cast out into the Earth and his angels were cast out with him

Book of Revelation 12:7,9

We glean from this that when the "morning star," that most highly-exalted of supernatural beings, decided to mutiny, he convinced one-third of the other "stars of heaven" to rebel with him. Thus one-third of the "sons of God," created spirit-men, made an eternal, binding decision to side with

Lucifer in his bid to usurp the throne of Yaweh, the Most High. But their coup was unsuccessful and they were cast out of Heaven. Now, as a result, these once holy servants of Yaweh became diabolically opposed to Yaweh.

In chapter one of the Book of Revelation we are given a description of the Son of Man, and he is seen here with seven stars in his right hand. Later on, in verse 20, we are told:

The seven stars are the angels of the seven churches.

In chapter nine of the same book, we are told of another "star" in action:

And the fifth angel sounded and I saw a star fall from heaven unto the Earth: and to him (i.e. to this "star," "angel") was given the key to the bottomless pit.
And he opened the bottomless pit ...

Book of Revelation 9:12

Because they are spirit, they can be invisible. For one cannot see spirit beings unless they take form and substance, which they of course do in many places throughout the Scriptures. But just because one cannot see them does not mean that they do not exist.

It is evident from the above that the original "sons of God" were created before the foundation of the world. It is also clear that these entities were party to the creation of the universe, for we are told that, on completion of the construction of the world, the "morning stars sang together and all the 'sons of God' shouted for joy." Job 38:7

Apparently these "sons of God" are associated with the actual stars, for they are called "stars" and Lucifer means "morning star." Perhaps each of the angels has a star and is thus named, for we are told that Yaweh both numbered and named the stars:

He determines the number of the stars,
and calls them each by name.

Psalm 147:4

We have established that there is a clear link between stars and the created spirit-men called angels. But why this obsession with Zodiacal constellations? To find out why these astronomical pictures appear in so many of the ancient monuments and temples, we must go back once again to the most ancient of the Hebrew texts and piece together the stellar information provided.

STAR WITNESS

Moses wrote the first five books of the Old Testament, known as the Pentateuch, circa 1490 BC. So for 2,500 years prior to this (see Appendix), there was no written record of the story of man's fall, his plight in the interim and his ultimate redemption. Did Yaweh leave no clue or witness to His plans for mankind in these intervening years or did He use some other means to communicate His blueprint for the generations?

The answer is given in the very first chapter of Genesis.

> And God said: "Let there be lights in the firmament to divide the day from the night; and let them be for signs and for seasons and for days and for years.
> And let them be for lights in the firmament to give light upon the Earth."
> And it was so.
> And God made two great lights: the greater light to rule the day and the lesser light to rule the night; he made the stars also.
>
> *Genesis 1:14-16*

The word signs comes from the Hebrew root *aveh*, meaning "to mark." So the stars are to mark or to signify someone or something to come. Thus at the first mention of the celestial bodies we are informed that one of their functions is to mark out or signify someone or something special to come.[38]

We have already seen that all the stars are named and numbered by Yaweh (Psalm 147:4). Most of these names are lost, but over 100 of them have been preserved down through the centuries in the Semitic languages. Originally, all these names and their meanings would have been known to the patriarchs of old and handed down by word of mouth. Josephus assures us that Biblical astronomy came down via Adam, Seth and Enoch and was passed on in this manner.[39]

Psalm 19:1-6 provides more information on the stars:

> The heavens declare the glory of God, the skies proclaim the work of His hands.
> Day after day, they pour forth speech.
> Night after night, they display knowledge.

There is no speech or language,
Where their voice is not heard.
Their voice goes out into all the Earth,
Their words to the end of the world.
In the heavens He has pitched a tent for the sun,
Which is like a bridegroom coming forth from His pavilion,
Like a champion rejoicing to run His course.
It rises at one end of the heavens and makes its circuit to the other.
Nothing is hidden from its heat.

Psalm 19: 1-6

A careful study of this passage shows that the stars in their courses do four things: they prophesy, they give knowledge, they illustrate the glory of Yaweh and they show forth His purposes.

It is the positioning and naming of the stars which gives us this knowledge and prophecy concerning the "one" to come and special events which are to occur. These groupings of stars are known as the Zodiac. The word Zodiac means *degrees or steps* which mark the stages of the suns's path through the heavens, corresponding with the 12 months of the year. We can only give a brief explanation here of Biblical astronomy and its meaning. (For further study, I would refer the reader to the sources listed at the end of this volume).[40]

So what is the special event or the special one that these signs were to point to in the stellar revelation? We have already spoken of this in a previous chapter, but now we need to look at it once more. Confronting the serpent and Adam and Eve, Yaweh said:

"And I will put enmity between thee (*serpent*) and the woman, and between thy seed and her seed:
It shall crush your head and you shalt bruise his heel."

Genesis 3:15

This is the first prophecy and promise of the Messiah, the seed of the woman. The heel of the Messiah would be bruised by the serpent. But the Messiah would ultimately crush the head of that same serpent. As has already been stated, this verse embraces all of the history of man's fall and ultimate redemption. In this one verse we are told that the coming seed of the woman would receive a temporary and non-fatal wound in his heel from the seed of the serpent, but that the Messiah would claim the final victory by crushing the head of the serpent under his heel, inflicting a fatal wound.

We are also given three of the main players in the saga, whose signs are to be found in all of the ancient Zodiacs. The woman is Virgo, the virgin from whose womb would come the Messiah. His star is *Leo (the lion)*, which can be seen in the planisphere of the heavens waiting to pounce and deal a fatal crushing blow to the serpent (*Scorpio*).

In Genesis chapter 49, we are given a prophecy which relates clearly to one of the constellations, *Leo*. In this passage, Jacob is on his death-bed and is speaking to his son Judah concerning his 12 sons and their offspring.

> Judah is a lion's whelp: from the prey, my son, thou art gone up; he stooped down, he couched as a lion, and as an old lion.
> Who shall rouse him up?
> The sceptre shall not depart from Judah, nor a lawgiver from between his feet (Hebrew: *regal*) until Shiloh come.
> Unto him shall the gathering of the people be.
>
> *Genesis 49: 9,10*

Here Jacob identifies Judah with a lion. This is a clear indication that Shiloh (another name for the Messiah) would come out of the lineage of Judah. But in astronomical terms he would come out of the sign of *Leo*. We are also told that "*the sceptre shall not depart from Judah nor a lawgiver from between his feet.*" In the Hebrew, Arabic and Aramaic this word is *regal*, meaning "foot." In the constellation of *Leo* the brightest star is *Regulus*. So in this one passage of Scripture we have the brightest star, *Regulus*, associated with the Messiah, the lawgiver, in the constellation of *Leo*, the lion. Furthermore, *Regulus* is associated with the future king (Messiah) and is strategically placed between the feet of *Leo*, the lion, ready to pounce and crush the head of the serpent, *Scorpio*.[41]

Further proof that the Messiah would come from the line of Judah is found in the Book of Revelation, whose prophecies are yet to be fulfilled.

> And one of the elders said to me: "Weep not, behold the Lion of the tribe of Judah, the root of David, hath prevailed to open the book, and to loose the seven seals thereof."
>
> *Book of Revelation 5:5*

It is evident here that the Messiah was to come through the line of Judah, which is linked to the constellation of Leo. There are many references in the Scriptures to show that the groupings of the stars and their names were given to communicate to mankind the plan and blueprint of Yaweh.

These star names and their groupings were well-known and rehearsed by the patriarchs and were handed down by word of mouth from generation to generation. When Moses finally wrote down the first five books, and these were followed by other Psalmists and prophets, there was no more need for the celestial writing. So, as time went on, their meanings were forgotten and lost. What we have today is astrology, which is a bastardisation of the original truths and a counterfeit of the true astronomy as originally given.[42] Furthermore, astrology and other so-called prognostications are to be strictly avoided, according to Isaiah and other prophets.[43]

Not all of this astronomical knowledge was lost all at once. The prophet Daniel was well versed in true astronomy and was charged with imparting this knowledge to the Magoi, who were in his care. It is most probable that this cult of Magoi were the predecessors of the Magi, who saw the star of the promised Messiah in the heavens and who came to Bethlehem seeking the "King of the Jews."

These wise men were Zoroastrians from Persia, which is present-day Iran. Down through the years from the time of Daniel (circa 500 BC), these Magi were initiated into the true meaning of the constellations and their stars. When they observed the various movements portending the birth of the promised "seed of the woman," they knew this to be the coming Messiah.

What exactly they saw and when it occurred is still a matter of much conjecture. In August of 3 BC Jupiter, known as the king planet, came into conjunction with Venus in the constellation of *Leo*. On September 11th 3 BC, the sun was directly in the midst of *Virgo* while at the same time the new moon was directly under the feet of *Virgo*. This is exactly as described in Revelation 12:12:

> And there appeared a great wonder in heaven: a woman clothed with the sun and the moon under her feet, and upon her head a crown of twelve stars.
> And she, being with child, cried, travailing in birth, and pained to be delivered.

Then, on September 14th 3 BC, there was a conjunction between the king planet Jupiter and Regulus in the constellation of *Leo* (which is the sign for Judah). This conjunction occurred a few times more over the coming months. So the most likely date for the birth of the Messiah, as prophesied in Genesis 3:15, was September 11th 3 BC. It is an established fact that he was not born on December 25th in the year zero.[44]

The Magi observed all of these unusual stellar displays and, because they were well aware of the prophecies concerning the coming seed of the virgin, they knew this to be the promised Messiah, the King of the Jews. On June 17th 2 BC, Jupiter was in conjunction with Venus, which formed a brilliant light in the western night sky in the constellation of *Leo*. This was the "star" which stood over Bethlehem and which guided these Persian astronomers there to pay homage.

It was over one year and three months (December 2nd 2 BC), by the time the Magi reached Bethlehem and found the child Messiah, who was a year old by then. This would have given the Magi enough time to observe the first movements of the relevant stars in their constellations, which convinced them that their calculations were accurate. Also, they had time to prepare for their journey to Jerusalem, the capital of Judah and the location of the throne of the promised king. This also explains why Herod, on learning from the Magi that a king was to be born, had all the children of two years old and under slaughtered. If the newly-born king was but hours old, why kill all children up to the age of two? Herod was taking no chances. He knew from the Magi that the child was over one year old; so, to be sure, he ordered his men to murder all children up to two years of age.

So the child was about one year and three months old when the Magi from the East finally found him and presented him with gifts. By the way, we are not told that there were three Wise Men. There may have been five or eight or ten. But these Zoroastrian astronomers, who were expert in the study of true Biblical astronomy, were watching out for the signs in the sky which would herald the birth of the seed of the woman, the promised Messiah. It was only a small few who knew of these prophecies. So, too, it will only be those who are aware of the prophecies concerning the second advent of the Messiah who will read the signs and discern what they portend.

There are other passages throughout the Scriptures which provide us with the names of various stars and refer to the Zodiac and the planets. But too much technical information can overburden the reader and lead to confusion. The above study is enough to show that the original story of the fall and redemption of man, from Genesis to Revelation, is recorded in the twelve signs of the Zodiac. These truths are written in the stars, where no man can touch or corrupt them. The twelve signs of the Zodiac are divided into three books of four chapters each. These twelve signs form a circle in the sky corresponding with the twelve months of the year. But where do we begin to read this book and where do we finish? Perhaps we may get a clue from the riddle of the sphinx. The Biblical scholar and author E.W. Bullinger suggests that the sphinx bears the head of a woman (*Virgo*) and the body and tail of a lion (*Leo*). So our story begins with the virgin and the promised seed and goes on through the whole Zodiacal story to end in the future with the king (*Leo*) in triumph over the arch-enemy (Scorpio: *the serpent*), just as Yaweh had predicted way back in Genesis 3:15.

Now here is the rub. Besides all those spiritual beings we have spoken of in this chapter who knew of these astronomical prophecies, there was another group of entities who also were extremely well-informed in this area. Lucifer, the original bright morning star, was keenly aware of these prognostications. Remember, he was the "anointed cherub who covereth." He was fully instructed and full of wisdom and splendour and knowledge. Furthermore, he and his host were all present when the Earth was founded.

The point is that Satan and all his supernatural allies are very familiar with the stars and their groupings. But they have managed to change the true meaning of Biblical astronomy into the false art of astrology and of the occult and other so-called related "sciences."

This explains to some degree why many of the ancient temples and monuments are decorated with Zodiacal configurations. For the persons who built them are intrinsically interwoven with the stars and their movements. And they are called "stars." Their original habitation was a place called "Heaven," which is somewhere among the stars, and more than likely they are named after individual stars. ("**He determines the number of the stars and calls them each by name.**" *Psalm 147:4*). So matters celestial are part of their heritage. Moreover, their leader, Lucifer, the Morning Star, was in Eden, the garden of God. He was upon the mountain of God and walked up and down in the midst of the fiery stones. Then he said in his heart: "**I will ascend into Heaven, I will exalt my throne above the stars of God ... I will ascend above the heights of the Most High**" ... (*Ezekiel 28 and Isaiah 14*).

But his rebellion was in vain and his plans came to nought. He and his host were cast out of "Heaven" to the Earth. But they remain obsessed with trying to return to their celestial habitation. Thus, the many monuments they constructed are often Earthly reflections of stellar configurations.

Here is a brief summary of the twelve signs of the Zodiac and their Biblical meanings. (I would refer the reader to E.W. Bullinger's *Witness of the Stars* for a more detailed and complete study). The twelve signs are divided into three books of four chapters (or signs). Each book, therefore, consists of four signs.

I Virgo
The Prophecy of the Promised Seed
1. Coma: Woman and child
2. Centaurus: The despised sin offering
3. Bootes: The coming one with branch

II Libra
The Redeemed Atoning Work
1. Crux: The Cross endured
2. Lupus: The Victim slain
3. Corona: The Crown bestowed

III Scorpio
The Redeemer's Conflict
1. Serpens: Assaulting the man's heel
2. Ophiuchus: The man grasping the serpent
3. Hercules: The mighty man victorious

IV Sagittarius
The Redeemed Triumph
1. Lyra: Praise prepared for the conqueror
2. Ara: Fire prepared for his enemies
3. Draco: The dragon cast down

V Capricornus
The Result of the Redeemer's Suffering
1. Sagitta: The arrow of God sent forth
2. Aquila: The smitten One falling
3. Delphinus: The dead One rising again

VI Aquarius
The Blessing Assured
1. Picis Australis: The Blessings bestowed
2. Pegasus: The Blessing quickly coming
3. Cygnus: The Blesser surely returning

VII Pisces
The Blessings in Abeyance
1. The Band: The great enemy
2. Andromeda: The redeemed in bondage
3. Cepheus: The Deliverer coming to loosen

VIII Aries
The Blessing Consummated
1. Cassiopeia: The captive delivered
2. Cetus: The great enemy bound
3. Perseus: The Breaker delivering

IX Taurus
Messiah Coming to Rule
1. Orion: The Redeemer breaking forth as Light
2. Eridanus: Wrath breaking forth as a flood
3. Auriga: Safety for His redeemed in the day of wrath

X Gemini
Messiah as Prince of Princes
1. Lepus: The enemy trodden underfoot
2. Canis Major: The coming glorious Prince
3. Canis Minor: The exalted Redeemer

XI Cancer
The Messiah's Redeemed Possessions
1. Ursa Minor: The lesser sheepfold
2. Ursa Major: The fold and the flock
3. Argo: The pilgrim's arrival home

XII Leo
The Prophecy of Triumph Fulfilled
1. Hydra: The old serpent destroyed
2. Crater: The cup of wrath poured out
3. Corvus: The birds of prey devouring

Thus end the Scriptures of the Heavens.
   At the beginning of this chapter, we quoted Psalm 19:1-6. Listen
again to the first four verses:

The heavens declare the glory of God;
and the firmament sheweth his handiwork.
Day unto day uttereth speech,
And night unto night sheweth knowledge.
There is no speech nor language,
Where their voice is not heard.
Their line is gone out through all the Earth
and their words to the end of the world.

The 36 constellations contain the Scriptures of the Heavens. This is the story they tell. This is the "speech" they "utter." This is the "knowledge" they "show forth." There is no articulate speech or voice and no words are heard; but their sayings have gone out into all the world.[45]

Conclusion:

From the very first mention of the stars in the first chapter of Genesis we are told that not only are they for light, but also as signs which would mark out something or someone to come. We have learned that this knowledge of the stars would have been passed down through the generations in the oral tradition. For the most part, this knowledge had been lost, as it was no longer needed due to the advent of the written word. We also learned that other spiritual beings are aware of this astronomical knowledge, as matters stellar are their heritage. Thus many of the pyramids and other monuments bear astronomical information and details which would be outside the realm of all but the initiates. We conclude this section with a quote from I Corinthians 15:39-41.

> **All flesh is not the same flesh: but there is one kind of flesh of men, another flesh of beasts, another of fishes, and another of birds.**
> **There are also celestial bodies and bodies terrestrial; but the glory of the celestial is one and the glory of the terrestrial is another.**
> **There is one glory of the sun, and another glory of the moon, and another glory of the stars: for one star differs from another star in glory.**

Today, we refer to famous actors, sports personalities and other celebrities as "stars." But other famous men, the stars and heroes of old, walked this earth in the dim distant past five and a half thousand years ago. It is to these we now turn our attention.

THE ANTEDELUVIAN AVATARS

We are now ready to consider the presence of the Nephilim on the Earth, prior to the Flood of Noah, and their effect on it. Very little information is provided in the texts, but I believe we can piece together the details provided through arcane sources and, along with the evidence left for us in hieroglyphs and other written records, we can reach an acceptable conclusion. Consider the following mathematical problem:

$$2 + 2 + 2 + ? = 8$$

By analysing the information to hand, we can fill in the blanks in a reasonable fashion and find the correct answer. But we must return to the original passage in Genesis 6 once more to begin this analysis.

> When men began to increase in number on the Earth and daughters were born to them, the sons of God saw the daughters of men were beautiful, and they married any of them they chose.
> Then the Lord said: "My spirit will not contend with man forever, for he is mortal; his days will be a hundred and twenty years."
> The *Nephilim* were on the Earth in those days and also afterwards, when the sons of God went in to the daughters of men and had children by them. They were the heroes of old, men of renown.
> The Lord saw how great man's wickedness on the Earth had become and that every inclination of the thoughts of his heart was only evil all of the time.
>
> *Genesis 6:1-5*

Because the Lord was grieved that he had made man, he decided to destroy all living things:

> "I will wipe mankind, whom I have created, from the face of the Earth: men and animals and creatures that move along the ground, and birds of the air, for I am grieved that I have made them."
> Now the Earth was corrupt in God's sight and full of violence. God saw how corrupt the Earth had become, for all the people on Earth had corrupted their ways.
>
> *Genesis 6:7,11*

What could man have done that was so bad that it would require Yaweh to totally obliterate all living creatures? Let us consider each verse and see if we can tease out the clues.

The "sons of God" married any of the daughters of men they chose. "Sons of God" in Hebrew is Beni-ha-Elohim. The word ben in Hebrew means "son." So Beni-ha-Elohim are the sons of Elohim (God). We have already concluded from a previous chapter that these "sons of God" are created spirit beings known to us as angels. These spirit-men were part of a band of angels which rebelled against Yaweh and became evil in their intent. It is said that they "married any of them they chose," the inference in the text being that these spirit beings were so powerful that the daughters of men could not resist them. Therefore they married any whom they chose. Again this phrase suggests more than one wife and probably very many.[46]

Now it would appear that there is a problem here in understanding how spirit beings can have intercourse with ordinary human women and produce children as a result? We are informed in Genesis chapter one that Yaweh created all manner of plants and trees, animals and fish, and they were all to produce seed "after their own kind." And, left alone in nature, animals and trees etc will automatically produce offspring after their own kind. Does this mean that the genetics of plants and animals cannot be interfered with to produce genetically-modified aberrations? No, it merely states that if you leave nature alone, it will produce seed after its kind.

So when the evil fallen spirit-men made the daughters of men pregnant, they may have done so by means of genetic engineering.

Is there any precedent for this in the old Hebrew texts? I believe that there is. Look at Genesis 3:17, where the context is Yaweh confronting Adam after the Fall:

"Cursed is the ground because of you:
Through painful toil you will eat of it all the days of your life.
It will provide thorns and thistles for you and you will eat the plants of the field."

Genesis 3:17,18

When Yaweh made Paradise, there was only perfection. Adam and Eve lived in a veritable Garden of Eden. No thistles, no mosquitos, no noxious plants or poisonous insects or snakes. The lion ate grass like the ox. But all that changed after the Fall. Because of the influence of the serpent, the Earth became cursed. Satan and his host of evil spirit beings changed Paradise into a hostile environment. Thorns grew on bushes which had none before.

Man now had to toil and sweat to eat. And all the time be bitten by insects or be on guard against other animals or creatures which could inflict harm.

We know that only good can come from the creator, Yaweh. Therefore the change in the environment had to be a result of the interference in the genetics of the whole universe by Satan and his entourage. Remember, we are dealing with a powerful foe. One who was so full of wisdom and knowledge that he thought himself to be on equal terms with the Most High, Yaweh.

But why would Satan want to produce such a race of evil people and have them populate the Earth? Remember the first promise and prophecy of the Messiah? When Yaweh pronounced that the seed of the woman would crush the head of the serpent?

Well, put yourself in Satan's shoes. Here the Most High is telling him that the lineage of the woman, Eve, will produce the offspring which will ultimately destroy him. So what is he going to do in order to thwart this plan? Well, the obvious thing to do is to kill off the line so that the seed cannot be born and the sentence can be averted. Satan begins to destroy the lineage when he has Cain murder his own brother, Abel. But this does not prevent the line continuing, since Adam and Eve produced many more children. So Satan decides to populate the world with his own seed and corrupt the Earth to such a degree that the line of Adam and Eve is wiped out completely. Thus the seed of the woman is extinguished and Satan preserves his own existence.

So Lucifer has some of his own band procreate with women and produce children. But these are no ordinary children. They are the offspring of superhuman and supernatural beings, half-human, half-demon, whose only intent is evil.

We are told that these *Nephilim* were on the Earth "in those days," i.e. the days of Noah. Now Noah was six hundred years old when the Flood finally came in the year 2348 BC (see Appendix). This means that the *Nephilim* were multiplying and living for at least six hundred years prior to the deluge taking place. So these genetically-engineered people were inhabiting the then known world only 1,000 years or so after Adam. We must realise that these *Nephilim* were totally evil. They were a hybrid of demons and men. They were evil and wicked by nature and could not be rehabilitated and made good, for the evil was in their genes. They were so corrupt and wicked that they had almost totally infected the whole human race at that time.

So what heinous crime could they have committed which would cause Yaweh to regret that he had made man and decide to destroy all living flesh on the face of the Earth with the exception of eight individuals? And, secondly, who were these people who so corrupted the ancient world? We

The Nephilim and the Pyramid of the Apocalypse

will now endeavour to answer these two important questions. Firstly, who were these *Nephilim* of old? Look again at verse four of Genesis six:

> The *Nephilim* were on the Earth in those days (the days of Noah) and also afterwards (after the Flood) when the sons of God went in to the daughters of men and had children by them. <u>They were the heroes of old, men of renown</u>.
>
> *(New International Version)*

The above verse contains all the detail we are given concerning these "heroes of old." But this passage is pregnant with information.

We are told that the *Nephilim* were the "heroes of old, the men of renown." In the Hebrew, "renown" means "the men of name," i.e. those men who got a name and were renowned as heroes. And what was the extent of their sin?

> The Lord saw how great man's wickedness on the Earth had become, and that every inclination of the thoughts of his heart was only evil all the time.
> Now the Earth was corrupt (Hebrew *shachath:* destroyed) in God's sight and full of violence.
> God saw how corrupt the Earth had become, for all the people on Earth had corrupted their ways.
>
> *Genesis 6:5,11,12*

Things must have been extremely bad when we are told that "every inclination of the thoughts of man's heart was only evil all the time," and that the whole Earth was full of violence. We go now to the New Testament, which sheds a little more light on the background to this situation. Speaking of the fallen angels, Jude 6 tells us:

> And the angels which kept not their first estate, but left their own habitation, He has reserved in darkness, bound with everlasting chains for judgment on the great day.
> In a similar way, Sodom and Gomorrah and the surrounding towns gave themselves over to sexual immorality and perversion...
>
> *Jude 6,7*

In the above verse we are told that these evil angels left their own habitation. In the Greek, this word is *oiketerion*, and it is used only here and in II Corinthians 5:2, where it refers to the "spiritual body." So these angels left their spirit body and came into physical form in order to produce the *Nephilim*, who were superhuman in size and in wickedness and evil. So heinous were their crimes that not only did Yaweh destroy all living creatures on the face of the Earth, but also the millions of people who had become totally evil and morally bankrupt as a result of the activities of the *Nephilim*. Their sin is likened to the perversion and sexual immorality of Sodom and Gomorrah and the surrounding towns.

The sin which these fallen spirit beings committed in debauching virtually the whole of the then known world was so vile that it precipitated the Flood. This worldwide deluge is well documented in the historical annals of most of the known ancient world. It destroyed all breathing things except for the eight souls preserved through the Flood and the animals Noah was instructed to bring along. But water cannot kill spirit beings. When we are told that these angels left their own spirit sphere, the inference is that they could not return there. So Yaweh, because of their sin, cast them into a place called *Tartarus*, there to await future judgment.

But was their crime merely excessive sexual immorality and worldwide violence or was there something more? I believe that there was something more. This theory is not spelt out in black and white in any of the Scriptures. But by examining the ancient written records pertaining to the period before the Flood, and even afterwards, I believe we can construct a good argument.

As was mentioned in an earlier chapter, it would appear that these spirit beings were involved in some form of genetic engineering. We observed how two of the Israeli spies carried one cluster of grapes between them on a pole from the land inhabited by the *Nephilim* in the days of Moses. Later, we encountered Goliath the Gittite, who had six fingers on each hand and six toes on each foot. In this chapter we considered how all the Earth was changed after the fall of man. Noxious plants and poisonous insects and other creatures appeared which were never part of the original Eden. Evil influences must have interfered with the DNA of all these plants, animals, insects etc to cause them to change and become as they are today. Consequently, when the fallen angels married the daughters of men, perhaps it was genetic engineering which was utilised to impregnate the women and produce the monstrous evil aberrations called the *Nephilim*. These in turn produced offspring who were genetically-engineered supernatural and superhuman evil monsters. Over the course of several hundred years, while the Ark was being prepared, these people contaminated the whole world with their immorality, perversion and violence. And only eight souls preserved their true nature and were saved: Noah and his family.

Let us take this a step further. If we examine many of the ancient writings and pictures, we see some peculiar images appearing in many of the countries surrounding the area where mankind dwelt during that time. We see pictures of beings who are half-human and half-animal. We see pictures of centaurs, who had the upper body of a man and the lower body of a horse. We have statues called sphinxes which show a man's or woman's head attached to the body of a lion (see **Figure 6**). In yet more reliefs we see other strange animals which appear to have human appendages (see **Figure 7**) as well as four-footed animals with men's heads and birds with the head of a man.

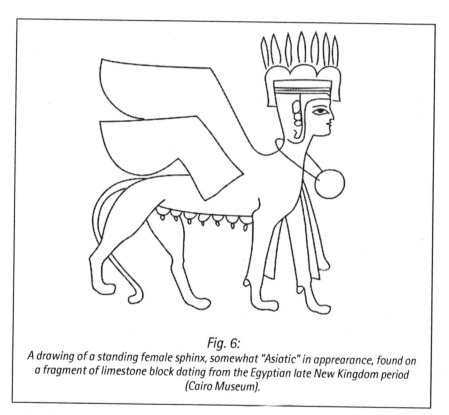

Fig. 6:
A drawing of a standing female sphinx, somewhat "Asiatic" in apprearance, found on a fragment of limestone block dating from the Egyptian late New Kingdom period (Cairo Museum).

An Egyptian historian named Manethos chronicled these times and wrote extensively on the legends of his country. He describes just such half-human, half-animal creatures and credits the gods with their creation. He wrote:

"And they [the gods] were said to have brought forth double-winged human beings, also others with four wings and two faces; and with one

Fig. 7:
A creature mostly animal in appearance but possessing some human features. Relief on a black obelisk dedicated to the Assyrian king Salamasar III (British Museam).

body and two heads, man and woman, male and female within one creature; still other human beings had thighs of goats and horns upon their heads; others had the feet of horses; others were horses behind and men in front; there were also said to have been man-headed bulls and four-bodied dogs, whose tails emerged like fish-tails from their backs; also horses with heads of dogs ... and other monsters, such as all kinds of dragon-like beings ... and a great number of wondrous creatures, variously formed and all different from one another, whose images they ranged one beside the other in the Temple of Belos, and preserved."[47]

Could all these be just myth or is there more to this than meets the eye? Many of these reliefs depict similar strange creatures, yet they are found in different regions such as Greece, Assyria, Italy and Egypt. Let us again look at the verse in Jude, this time taken from the King James Version. Speaking of these fallen angels and the activities of the people in Sodom and Gomorrah and those prior to the Flood, we read:

> ... in like manner giving themselves over to fornication and going after strange flesh ...

The word "*strange*" here is *heteros* in the Greek, which means "*another of a different kind, usually denoting generic distinction.*"[48]

By the way, the word "*fornication*" here is *ekporneuo*, which is the intensive form of *porneuo*, from which we derive our English word "pornography." So intensive, extreme pornography is what they were involved in. The sin of these people was an unnatural one, breaking through the natural bounds which Yaweh had set. Could this mean cross-breeding between man and animals, or humans breeding with birds etc?

In reading Genesis six one is struck by the way Yaweh pronounces judgment not only against mankind, but against the animals and other creatures as well. Observe:

> "I will wipe mankind, whom I have created, from the face of the Earth, men and animals, and creatures that move along the ground and birds of the air ..."

One can understand why such a judgment is passed upon human beings, for they have minds and can reason. But why destroy the poor dumb animals, who are blameless? Or is there more to this? Let us consider a passage from the Book of Romans.

> For since the creation of the world God's invisible qualities – His

eternal power and divine nature – have been clearly seen, being understood from what has been made, so that men are without excuse.

For although they knew (Greek: *ginosko: to know by experience*) God, they neither glorified Him as God nor gave thanks to Him, but their thinking became futile and their foolish hearts were darkened.

Although they claimed to be wise, they became fools, and exchanged the glory of the immortal God for images made to look like mortal man and birds and animals and reptiles.

Therefore God gave them over in the sinful desires of their hearts to sexual impurity for degrading of their bodies with one another.

They exchanged the truth of God for a lie, and worshipped and served created things rather than the creator.

Romans 1: 20-25

The context of this verse is the "*creation of the world.*" Well, the only ones who have been around since the creation of the world are the "sons of God," who "shouted for joy," and the "morning stars," who sang together when Yaweh laid the foundations of the world. Next, we are told that they knew God. This word in the Greek is *ginosko,* meaning to know by (personal) experience.

Furthermore, we are told that these "people" changed the glory of the immortal God to images made to look like – wait for it – *mortal man, birds, animals and reptiles!* This is the exact same phrase we just read in Genesis six, where Yaweh is quoted as saying that he would destroy *men and animals, and creatures that move along the ground, and birds of the air!*

Could it be that this passage is referring to the fallen angels of the time of Noah and to their immoral and indecent behaviour? Not only were they morally depraved, but they interfered genetically with animals and birds and reptiles and changed them into objects of worship. Is this why so many of the reliefs, pictures and hieroglyphs depict animals, birds and reptiles as being half-human, half-animal? I cannot categorically state that this is exactly how it was. I am presenting the evidence as I find it and I encourage readers to reach their own conclusions. If this was the case, it would be highly understandable that Yaweh would pronounce judgment against the *Nephilim* and their offspring and mankind in general by way of the Flood. Furthermore, we can understand why it was necessary to imprison the fallen angels who perpetrated these heinous sins, and to contain them in *Tartarus,* awaiting a day of judgment.

Now let us address the other great question posed at the beginning of this chapter. Who exactly were those "**mighty men of old, who were renowned and got the name of heroes**"?

Many scientists, historians and academics now believe that much of what is called "mythology" has its basis and foundation in facts. The writings we have from Greek and Roman mythology as well as the extensive texts from Egypt, as in the "Book of the Dead," and the Babylonian "Creation Tablets" and other cosmogonies, provide us with reliable records.

Do any of these writings describe a situation where the gods came down from heaven, took women as wives and produced sons and daughters who were to reign in their stead? Of course they do. In fact, all the legends and memories of these mythologies were no mere invention of the human brain. Most of these stories and traditions grew and evolved from the real doings of these "**mighty men of renown, the heroes of old**" of Genesis six. Furthermore, all these stories and legends, from Greek, Roman and Egyptian mythology and, indeed, Vishnu and others, are corrupt versions of primitive truths which have been distorted as they passed from generation to generation, the memory of the original meaning being gradually lost as they did so.

Can we name any of these "gods" or "heroes" and do we know anything of their origin? Insofar as there is information at our disposal, we have a surfeit of details. Let us begin with the gods of Greece, who are the same entities as appear very often in Roman history. Please note in their various names the association with celestial and astronomical bodies, considering at the same time the background of the original "morning star" and the other "stars of God."

The major Olympians (for such is the name given to the ancient gods) are very often the same entities but with differing names in Greek and Roman legend. They are as follows:

Apollo (*star*)	Aphrodite
Ares (Aries: *star*)	Artemis
Dionysus	Athena
Hades	Demeter
Hermes	Hera
Poseidon (Neptune: *planet*)	Janus
Oedipus	Juno
Zeus	Jason
Jupiter (*planet*)	Prometheus
Atlas	Romulus
Charon	Remus
Cronos	Saturn (*planet*)

Deucalion	Selene
Heracles (*star*)	Eos
Icarus	Uranus (*planet*)
Vulcan	Pluto (*planet*)
Mars (*planet*)	Mercury (*planet*)
Orion (*star*)	Orpheus
Pegasus (*star*)	Perseus (*star*)
Centaurus (*star*)	Andromeda (*star*)

There are many more gods and I shall not delve into the stories which detail their adventures.

Mount Olympus was the ancient site where many of the gods lived. The most ancient of these gods are known as Titans, who were reputed to be the children of heaven and earth. These are defined as a race of gigantic primeval gods who were of great physical and mental strength.

Apollo was the son of Zeus and Leto, who was a daughter of the Titans, her parents being Phoebe and Coeus. Apollo was the god of medicine, music and prophecy and Delphi in Greece is the site of his shrine and oracle.

There was a city of Macedonia called Apollonia, meaning "Place of Apollo," which is situated about 35 miles from Thessaloniki. Interestingly, there is a passage in the Book of Revelation describing a "star" (angel) having the key to the "bottomless pit." On opening this pit, a great cloud of "locusts" of fearful appearance ascended. Then we are told that these locusts have a king reigning over them whose name in the Hebrew is Abaddon and, in the Greek, Apollyon. Could this be one of the original *Nephilim*, thrust down into *Tartarus* for causing the heinous crimes which precipitated the Flood? We shall return to this later. Incidentally, the meaning of both Abaddon and Apollyon is "Destroyer."

Paneas is another site which still exists. It was later called Caesarea , but in ancient times it was a shrine to the god Pan. This god was half-human, having the legs and horns of a goat, and he spent his time pursuing and fornicating with women (nymphs). Often his drunken orgies would turn into bloodshed, as he was prone to suddenly become violent. Thus we get the word "panic" from this particular demi-god. This sanctuary to Pan was also called Baalgad and it is close to Mount Hermon on the border of Lebanon and Syria where, according to the Book of Enoch, the original fallen angels landed after descending from heaven.

Huge palaces were constructed in the era of these gods at many sites around the then known world and the descendants of the people of these regions believed that these had been built by the Cyclopes, a race of giants known as Cyclopeans. Some of the earliest fortifications are said to have been built by Perseus, the legendary founder of Mycenae. These Cyclopes were sons to Uranus and Gaia: Brontes (meaning thunderer), Steropes (lightener) and Arges (bright). These savage one-eyed monsters were identified with the island of the cyclops (Sicily).

As was mentioned earlier, historians and scientists now admit that many legends and so-called mythologies have their basis in ancient truths. We have learned from Genesis that the whole world was filled with violence and immorality and that "**every inclination of the thoughts of his (man's) heart was only evil all the time**" *(Genesis 6:5)*.

Based on the evidence of the impressive temples and other advanced buildings of these ancient times, and considering the many written accounts of the identity of the gods and their exploits, it takes only a small step to identify these people with the *Nephilim* of Genesis six. For in the Greek and Roman legends we have the gods coming down to Earth, taking mortal women as wives, and bearing many children who were demi-gods, half-human, half-divine. Even if only some of the stories about these gods and their offspring are true, then we have a most bloodthirsty lot. For throughout the legends concerning these people we have debauchery, infanticide, matricide, patricide, rape, murder, adultery, incest, treachery and even cannibalism. You name it, they did it. This fits in exactly with the Genesis record, which tells us that the entire world was filled with violence.

Human sacrifice was a significant feature of these times both before and after the Flood of Noah. One god was called Moloch. His image was of a creature who had a fire burning in his lap as he sat upright with hands extended (see **Figure 8**). Young babies and infants were burned in this fire to appease the god and ensure grace and favour. Grossly immoral behaviour, including bestiality, drunkenness and orgies, was normal and, as with any such liberal behaviour, murder and violence followed. If we take these primeval stories at their face value, they fit right in with the picture painted in Genesis six, where the *Nephilim* reigned:

"**These were the heroes of old, men of renown.**"

(NIV)

Apart from the fact that these gods bore the names of stars and planets, also remember that the *Nephilim* and their offspring were exceedingly depraved and wicked and could be no other way, since this was their genetic make-up and nature. They so infected the entirety of the people with their sin and behaviour that all of mankind had to be destroyed, for they were beyond redemption. Only eight souls – Noah and his family – were saved.

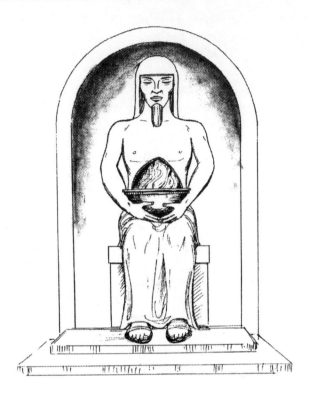

Fig. 8:

An artist's impression of Moloch. This deity was often represented as a horrible idol from whom flames came forth to consume whatever offerings or sacrifices were placed in his arms. Babies and young children were frequently sacrificed to Moloch.

The prime *raison d'être* of the chief archangel, Lucifer, was to kill all people so that the line of the seed of the woman could not survive and hence Yaweh's prophecy could not be fulfilled. By filling the world with the *Nephilim* and their wanton brood, Satan almost succeeded. But the line of the promised Messiah, the seed of the woman, was maintained through Noah, and the nefarious plan of Lucifer came to nought.

The fallen angels, these sons of God, who infiltrated the people of the Earth and who were the gods of old, the heroes and men of renown, are all now kept in *Tartarus*, awaiting a future judgment day. And I shall now show you something quite amazing concerning these same fallen angels, the gods and heroes of old.

TARTARUS AND THE UNDERWORLD

Such was the extent of the violence and immorality being practised by practically all the population of the entire world that Yaweh had to destroy it. So all the living, breathing things were drowned in the Flood of Noah. But the original fallen angels are not mere flesh and blood and cannot be drowned as ordinary people can. So Yaweh had to detain these spirit-men in a place from whence they could not escape. We are told of these beings in just three verses in the latter end of the New Testament. First in the Epistle of Peter. Speaking of the risen Messiah, he tells us:

> He was put to death in the body but made alive by the spirit, through whom also he went and preached (Greek: *kerusso)* to the spirits in prison who disobeyed long ago when God waited patiently in the days of Noah while the Ark was being built.
>
> *1 Peter 3:18,19*

The Greek word for "preached" here is *kerusso,* which means "to herald." This is a phenomenal revelation. We are told here that the risen Messiah, in his new spiritual body, went to this prison where these fallen spirit beings are kept and heralded or announced his triumph to these evil spirits.

In essence, we might assume that he appeared triumphantly to these evil spirit-men and said to them, in our present-day vernacular, something like: "Here I am boys. All your plans have failed and have come to nothing. I am risen from the dead and, in short, your number is up and you're history ... I'll be back!"

This passage states that these spirits are those who "disobeycd" in the days prior to the Flood and that, as a result of their sin, they are held in this place awaiting a future judgment. In the second Epistle of Peter we are given some further details:

> If God did not spare the angels that sinned, but cast them down to hell (Greek: *Tartarus),* putting them into gloomy dungeons to be held for judgment.

73

> **If he did not spare the ancient world when he brought the flood on its ungodly people, but protected Noah, a preacher of righteousness, and seven others ...**
>
> *II Peter 2:4,5*

This tells us that these angels who committed the sin which precipitated the Flood are *"thrust down to Tartarus."* What makes this interesting is the fact that the word *"Tartarus"* is used only once in the entire New Testament. The only other place it is found is in Greek mythology. The *Tartarus* described by Homer is the subterranean prison of the Titans or giants, who rebelled against Zeus. In a similar way, Egyptian writings speak of the *"Underworld."* Could it be that these ancient "mythologies" are describing the place where the *Nephilim,* the fallen evil angels who perpetrated all the violence and heinous crimes in the days of Noah, are kept?

Jude 6 gives another mention of this particular band of fallen angels:

> **And the angels who did not keep their positions of authority, but abandoned their own home – these He has kept in darkness, bound with everlasting chains for judgment on the great day.**
>
> *Jude 6*

Without delving too much into the Greek text, the above phrase *"They ... did not keep their positions of authority but abandoned their own home ..."* means that they left their spiritual realm and became manifested in the realm of the earthly. The inference is that, having abandoned their spiritual state, they could no longer go back there and were permanently obliged to remain on this Earth. But, because they are not flesh and blood but are celestial beings (even though they are in physical form and can be seen), they do not die as mortals and therefore have to be imprisoned in these gloomy dungeons known as *Tartarus.*

Now I would like to change tack slightly and introduce another idea.

In the Gospel of Mark, chapter five, we have an account of a meeting between the Messiah and a man who was possessed by many demons. This man was wild. If they bound him with chains or ropes, he would break them asunder. He lived in the tombs and would cry aloud and cut himself with stones. When he was confronted by the Messiah, the evil spirit speaking through the man said that his name "was legion ... for we are many." And they begged the Messiah not to cast them into the "Abyss." (By the way, there are about 6,000 men in a Roman legion).

The Greek for "Abyss" is *abussos* and it is sometimes rendered "The Deep" and sometimes "Bottomless Pit." But before looking at this passage, let us briefly recap some of the points already made.

We are told that these fallen angels of old were called the *Nephilim*, the "fallen ones." These beings and their offspring inhabited this world both before and after the Flood of Noah. We are told that, in ancient days, these were the men of renown, the heroes of old, the mighty men who had made a reputation for themselves. Putting this information together with the ancient Greek and Roman mythologies, we can hazard that the gods of old were actually these *Nephilim* and their offspring. And that these old myths actually have their foundation in primitive truths which have changed into legends that have been passed down to us today.

We have also named many of these gods, illustrating that, just as they are known in the Hebrew texts as "stars" and "angels" alike, so they have been given the names of actual stars and planets, which star names date back to antiquity. So these *Nephilim* go by such names as *Apollo, Hercules, Orion, Pegasus, Perseus* and planets such as *Mars, Jupiter, Mercury, Saturn, Neptune, Pluto, Uranus* etc. Only about a hundred of these ancient star names are known to us today. However, I would not be surprised if all the other so-called gods of Greece and Rome were not also the actual names of stars now long lost or forgotten.

It has been established that these fallen spirit beings which came to Earth and corrupted the whole of mankind are now imprisoned in a place called *Tartarus*. We have also noted how the risen Messiah went and visited these evil beings in their present prison and proclaimed his triumph to them. Now let us jump forward into the future, to the middle of the events described in the Apocalypse, the Book of Revelation:

> **The fifth angel sounded his trumpet, and I saw a star (*angel*) that had fallen from the sky to Earth. The star was given the key to the shaft of the Abyss.**
> **When he (*the star or angel*) opened the Abyss, smoke arose from it like the smoke of a gigantic furnace. The sun and sky were darkened by the smoke from the Abyss.**
>
> *Book of Revelation 9:1,2*

Notice once again that an angel is here referred to as a "star." This angel, on opening the *Abyss*, lets loose smoke similar to that of a huge furnace. The passage goes on to describe "*locusts*" which also emerge from the *Abyss*. These locusts are given power to torture people like scorpions but not to kill them. The agony suffered by those stricken by these locusts is like that of the sting of the scorpion when it strikes a human. But now comes a very interesting vignette. We are told regarding these locusts:

They had a king over them, the angel of the Abyss, whose name in Hebrew is *Abaddon*, and in Greek *Apollyon*.

Book of Revelation 9:1,2,11

The meaning of both *Abaddon* and *Apollyon* in English is *The Destroyer*.

Could it be that the *Abyss*, also called the Bottomless Pit or the Pit of the Abyss, is that same place called *Tartarus* in the Epistle of Peter? Could it be that this is the present abode of the evil angels who inhabited the world before the Flood? And is there not a distinct etymological similarity between the Greek god of old called *Apollo* and the angel here described as being the king reigning over the locusts of the Abyss whose name in Greek is *Apollyon?*

I am not saying that the above conjecture is the definitive truth. But, by putting together all the pieces of the jigsaw based on the Scriptures, Greek and Roman mythology plus the other pieces of information we have examined, it would appear that the *Apollo* of old is one of the chief *Nephilim* who sinned in the days of Noah and was thrust down to *Tartarus* for his offence. And that this same evil spirit-man is none other than *Apollyon*, the king reigning over the "locusts" which are to emerge, in the future, from the *Abyss*, the Bottomless Pit, to bring agony and destruction to the people of the Earth.

In the latter half of this book we shall delve into the events of the Apocalypse more closely. But for now I believe that this passage is pertinent to the context we have been pursing thus far.

If this surmising proves to be the truth, then it verifies that the gods of old, the gods of Greece and Rome, were indeed the *Nephilim* and their offspring, and that these men are now held in *Tartarus*, the underworld of myth and the Bottomless Pit or *Abyss* of the Scriptures, awaiting a future day of judgment. Furthermore, in the passage quoted from Revelation chapter nine, it is stated that the angel who was given the key to open the Pit of the Abyss had fallen from heaven to Earth. This would suggest that the *Abyss* or *Tartarus* out of which *Apollyon* and the "locusts" arise is on this Earth. This would tie in with those mythologies which speak of a subterranean underworld. *Hades*, a brother to *Zeus* who was married to *Persephone*, was the keeper of the nether world, the abode of the dead. In Roman mythology, he is called *Pluto*. In Egypt, the god who was the ruler and judge of the underworld is *Osiris*, who was the brother and consort of *Isis*.

In an earlier chapter, a list of the 12 signs of the Zodiac and the 36 constellations was given. The Hebrew and Arabic names of these and the principal stars contained in them provide much information. In the context of this chapter it is most interesting that in the sign of *Gemini*, which means "the twins," the two principal stars are of the same magnitude. They are named in Greek as *Apollo* and *Hercules* and the Latins called them *Castor* and *Pollux* (which was the name of a boat Paul sailed in from Malta after being shipwrecked there: Book of Acts 28:11).

Apollo and *Hercules* were the twin sons of *Jupiter (Zeus)* and *Leda*, although some hold that *Artemis* (or *Diana*) was the twin sister of *Apollo*. *Artemis* is the Greek goddess of sex and fertility. She was *Diana* to the Romans. *Artemis* and *Diana* are both identified as *Ashtaroth*, who was a goddess and idol of the *Phoenicians, Philistines* and *Zidonians*. These peoples fashioned trees and bushes in the shape of female genitalia for worship purposes.

However, the main point here is that one of the two brightest stars in the sign of *Gemini* is named *Apollo*, which means "ruler" or "judge." (In Revelation 9, *Apollyon* is the king [ruler] of the "Locusts"). This again gives credence to our thesis that the original "fallen ones," the rebel angels, were named after stars and kept these names with their arrival on Earth. These names survived through the myths and legends of yore and we recognise them here as being the **"mighty men of renown, the heroes of old who got themselves a name,"** the *Nephilim*. Also note that the other brightest star in Gemini is *Hercules*, who is twinned with *Apollo*. These two stars (angels) fell to Earth and are two of the principal gods of early prehistory.

Incidentally, we know that, in a secluded glade overlooked by Mount Parnassus about 10 kilometres from the Gulf of Corinth, lies *Delphi*. This was the most important sanctuary of *Apollo* and included his temple, theatre and treasures. At *Delphi*, the oracle of Apollo was consulted. It was discovered in 1890.[49] What is intriguing is the fact that *Delphinus* is a constellation in the star sign *Capricornus*, which is in the Northern Hemisphere near to *Pegasus* and *Aquila*. This is further proof of the astronomical knowledge and association of the *Nephilim* with the celestial bodies and their movements, as *Delphi* obviously derives its name from the constellation of *Delphinus*.

Now, riddle me this. Earlier in this chapter we examined passages in both the first and second Epistles of Peter and one in Jude six concerning the angels or spirit beings who are kept in a gloomy prison called *Tartarus*, awaiting a future judgment. We were told that the risen Messiah, in his new spiritual body, went and "heralded his triumph" before these evil demonic men. I Peter 3:19 identifies these spirit beings or angels as being those who sinned in the days of Noah. In other words, it specifically states that the Messiah appeared to these spirit beings, the *Nephilim*, who had brought about all the chaos prior to the Flood. Now here is the conundrum. If the spirit beings who were responsible for the first irruption on the Earth are held in this prison called *Tartarus,* then where are the fallen angels who caused the second irruption some time after the Flood?

A careful study of the three short passages reveals that the angels who sinned are kept in this prison. But these texts only specifically identify the Messiah as visiting those fallen ones who were responsible for all the violence and evil on the Earth prior to the Flood. So this begs another question: where are the *Nephilim* who materialised after the Flood and proceeded to multiply and fill up the land of Canaan for several centuries from the time of Abraham, circa 1912 BC, to the time of David, almost 1,000 years later?

It could be that it was the same "sons of God" who caused both the first irruption prior to the Flood and the second irruption sometime afterwards. This seems both illogical and implausible, since the spirits who were active before the Flood were cast into prison for their sins. But if a second band of these spirit beings, having once left their original spiritual abode and having materialised in the realm of the senses, cannot return, then this must mean, if our deductions are accurate, that this same band of *Nephilim* are still wandering or in hiding somewhere in our world today!

I would again like to emphasise that this is mere conjecture on my part. But it might explain how some of the pyramids in distant lands appear to be relatively recent compared to the pyramids of ancient Egypt and other such buildings and temples which populate the region surrounding the Mediterranean Sea. The pyramids of Mexico and Guatemala and the temples of Angkor Wat, if we are to believe our historians, were all built after the time of the birth of Christ. In fact, we are told that some of these buildings, (i.e. Angkor Wat),may have been inhabited by their builders as recently as just a few hundred years ago.[50]

Could it be that these *Nephilim,* who caused the irruption with humans after the Flood, are now on the run? Is this why their trail begins in Canaan and the Middle East and then spreads out to distant lands such as Peru, Bolivia, Guatemala, Mexico and on to Cambodia?

We have no reason to believe that these avatars did not travel far and wide even in the pre-Flood era. For we have ample evidence for this in the buildings they left at Stonehenge, for instance, as well as neolithic buildings in Ireland such as Newgrange. This also accounts for the many other strange constructions, such as the giant statues on Easter Island. It also explains why many similarities in construction can be seen between the monuments in Egypt and those in Guatemala, Peru and Mexico.

For instance, the builders of the temples of Egypt hewed out dovetails at both ends of the large blocks which were to be fitted together. Into these dovetails would be poured molten bronze or iron in order to "copperfasten" the two blocks together (see **Figure 9**). Yet the dovetails used in the temples of Egypt are similar to those used in the huge edifices located high in the Andes at Tiahuanaco. These metal clamps are also employed in a similar fashion at Angkor Wat in Cambodia. This would suggest that the same builders were involved at all these differing sites even though they are thousands of miles and thousands of years apart.

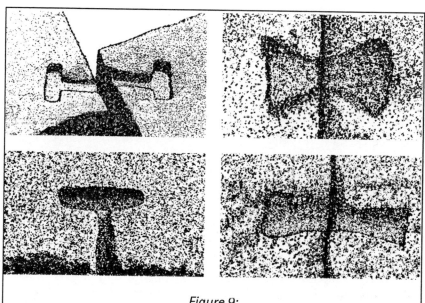

Figure 9:
Imprint of metal clamps used by the builders of the ancient world to join gigantic blocks together. Clockwise from top left: Puma Punku, Tihuanaco, Bolivia; Angkor Wat, Cambodia; Dendera, Egypt; Ollantaytambo, Peru.

We are familiar with the tales of the travels of Jason and his Argonauts. Argo happens to be the third constellation in the sign of Cancer. Argo means "the ship." In legend, Jason encountered many adventures on his journeying in search of the elusive Golden Fleece. His Argonauts take their name from the constellation Argo, which provides more evidence of the connection of the ancient gods with the stars and their signs. It also tells us that these ancient travellers journeyed far and wide, probably using the celestial bodies to chart their courses. Because these men were supernatural in intelligence, it is more than feasible that they travelled extensively both before the Flood and after it.

Conclusion:

Because of the nature and seriousness of their crimes in the days of Noah, the *Nephilim* are imprisoned in an earthly abyss known as *Tartarus*. This may be the same location that is referred to in Roman, Greek and Egyptian mythology when these peoples speak of the *"underworld"* and *"Hades"* and the *"abode of the dead."*

The risen Messiah visited these spirit prisoners in their place of detention. We are told that those he visited were responsible for the irruption with humans which precipitated the deluge. Because the Scriptures only mention these pre-Flood fallen beings, we can deduce that the angels responsible for the second irruption, after the Flood, may still be at large. This would explain some of the edifices in question in the Americas and in Cambodia which were built much more recently.

One of the main rulers of the pantheon of the early antedeluvian avatars in Greek legend is named *Apollo*. In the midst of the coming Apocalypse, the Pit of the Abyss is opened and an infernal horde of spirit beings emerge. This band has a ruler and king over them whose name in Hebrew is *Abaddon* and in Greek *Apollyon*. There is a clear etymological connection between the Greek god of yore, *Apollo*, and this future destroyer who is to be released from the Abyss in the Apocalypse, *Apollyon*. (Incidentally, Apollo in French is *Apollon!*).

This would prove that the gods of old, the heroes of legend, were indeed the *Nephilim* and their offspring. These are the "stars" who fell from heaven and contaminated the purity of the whole human race to such a degree that they had to be completely destroyed.

Further astounding and conclusive evidence will be provided in the chapter on the Book of Enoch, titled *The Watchers*, which will show beyond doubt that this scenario is indeed the correct one.

CHILDREN OF A LESSER GOD

Of all the places where the gods of old left their fingerprints, Egypt is probably the most pronounced. In fact, not only did they leave their fingerprints, but also their wardrobes, diaries, photo albums, religious rituals, architecture etc. It is apparent on reading the *avant garde* writers on this subject that the so-called experts on Egyptology dismiss as mere rubbish much of the evidence pointing to a superior race being the builders of these monuments. According to these experts, the ancient Egyptians possessed all this information, technical ability and astronomical knowledge, with absolutely no explanation as to how they acquired same. Neither can they determine how such a primitive people manoeuvred huge stone blocks, some weighing over 100 tons, into position at heights of close to 50 metres when, apparently, the wheel had not then been invented.

Nor can these same "academics" admit that perhaps there was an Ark in existence at all, despite the fact that eleven large round stones with holes in them have been found in and around the area of Mount Ararat in Turkey (the Biblical landing site of the Ark). These were obviously used as ballast stones on a large vessel. There is also evidence that the bow of just such a large ship is buried high up on this same mountain and is visible under the shallow grave in which it lies.[51] The Turkish government has prevented further investigation at this site and fenced it off. Presumably, it has its own political and religious reasons for doing so. But if scientists admitted that the remains of an Ark had been found, then they may have to admit also that perhaps other Biblical stories have credence, and this would fly in the face of science, so-called, and open up a whole new Pandora's Box, if you will excuse the pun.

Such an ostrich mentality will lead nowhere. The pyramids and temples of Egypt did not suddenly fall out of the sky or just materialise with apparently no history or precedent. To simply allow that the ancient Egyptians built them, and leave it at that, is totally incongruous. On a recent trip to Egypt to view some of the sites, we were accompanied by a very enthusiastic tour guide. According to him, Egypt was the centre of the world and all culture began there. Mathematics began in Egypt. Plato and Socrates studied there. Even Christianity began in Egypt. When I asked him who built the pyramids, he said, of course, that they had been built by the Egyptians. In my own mind, however, I tended to disagree, as the evidence would seem to point elsewhere. For the pyramids and temples of this country are simply awesome in detail and character. Stretching back over three, or maybe more millennia BC, these structures are elegant and quite inspiring, and they awake in one a sense of wonder. Yet here we were in almost 2004 AD and this same people, who were supposed to have built these fantastic monuments, seemed to have great problems in constructing the most basic of dwellings. In fact, if the Egyptians were the builders of the pyramids, then they have been regressing ever since, while much of the rest of the world has gone on to achieve the benefits of the technical and other advances of our modern era.

I do not wish to denigrate Egypt or its people. But to imagine that this or any other primitive race, perhaps earlier than 3000 BC, had the abilities required to plan and construct such buildings is simply implausible. No. The evidence staring us in the face suggests that an incredibly advanced civilisation of beings, with a fascination for astronomical matters, and possessing great strength and mathematical abilities, were the builders.

Only one group can qualify as the potential candidates. The primeval gods of prehistory. Not a bunch of mythological characters forged from the traditions or legends of archaic religious ritual. But a caste of sophisticated super-intelligent and supernatural beings. Men who were of a divine background and whose former abode was of a celestial nature. Spirit-men who, in the course of ancient time, changed and became wicked and evil. These are the architects of the buildings, the founders of the religious rites and the original high priests of Egyptian antiquity.

Do the writings of the Egyptian "Book of the Dead" or the Pyramid Texts substantiate such a theory? The answer is a resounding affirmative. Just as the writings and buildings of Greece and Rome (and elsewhere) subscribe to this truth, so also do the monuments and writings of Egypt fit, like a hand in a glove, with the Hebrew texts, which testify of a fallen race of angelic spirit beings who populated this Earth before being wiped out in a worldwide deluge.

It is not for me to investigate every nook and cranny of the various texts of Egypt. I am neither qualified to do so, nor am I thus inclined. However, suffice to say that all of these same profane scriptures will support and prove the thesis that these same gods of old are the perpetrators and initiators of all the enigmas pertaining to, and associated with, Egypt and its mysterious past.

But let me sound a note of caution. These beings are in the business of deceit. What you see is not always what you get. I have no doubt that much of the funerary rites and religious rituals and doctrines of Egypt are nothing but red herrings, designed to confound, trick and enslave the naive and ignorant mortals who were under the spell of these semi-divine potentates.

So they do not show their true nature and identity. Secrecy and sleight of hand are their intimate friends. Even as it was in ancient Egypt and elsewhere, so it is all the way through history in all nations, right up to and including the present day. These beings conceal themselves behind religious doctrines and pious platitudes designed to lead the blind majority of their devotees down the wrong path, which ultimately and inevitably ends in despair and destruction.

That is not to say that they do not have power. For they possess vast influence and authority and strength, which shall be demonstrated in these pages in due course. But for now let us be aware that the gods of Egypt are exactly what their writings say they are. Just as the "myths" and "legends" and scriptures and monuments of other parallel eras are telling us of their origins, so too the artefacts of Egypt are screaming at us at the top of their voices to tell us of their past. But do we have ears to hear? Or are we to be as the self-styled experts and scientists who cannot recognise an ostrich until one falls on their heads?

Let us now name some of the primary gods and goddesses of Egypt, all the time bearing in mind their counterparts who dwelt in nearby Greece and other Mediterranean regions around the same time periods.

Re: *Re* or *Ra* was the creator sun god (see **Figure 10**). His centre of worship was at Heliopolis. He is depicted with the head of a falcon, which has a sun disc and a cobra surrounding it. *Re* or *Ra* is said to have fused with the fertility god *Amun* to become *Amun-Re,* the king of the gods.

Amun (the *"hidden one"*) was the empire's main war god and often appears wearing two tall plumes and carrying a spear. *Amun-Re* was supposed to have come from the dark primordial waters of Nun. He created both light and land and then conceived the first of the gods, who were called *Shu* and *Tefnut.* These brothers and sisters married and produced *Geb* and *Nut,* who in turn gave birth to four of the principal gods: *Osiris, Isis, Seth* and *Nepthys.* These nine gods were based at Heliopolis and are known as the Great Ennead.

Horus is another belonging to this pantheon. The son of *Osiris* and *Isis,* he plays a major role and appears throughout the history of the different ages of the Old, Middle and New Kingdoms of Egypt. The followers of *Horus* were known as the "mystery teachers of the heavens." [52]

Osiris was the god of death and rebirth and the brother and wife of *Isis.*

Figure 10:
An artist's impression of some of the more prominent deities in the Egyptian panteon.
Clockwise from bottom left: Khnum; Ra; Sobek; Anubis; Horus.

The supreme god of the underworld (*Hades?*) and the first-born of *Geb* and *Nut, Osiris* was murdered by his jealous brother, *Seth.*

Nepthys was the wife of *Seth,* but when he murdered *Osiris,* she aligned herself with *Isis.*

Portrayed as a hawk or falcon, *Horus* fought against *Seth* to reclaim his father's inheritance. He is represented as far back as predynastic times and always appears as a falcon or hawk-man.

Hathor was the goddess of love (sex) and drink. She was a fertility goddess and was portrayed either as a woman with a cow's head or having horns.

Anubis was the god of embalming and the son of the gods *Nepthys* and *Osiris,* who admitted the dead to the Underworld. *Anubis* was a god with the head of a jackal and a man's body. He was the "one in front of the gods' pavilion" and the "lord of the tombs." After the weighing-of-the-soul ceremony, *Anubis* guided the dead to the throne of *Osiris.*

Thoth was known as the recording angel and is said to have been the inventor of astronomy, science, mathematics, magic and writing. He was an arbiter between the gods and healed both *Horus* and *Seth* after their battle.

Both *Thoth* and *Maat* are present in all the earliest writings, including the Pyramid Texts, which are dated to 3000 BC or perhaps earlier. In the "Book of the Dead," *Thoth* is referred to as he **"who reckons in heaven, the counter of the stars, the enumerator of the earth and of what is therein, and the measurer of the earth."** (Perhaps Thoth was the chief architect of the Great Pyramid!).

Maat was the wife of *Thoth* and the goddess of truth and justice.

Ptah was among the most ancient of the gods and was the supreme god of creation at one time. He was the god of architects, artists and masons and was the creator of design skills and sculpture. He was portrayed as a shaven-headed god-man holding a sceptre.

The deity known as *Khnum* was represented as a man with a ram's head. He was said to control the annual flood on the Nile. *Khnum* was also one of the primeval god-men; he is said to have created man on his potter's wheel.

Sobek was a god with the head of a crocodile. His temple is at Kom Ombo on the banks of the Upper Nile, where he resided with his wife *Hathor* and their child *Khonsu*. Any enemy of the gods was immediately destroyed by this fearsome deity.

Sekhmet ("Powerful One") was a fierce goddess with the head of a lion. She was the daughter of *Re* (or *Ra*) and was consort to *Ptah*. She was used by *Hathor* in the destruction of mankind until *Hathor* was tricked into drinking beer which she thought was blood. This made her drunk and, as a result of this, *Hathor* ceased from her destruction. *Sekhmet* was a ferocious war goddess used by the vengeful sun god against the human race.

Sometime during the Old Kingdom period, the first three pharaohs are said to have been conceived by a priest of *Ra* after intercourse with the god himself. Because of this, all the pharaohs believed themselves to be direct descendants of the gods; thus pharaoh means *"son of Ra."*[53]

In our study of the irruption of the *Nephilim* after the Flood, we pointed out that some of the offspring were known as *Rephaim*, after one *Rapha*. Could this *Rapha*, from the area of Canaan, be the same *Ra* who fathered the first three pharaohs? After all, these areas were but a couple of hundred miles from each other, making travel and access relatively simple. These descendants of *Rapha* (Hebrew: *fearful*) and their close comrades the *Anakims*, the descendants of *Anak* (Hebrew: *giant, long-necked*), along with other descendants of the *Nephilim*, had populated the whole area of Canaan by the time Abraham and Sarah passed through there circa 1912 BC (or 436 years after the Flood). Remnants of these "giants" still remained in the land when David defeated Goliath circa 974 BC. So for the intervening 938 years we have evidence to show that these descendants of the *Nephilim* were in the general area of Canaan, which was close to, and a province of, Egypt at one time. It needs no stretch of the imagination to conclude that these beings were heavily involved therefore in the affairs of Egypt throughout this entire period.

Rafah is a town about 20 miles south of present-day Gaza on the border between Israel and Egypt. Its ancient name was *Rapha*. It is likely that the *Rapha* after whom the original town was named was a post-Flood *Nephilim* or one of their descendants.

Incidentally, *Anak* was the son of one *Arba*. In Hebrew, *Arba* means "*strength of Baal*." Baal was the chief male deity of the Phoenicians and Canaanites and Ashtaroth was their chief female goddess. Baal in the Hebrew means "*master, possessor*" or "*the lord who possesses*." This *Anak* was a *Nephilim* and his name suggests a direct link with *Baal*, which is another alias for Satan.

Arba built a city which was called "*Kirjath-Arba*" or "city of *Arba*." We are told that this city was built seven years before the building of Zoan in Egypt (Numbers 13:22), which was constructed by the first kings of the 19th dynasty. Rameses II made this his capital and Zoan was the scene of the Exodus and was noted for its wisdom.

In the name *Anak* we find another link with the stars. For in the sign of *Scorpio* and in the constellation of *Serpens* the brightest star is called *Anak*, which means "encompassing."[54] In the Book of Numbers, 13:33, we are told that the spies sent in by Moses said **"there we saw the *Nephilim*, the sons of *Anak*, which come of the *Nephilim*."**

It would appear that yet again, as with the Greek and Roman gods, we find this stellar thread associated with the *Nephilim* and their offspring in Egypt.

It has also been established that the descending shafts in the Great Pyramid of Giza align with four distinct stars at certain times. The north shaft from the King's Chamber aligns with *Alpha Draconis* while the south shaft from the King's Chamber aligns with *Zeta Orionis*. The north shaft from the Queen's Chamber aligns with *Beta Ursa Minor* and the south shaft from the same chamber aligns with *Sirius*.

While no direct connection has yet been discovered for *Beta Ursa Minor* which can connect us with an Egyptian god, we have definite associations for the other three. *Sirius* is the celestial counterpart of the goddess *Isis* and is identified with her. *Zeta Orionis* is the brightest and lowest star in Orion's belt and is associated with *Osiris*. The ancient

Egyptians referred to *Osiris* as the high god of resurrection and rebirth in the remote epoch known as the "Zep-Tepi" or "First Time." *Osiris* is spoken of in one coffin text thus: "*Osiris, Lord of the Doubles ... who threads his two lands, who navigates in front of the stars of the sky.*" And pyramid text spell 882 states: "**O king, thou art this great star, the companion of Orion.**" Could *Orion,* the great hunter of Greek mythology, be *Osiris,* who reigned in Egypt a short distance away?

So here we have two more of the primeval gods of prehistory, *Osiris* and *Isis,* associated with, and named after, prominent stars. But what of *Alpha Draconis?*

Draco is the third constellation in the sign of *Sagittarius* and is in the northern sky. The brightest star in it is called *Thuban,* which means "the Subtle." *Draco* means "the Dragon" and is depicted in the pictures of the planisphere of the heavens as a serpent. Draco was the pole star in 2170 BC. In many places in both the Old Testament scriptures and in the Apocalypse, the dragon is directly associated with Satan. So here in this so-called star shaft of the King's Chamber we have a direct link with *Draco,* who is the dragon, who is the serpent or Satan, who is the devil, who is more subtle than any beast of the field. It is of him that we read in the Apocalypse:

> **The great dragon was cast out, that old serpent called the devil and Satan which deceives the whole world: he was cast out into the Earth, and his angels with him.**
>
> *Book of Revelation 12:9*

This leaves us in no doubt as to who the dragon is. And now we have a major clue and connection between the Great Pyramid of Giza and the chief prince and ruler of the rebel band of fallen angels, Satan, and two of his earthly subordinates, *Osiris* and *Isis.*

If we cast our minds back to the original fall of Lucifer, as recounted by the prophet Isaiah, we will recall that prideful ambition led to his fall from grace. But this passage reveals another interesting vignette:

> **For thou hast said in thine heart: "I will ascend into heaven; I will exalt my throne above the stars (*angels*) of Yaweh; I will sit also upon the mount of the congregation, in the <u>sides of the North</u>."**
>
> *Book of Isaiah 14:13*

Draco is in the northern sky and it would appear from this verse that the habitation of Yaweh and his congregation is also in the north.

In verse 519 of the pyramid texts we find another celestial link between these primordial avatars, *Isis* and *Osiris*, and their offspring, *Horus*.

"O Morning Star, Horus of the nether world, divine falcon."

Lucifer literally means "Morning Star," here used as an appendage to one of the principal heroes of the gallery of gods stretching back to the first epoch of ancient Egypt. *Horus* plays a major role all through the history of the pharaohs and beyond and is clearly identified in engravings in many of the temples of Egypt. Often he is a large man, over twice the size of his captives, and often he is depicted holding a number of slaves or prisoners by the hair with one hand, his other arm raised with a weapon in readiness to slay his prey.

Can there be any doubt that the Pyramids of Giza, known by the ancient Egyptians as the "gateway to the other world" and dating to the time of the primeval age, the *"Zep-Tepi"* or *"First-Time"* of the gods *Horus*, *Isis* and *Osiris*, were related directly to the activities of the *Nephilim*, the fallen ones, and to their offspring? In his fine book *Heaven's Mirror*, Graham Hancock assures us that the Edfu Texts declare that the development of these sites should bring about "the resurrection of the former world of the gods." He also informs us that the time of the "seven sages" was an era when divine beings settled along the banks of the Nile; these divine beings were known as the "builder-gods." This primeval land was where the earliest mansions of the gods were founded, but this ancient domain was destroyed by a huge deluge and the majority of its divine inhabitants were drowned and their mansions were inundated.[55]

By this stage it should be glaringly obvious to the reader that there is a clear and distinct connection between much of the extant evidence in the Egyptian texts and the Biblical records of the Flood of Noah and the activities of the *Nephilim*. But the connections become stronger and the picture becomes clearer still as the evidence continues to unfold.

Another illustration of the obsession which the gods of Egypt had with the stars and their courses is found in the ceiling of the Temple of Hathor at Dendera (see **Figure 11**). Here we find not only the 12 signs of the Zodiac and their principal characters, but also depictions of the gods themselves apparently strolling among the constellations, including *Mercury, Venus, Mars, Jupiter* and *Saturn. Sirius*, the *Dragon (Draco)*, and *Orion* are also clearly visible.

In endeavouring to determine the reasons for this obsession with the

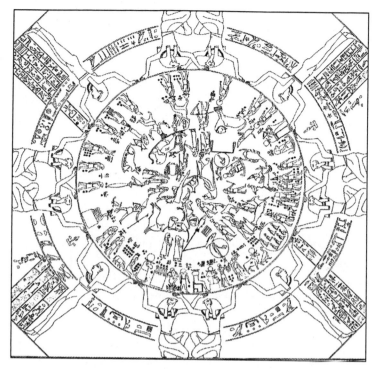

Figure 11:
Zodiac from the ceiling of the Temple of Hathor at Dendera showing many
of the gods strolling among the constellations.

celestial bodies and also with a never-ending quest for immortality and eternal life (as evidenced by their various religious rituals and rites), it must be remembered that these spirit-men once owned these treasures. Before their rebellion and their free-will decision to vote with Lucifer and attempt to usurp the throne of Yaweh, these angels possessed both immortality and a heavenly abode among the stars. But their reward for believing in the lie of the serpent was to be ejected from the presence of Yaweh and cast down to Earth.

Having once lived among the celestial bodies and having possessed immortality, they are now exiled in a distant land. But, like most exiles, they yearn for restoration to their original state and hanker for a return to their former homeland. Also, they now face the prospect of the ultimate sanction, as prophesied and promised by Yaweh when he said "He (the Messiah) will crush your head" (and, by extension, the heads of your associates). *Genesis 3:15.*

So it is little wonder that, having backed the wrong horse and lost, these forces of evil should try everything in their power to kill the Messiah, thwart the plan of Yaweh and thereby avert their own doom and regain immortality. This is the reason why the *Nephilim* infiltrated the Earth in the first place and filled it with violence. The plan was to kill off all human life, thus ending the "line of the seed of the woman," so that the Messiah could not be born. But Yaweh always seems to be one move ahead in this eternal chess game, and He maintained the line through Noah and his family.

After the Flood, when it became known to the princes of darkness that Abraham would possess the promised land, and that the seed would continue through him, Satan again endeavoured to prevent this prophecy by flooding the entire area of Canaan with a second irruption of *Nephilim* so that Israel could not possess the land and the line would be broken once more. But, alas, his scheme failed yet again and, as ever, Yaweh's prophecy was realised.

And so the contest continues. Many times down through the ages Satan has interfered with Israel and the line of the seed of the woman in order to frustrate the prophecy and destroy the promise of a redeeming Messiah. When the Messiah was crucified and placed in a tomb, Satan and his host thought that they had finally won and averted their own demise. I am sure they had a big celebration that night. And perhaps that is why the Messiah, in his new risen spiritual body, went forth and appeared before those fallen angels who are kept in prison in *Tartarus*. This must count as one of the best party-poopers in history.

But I digress. In the latter part of this book, the questions pertaining to the bigger picture of exactly what is going on, and why, will be answered in some detail. As a result, the reader will be better able to understand the reasons for this cosmic battle and where it is leading us and how it will all end. But, for now, back to the past.

Blood sacrifices seemed to be an important part of the ritual in many of the temples and monuments of the gods of eras past. In the pyramids of the Maya in Mexico and elsewhere it would appear that the gods had an insatiable appetite for fresh blood.

The Aztecs reputedly sacrificed up to 60,000 humans per year, often plunging knives into the victim's chest and pulling the heart out while it was still beating in order to appease the gods.

Munoz Camargo, a historian, described one such sacrifice: "One who had been a priest of the devil told me that when they tore the heart from the wretched victim, the strength with which it pulsated and quivered was so great that it used to lift three or four times from the ground before the heart grew cold."[56]

In the time of Abraham we know that many of the surrounding peoples practised human sacrifice. For when Yaweh told Abraham to take his son Isaac up to Mount Moriah, and offer him there as a sacrifice, one of the reasons why Abraham did not hesitate to do so was because he was very aware that human sacrifices were the norm in the areas surrounding him. This was the place where the Messiah was eventually sacrificed two thousand years later. And, as Abraham had been prevented from killing his son and a lamb was substituted for the sacrifice, on Calvary, the Messiah, the Lamb of God, was provided as the ultimate sacrifice for mankind.

In Egypt, however, according to my erstwhile guide, human sacrifices had never been offered to the gods. I presume that the guide did not want anything to reflect badly on Egypt or its culture. But the pictures and engravings tell a different story. In the Valley of the Kings, for instance, there is a relief depicting a line of prisoners, many with their heads chopped off and blood spurting freely in all directions. In another relief, a captive kneels before one of the pharaohs. His hands are tied behind his back and the king, his arm aloft with weapon in hand, is poised to strike.

Behind the captive, one of the gods looks on approvingly, a wry smile on his lips. When I quizzed my guide on the meaning of this relief, he replied that it was "symbolic."

On the huge wall beside the entrance to the mighty temple at Edfu there is a relief of *Horus* with five Nubian captives in his left hand, his right arm held aloft ready to slay the poor wretches. *Narmer*, reputed to be the first of the kings of Egypt, lived in the predynastic period of 3,000 BC or before. He is reputed to have been a "knocker of heads" (see **Figure 12**). In a much later period, probably circa 1200 or 1300 BC, we see another pharaoh receiving offerings from his subjects (see **Figure 13**). But we should look more closely at these two figures, separated by almost 2,000 years. The first, Narmer, is around the time of the gods of Greece and Rome, the era of the Titans, who were huge superhuman beings of great size and strength (hence the ship, *Titanic*). Some 2,000 years later, in the days of Ramesses II, we had the "war of the land" between Joshua and the "giants" who inhabited the entire area of Canaan. If we look at the size of both Narmer and this second pharaoh, compared to the other men, we can see that they are at least twice as big. Look also at the size difference in **Figure 14**.

This is the case in scores of ancient Egyptian paintings and sculptures. Invariably, the gods or the pharaohs are huge compared to the ordinary people around them. This holds true for many of the pictures of ordinary scenes in religious rituals, or scenes of hunting or of war. Of course, it will

Figure 12:
A section of the Narmer Palette, dating to circa 3200 BC, showing the pharaoh of the same name making a notive or gift offering to his "father", the god Amun-Ra. The palette, which is decorated on both sides, was at one time displayed in the Temple of Horus at Nekhen (CairoMuseum).

be said that this was to indicate that the kings and gods were superior to the mere mortals depicted in the same scenes. Academics will scorn any idea that perhaps these gods and their offspring were actually at least twice the size of ordinary men. As in the case of Goliath, who was $13^1/_2$ feet tall, and Og, the king of Bashan, whose bed was $18^1/_2$ feet long and more than 9 feet wide (see **Figure 5**), these pictures, if taken at face value, also put Narmer and the second pharaoh at around the same height (i.e. 13 to 15 feet tall).

Is it not improbable to suppose that these gods and rulers, who master-minded and built with immaculate detail the temples and pyramids of Egypt, were totally inaccurate in depicting their own size and height? No, for those with eyes to see it is obvious that, just as the Titans of old were great in stature and strength, so too their counterparts, the *Nephilim* of Egypt and their descendants, were monsters and giants of men. This huge size advantage enabled them to enslave ordinary people and lord it over them so that the gods and kings were in complete control. This holds true at every site where these extraordinary temples and pyramids are found around the globe. If it were not so, and the *Nephilim* and their offspring were the same as ordinary mortals, then they would have been quickly defeated and eliminated and we would have no records or monuments testifying to their existence.

Figures 13/14:
Reliefs from Egypt showing the huge difference in size
between these two pharaohs and their subjects.

Immense physical strength was obviously an attribute of these super-men. But they had more than just physical strength at their disposal in the construction of buildings, some of which contain huge stone blocks which were set in place at great heights. At one such site at Sacsayhuaman in the Andes, one stone is estimated to be 355 tons in weight and is situated at a height of $8^{1}/_{2}$ metres.[57] Consider also the 2.3 to 2.5 million blocks of the Great Pyramid and the cutting and placing of these to provide for the various chambers and passageways therein. The sheer scope and magnitude of this structure almost defies logic and today there is no way such a feat could be replicated. So how did the builders accomplish these mighty tasks and do so with such mathematical accuracy?

This enigma we shall endeavour to answer now.

The legends of Viracocha and the myths of the Andes tell of the white-skinned god and his compatriots, described as "the messengers, the shining ones," who arrived in primordial times and were responsible for building the great temples by means of magic. Viracocha was said to have created giant men from the heavens to build the temples.[58] But then he drowned them all and overran the world with water (sound familiar?). The Incas also believed that they were exiled from the world above and strove to return to their former abode.[59] It is because of their spiritual connections that the gods of yore could accomplish such enormous physical feats. To demonstrate some of these strengths, we return to the Scriptures. First to a passage already cited concerning a man possessed with a "legion" of demons:

> They went across the lake to the region of the Gerasenes.
> When Jesus got out of the boat, a man with an evil spirit came from the tombs to meet him. This man lived in the tombs and no one could bind him any more, not even with a chain. For he had often been chained hand and foot, but he tore the chains apart and broke the irons on his feet. No one was strong enough to subdue him.
>
> *Gospel of Mark 5:1-4*

This is an example of spirit power on the negative side. For here we have a man who in normal circumstances would in no way be able to "tear apart" chains and break irons off his feet. What enabled him to accomplish this feat of strength was the spiritual power with which he had been imbued. In other words, it was the demonic spirit power working through him which tore the chains apart and broke the irons off his feet. These were the same spiritual powers as were used by the *Nephilim*, the Titans etc.

Next we have the story of the seven sons of a chief of the priests. The background to this is that the apostle Paul was healing many people and exorcising demons as he preached among the Gentiles. Then a few impostors decided to try their hand at it:

> Then certain of the vagabond Jews, exorcists, took upon themselves to call over them which had evil spirits in the name of the Lord Jesus, saying: "We adjure you by Jesus, whom Paul preaches."
> And there were seven sons of one Sceva, a Jew, and chief of the priests, which did so.
> And the evil spirit answered and said: "Jesus I know and Paul I know; but who are you?"
> And the man in whom the evil spirit was leaped on them, and overcame them, and prevailed against them, so that they fled out of the house naked and wounded.
> *Book of Acts 19:13-16*

This seems quite humorous on one level. But the point is that one man here possessed with an evil spirit was stronger than seven others.

In Luke 4 we have one of the records of the temptations of the Messiah. And in verse 5 we read:

> Again the devil led him up to a high place and showed him, in an instant, all the kingdoms of the world.

I confess that I do not understand exactly what occurred here. But it remains that the devil was able to show the Messiah all the kingdoms of the world "in an instant." Spiritual power was surely involved in this and it is another example of the resources available in the spirit realm.

Exodus chapter 7 provides another example of the negative spiritual power available to the demonic world:

> So Moses and Aaron went to Pharaoh and did just as the Lord commanded. Aaron threw his staff down in front of Pharaoh and his officials, and it became a snake.
> Pharaoh then summoned the wise men and sorcerers, and the Egyptian magicians also did the same things by their secret arts.
> Each one threw down his staff and it became a snake. But Aaron's staff swallowed up their staffs.
> Yet Pharaoh's heart became hard and he would not listen to them...
> *Book of Exodus 7:10-13*

This is a perfect example of the power of both good and evil. Also, this scene is set in Egypt before the Exodus circa 1490 BC. It is interesting to note that the magicians and sorcerers caused their staffs to change into snakes by using their "secret arts." What makes this noteworthy is that only very sketchy information exists about the people who built many of the great monuments around the world. They seem to have consciously covered their tracks and hidden their intentions. The Druids, for instance, left no written texts and passed their traditions orally and in secret. (Blood sacrifices were also part of their mystical rituals).

The activities of these sects were invariably shrouded in mystery. So, too, with the black, secret arts of the sorcerers of the pharaohs. Only those who were initiates were allowed access to the deeper, clandestine rites of the inner cabal.

So when we ponder how these gods of old fashioned and assembled these gigantic stones in the monuments they built, we must remember that we are dealing with beings who had great spiritual power at their disposal.

Not only were the Titans and other *Nephilim* great in physical stature and strength, but the infusion of spiritual power available to them empowered them to even mightier feats. And their leader was the most exalted spirit being of all when first created. Remember how he is described in Ezekiel:

> You were the model of perfection, full of wisdom and perfect in beauty ...
> Your settings and mountings were made of gold. On the day you were created they were prepared.
> You were anointed as a guardian cherub, for so I ordained you.
> You were on the holy mount of God: you walked among the fiery stones.
> You were blameless in your ways from the day you were created till wickedness was found in you.
> Your heart became proud on account of your beauty, and you corrupted your wisdom because of your splendour.
>
> *Book of Ezekiel 28:12-17*

Nowhere else do the Scriptures speak of any of the "*sons of God*" or any other angelic being as they speak about Lucifer. We are dealing with no ordinary being here. He was so powerful that he thought he was above the Most High and could overthrow Yaweh. This is the power which has lain behind the "secret arts" of all sorcery and black magic ever since the dawn of time. Lucifer, in one of his aliases, is the "deceiver." He is in the business of secrecy and concealment. His *modus operandi* is to keep us off the scent and going on wild goose chases down the wrong path. The main reason why authors and investigators have not discovered the perpetrators of these secret arts and the builders of the temples we speak of is because, for the most part, they are digging in the wrong places. And so successful have Lucifer and his lot been at covering their tracks that very few artisans are skilled enough to be able to turn over the stone and reveal the snake hiding underneath.

We cannot say for sure what tools they used or by what means they shaped these great monuments. But when Lucifer's denizens and agents are able to accomplish such feats as changing staffs into snakes, or causing a man to break through leg irons and chains as though they were mere paper, can it be such a task for them to build a pyramid or erect large temples? As I have already said, we are dealing with beings who considered themselves equal with Yaweh himself. And we only have to look at the power exhibited by the Messiah when he walked on this Earth for more examples of spiritual strength, albeit this time in a totally positive vein. For instance:

> For verily I say unto you, that whosoever shall say unto this mountain "Be thou removed and be thou cast into the sea" ... He shall have whatsoever he saith.
>
> *Gospel of Mark 11:23*

The Gospels are littered with examples of spirit power as exemplified by the Messiah. In the Acts of the Apostles there are again many examples of the disciples of the Messiah carrying on this work and emulating what he had previously done. So is it really any wonder that the precursor to the Messiah, who was around before the foundation of this world (and probably played a prominent part in its design and construction), is able to engineer and construct mere pyramids and temples? It is no big deal for him or for his minions to construct puzzling lines all over Nazca. But what *is* amazing is how Satan and his infernal band have managed to keep practically the whole world in darkness and ignorance for such a long time.

When considering the mathematical and astronomical alignments of the pyramids and the temples of Mexico, Guatemala, Cambodia and Egypt (and other places), let us remember that these spirit-men are intimately familiar with the stars and their courses. They are also keenly aware of the signs and seasons which mark the precession of the equinoxes. And I am sure that they are carefully watching for any conjunctions or other signs in the stars which may announce the next major happening on the prophetic calendar. For they are very aware of what lies ahead.

We remember *Thoth* and his description of being a master of mathematics and astronomy and "a recording angel." We remember that the devil was able to show the Messiah all the kingdoms of the world "in an instant." We are aware that, by his schemes and deceits, the whole world is ensnared in delusion and despair. So it is manifestly clear that the architect and sponsor behind all the massive pyramids and temples around this world, and the dark deeds which distinguished those ancient times, is none other than Satan, the devil, that ancient serpent who deceives the whole world. He is the brains and motivator behind his lesser gods, the *Nephilim*.

But why choose the pyramid shape? Would it not be more practical to build a temple or a tower or a statue or some other icon. But a pyramid? The shape is so unusual and incongruous. Or could there be another reason why the gods chose the pyramid? I believe that there is great significance in this shape and a good reason why the pyramids were constructed. We shall answer this riddle in due course.

THE WATCHERS

I would like to tie up this section by mentioning other items of information which may throw more light on the subject under discussion. We spoke in the earlier chapters of the possibility that genetic engineering or genetic modification may have been practised in ancient times. In Egypt we also have evidence to suggest that this was probable if we take the engravings and other records at face value. The same can be said for many of the empires which existed both before and after the Flood.

Look at **Figure 15**. These carvings date from the time of Salamasar III, an Assyrian king, and are engraved on an obelisk. If these beings are not real, then why would the engravers and their rulers go to so much trouble to produce them? After all, it must have taken a skilled stonemason a long time to carve out these images in such great detail. It must have been an expensive undertaking also. The same can be said of the other figure from the same source (**Figure 16**).

There are many other illustrations depicting various half-animal, half-human creatures. These are from roughly the same era and from countries in relative proximity to one another. Why would the artists and their sponsors go to the bother of producing such images if they were not trying to communicate an idea? And why are so many of the images similar, given that they come from differing areas and societies? I am sure that these artists could have utilised their time and effort creating images of beauty from hundreds of different subjects. And why would they produce these images if they were not attempting to convey something which was real?

In the Temple of Isis at Philae in Egypt I was amazed by an engraving on a wall close to the sanctuary. This showed one of the pharaohs offering a baby sphinx to one of the gods. What was striking about this image was that everything looked so real. The sphinx looked like a young child with the body of an animal. If this was a mere statue which was being presented to the god, then why go to the trouble of carving this engraving on the wall? After all, there are hundreds of very large statues depicting sphinxes all over the Egypt. So why make such a big deal of a miniature statue?

If these people had used cross-breeding to produce an animal with a human head, this might indeed have been an offering befitting a god. But a statue! If this was truly a half-human, half-animal aberration which had recently been "born," then perhaps it would be worthy of such an elaborate sculpture.

Figure 15:
This small creature being led away by King Salamasar III is supposed to be an "ape," but neither the feet nor the spread fingers belong to an ape. Engraving from the black obelisk of King Salamasar III (British Museum)

Then we have the gods themselves. *Horus* had the head of a falcon or hawk. *Anubis* was the jackal-headed god of embalming. *Thoth* was an ibis, while *Sobek* was the god with the crocodile head. *Seth* had a peculiar head similar to that of an ant-eater. And on it goes. This begs the question of why these people are always represented as half-human, half-animal? The experts will say that this is all symbolic and is an indication of the gods' authority and power. But is there more here than meets the eye?

Could it possibly be that these beings were indeed just as they appear. Could it be that the *Nephilim* used their powers of creation in engineering these demonic demi-gods in order to gain power and maintain control over the mere mortals who populated the Earth? Look at the overall images we have of the pantheon of the gods. There is the Greek *Pan*, who was half-man, half-goat. The half-human, half-horse *Centaurs* are depicted widely in ancient art. The *Minotaur* was the monster with the head of a bull and the body of a man who inhabited the Labyrinth. He would have fitted right in with his compatriots in Egypt.

Figure 16:
These mixed-breed creatures are found on the black obelisk of King Salamasar III (British Museum).

We know that these gods of Egypt were extremely advanced in the art of medicine. In the Temple of Sobek at Kom Ombo, overlooking the Nile, we find evidence of this. For engraved on one wall is a set of medical instruments which, according to a leading surgeon, are equal to many of the surgical instruments available to us today. This surgeon told me that the cosmetic surgery practised by these ancient peoples was as advanced if not more advanced than our modern techniques.

Note also that the main temple of Angkor in Cambodia comes from the words "Ankh," meaning life, and "Hor," after *Horus*. In other words, "Horus Lives."[60] Well, if he does live, this would fit right in with our theory that perhaps the *Nephilim* who caused the second irruption with humans after the Flood are still at large. For, as was stated earlier, the pyramids in Mexico and Central America are believed to have been built much later than those of Egypt. And the temples of Cambodia are relatively recent, believed to have been erected between 800 and 1200 AD. If these dates are accurate, then perhaps Horus does live, and he and his merry band of post-Flood *Nephilim* have been staying one step ahead of civilisation for the past couple of thousand years!

I may be wrong in these particular speculations. Nothing is carved in stone, if you will forgive the metaphor. But it is good to examine the evidence we have from a different perspective in order to hopefully find the truth.

Book of Enoch

Enoch was a seventh-generation direct descendant of Adam and was born in 3382 BC (see Appendix). Although the *Book of Enoch* is not part of the canon of the Old Testament, fragments of it were found among the Dead Sea Scrolls, which are reckoned to date back to circa 300 BC. Even though this book is not part of the Old Testament, nevertheless it is quoted in the New Testament by Jude, who was the brother (or half-brother) of the Messiah. Enoch writes extensively regarding both the fallen angels, whom he refers to as the "Watchers," and the Apocalypse. The following quotes are from the Book of Enoch and I shall offer comment as we go through it.[61] It is important to consider these excerpts in the light of the information we have already covered.

> And it came to pass when the children of men had multiplied that in those days were born unto them beautiful and comely daughters. And the Angels, the children of the heaven, saw and lusted after them, and said to one another: "Come, let us choose us wives from among the children of men and beget us children."
>
> And Semjaza, who was their leader, said unto them: "I fear ye will not indeed agree to do this deed, and I alone shall have to pay the penalty of a great sin." And they all answered him and said: "Let us all swear an oath, and all bind ourselves by mutual imprecations not to abandon this plan but to do this thing."
>
> Then swore they all together and bound themselves by mutual imprecations upon it. And they were in all two hundred; who descended in the days of Jared on the summit of Mount Hermon, and they called it Mount Hermon, because they had sworn and bound themselves by mutual imprecations upon it. And these are the names of their leaders: Semiazaz, their leader, Arakiba, Rameel, Kokabiel, Tamiel, Ramiel, Danel, Ezeqeel, Baraqial, Asael, Armaros, Batarel, Ananel, Zaqiel, Samsapeel, Satarel, Turel,

Jomjael, Sariel.
> These were their chiefs of ten.

Book of Enoch VI 1-8

Jared (born 3544 BC) was the father of Enoch and was 162 years old when his son was born. This would place these renegade angels on Earth around the time many experts believe the Great Pyramid was built. It would also allow plenty of time, about 1,000 years, for the population of the Earth to become polluted and corrupted by them prior to the Flood in 2348 BC.

> And all the others together with them took unto themselves wives, and each chose for himself one, and they began to go in unto them and to defile themselves with them, and they taught them charms and enchantments, and the cutting of roots, and made them acquainted with plants.
> And they became pregnant, and they bare great giants, whose height was three thousand ells: who consumed all the acquisitions of men. And when men could no longer sustain them, the giants turned against them and devoured mankind.
> And they began to sin against birds, and beasts, and reptiles, and fish, and to devour one another's flesh and drink the blood.
> Then the Earth laid accusation against the lawless ones.

Book of Enoch VII 1-6

This passage copperfastens all the prior Scriptural evidence, which states that fallen angels came to Earth and bred with ordinary women, who then gave birth to giants, who become the **"heroes of old, mighty men of renown."**

In a previous chapter we surmised that the fallen angels, the *Nephilim*, interfered in some way with the animals and birds of the Earth, for it seemed unusual that Yaweh would pronounce judgment against **"the beasts, the creeping things and the fowls of the air"** (*Genesis 6:7*). Yet, here again in the Book of Enoch, we are told that these reprobate angels began to *"sin against birds and beasts and reptiles and fish ..."* The context of this passage is sexual sin, for how else can you "sin" against such creatures. Is this another allusion to genetic engineering? Is Enoch here intimating that these *Nephilim* were involved in creating the half-human, half-animal creatures which appear in numerous images in many countries during this same era?

Also note that it was these angelic beings who taught them "enchantments and charms and the cutting of roots," i.e. witchcraft, black magic, call it what you will. It is all proceeding from the same source. "And made them acquainted with plants." Could this mean that they introduced them to cultivating and producing drugs such as opium and heroin? For such could not possibly emanate from Yaweh. We are also told here how these giants, the offspring of the *Nephilim,* began to devour one another's flesh and to drink blood. This fits in with many of the stories of the Greek gods who, we are told, indulged in all these activities.

> And Azazel taught men to make swords, and knives, and shields, and breastplates, and made known to them the metals (of the Earth) and the art of working them, and bracelets, and ornaments, and the use of antimony, and the beautifying of the eyelids, and all kinds of costly stones, and all colouring tinctures.
> And there arose much godlessness, and they committed fornication, and they were led astray, and became corrupt in all their ways.
> Semjaza taught enchantments and (the use of) root-cuttings, Armaros the resolving of enchantments, Baraqijal astrology, Kobabel the constellations, Ezeqeel the knowledge of the clouds, Araziel the signs of the Earth, Shamsiel the signs of the sun and Sariel the course of the moon.
> And, as men perished, they cried, and their cry went up to heaven ...
> *Book of Enoch VIII 1-4*

In the naming of these fallen "sons of God" and the things they imparted to men, we find astrology, the constellations, the courses of the sun and the moon. This provides more evidence that the Zodiac and its signs were not merely invented by the imaginations of ordinary men over time, but were known to these fallen "stars," and the knowledge of them was transferred, along with other magic formulae, to humans. It is also evident that astrology, considered by some to be the false counterpart of astronomy, has its basis in evil and issues from the forces of darkness.
The *Book of Enoch* continues:

> And then Michael, Uriel, Raphael and Gabriel looked down from Heaven and saw much blood being shed upon the Earth, and all lawlessness being wrought upon the Earth.
> And they said to the Lord of the Ages: "Thou seest what Azazel hath done, who hath taught all unrighteousness on Earth and revealed the eternal secrets which were (preserved) in Heaven, which men were striving to learn.

And they have gone to the daughters of men upon the Earth, and have slept with the women, and have defiled themselves, and revealed to them all kinds of sin.

And the women have borne giants, and the whole Earth has thereby been filled with blood and unrighteousness."

Book of Enoch IX 1-11

Michael and Gabriel we are familiar with. They are named in the Scriptures often, appearing in many places. Uriel and Raphael were never named in the Scriptures and are new to us. In reading this passage we can contemplate the original story from Genesis 6 of how the Earth was filled with violence and blood caused by the giants, or Titans, the *Nephilim* and their offspring. The Book of Enoch adds yet more detail and insight. But what is Yaweh to do concerning this great sin? The story goes on:

Then said the Most High, the Holy and Great One spake, and sent Uriel to the son of Lamech, and said to him:

"Go to Noah and tell him in my name 'hide thyself' and reveal to him the end that is approaching: that the whole Earth will be destroyed, and a deluge is about to come upon the whole Earth, and will destroy all that is on it. And now instruct him that he may escape and his seed may be preserved for all the generations of the world."

Book of Enoch X 1-3

Enoch had a son whose name was Methuselah, which means "when he is dead it shall be sent" (i.e. the deluge). Methuselah died at the age of 969 in the first month of the Flood year of 2348 BC (see Appendix).[62] He was the only man ever to live to such an age. When Methuselah was 187 years old he had a son whom he named Lamech. When Lamech was 182 years old he had a son and called him Noah. Noah literally means *rest, comfort or consolation*. For Noah was to give rest and comfort from the evil deeds which were being perpetrated all around him.

In the beginning of this section devoted to the Book of Enoch we are told that it was "in the days of Jared" that the fallen angels descended on Mount Hermon and began their evil doings. Jared was born in 3544 BC and Noah in 2948 BC, so the activities of the fallen ones, or the "Watchers" as Enoch refers to them, occurred sometime during the 596 years between Jared and Noah. And there is yet another 600 years of Noah's life before the deluge strikes. Ample time for the gods of Greece and Rome and Egypt to erect their temples and other edifices and establish their legends.

> And again the Lord said to Raphael: "Bind Azazel hand and foot, and cast him into the darkness; and make an opening in the desert, which is in Dudael, and cast him therein. And on the day of the great judgment he shall be cast into the fire. And the whole Earth has been corrupted through the works that were taught by Azazel: to him ascribe all sin."
> And to Gabriel said the Lord: "Proceed against the bastards and the reprobates, and against the children of fornication; and destroy the children of fornication and the children of the Watchers from amongst men and cause them to go forth; send them one against the other that they may destroy each other in battle, for length of days shall they not have."
> And the Lord said unto Michael: "Go, bind Semjaza and his associates who have united themselves with women so as to have defiled themselves with them in all their uncleanness ...
> In those days they shall be led off to the abyss of fire; (and) to the torment and the prison in which they shall be confined forever.
> And destroy all the spirits of the reprobate, and the children of the Watchers, because they have wronged mankind."
>
> *Book of Enoch X 4-15*

In this passage the past and the future are linked in the same notion. We see the Watchers, the fallen angels, being condemned for their corruption of mankind and sent to a prison which sounds not unlike *Tartarus*, there to be held until a future judgment, which is set at the end of the Apocalypse and will be discussed in the latter part of this book. The Abyss is also mentioned, but this is a future abyss which is spoken of as a place of torment and confinement for all the evil host of heaven and their mentors and the godless in the final chapters of the Book of Revelation.

The Book of Enoch continues with the pronouncement of blessings and joy for the righteous in a future Paradise. But other mentions are made of the angelic host, both good and evil, and it may be beneficial, in light of the thesis thus far, to briefly quote some of these passages.

This next passage is from the Book of Enoch XV and XVI. In it, Enoch is asked by the aforementioned condemned angels to bring a petition to the Most High, asking for their sentence to be remitted. Enoch reads the petition and then falls asleep. In his sleep he has a vison and recounts the words given to him. In this section he quotes the Most High himself:

"And go, say to the Watchers of Heaven, who have sent thee to intercede for them: You should intercede for men, and not men for you.

Wherefore have ye left the high, holy and eternal Heaven, and lain with women, and defiled yourselves with the daughters of men and taken to yourselves wives, and done like the children of Earth, and begotten giants (as your) sons.

And though ye were holy, spiritual (beings) living the eternal life, you have defiled yourselves with the blood of women, and have begotten (children) with the blood of flesh and blood as those (also) do who die and perish.

And now, the giants, who are produced from the spirit and flesh, shall be called evil spirits upon the Earth, and on the Earth shall be their dwelling.

And the spirits of the giants afflict, oppress, destroy, attack, do battle and work destruction on the Earth, and cause trouble: they take no food, but nevertheless hunger and thirst, and cause offences.

And now as to the Watchers who have sent thee to intercede for them, who have been aforetime in Heaven (say to them): 'You have been in Heaven, but all the mysteries had not yet been revealed to you, and you knew worthless ones, and these in the hardness of your hearts you have made known to the women, and through these mysteries women and men work much evil on Earth.'

Say to them therefore: 'You have no peace.' "

Book of Enoch XV 2 to XVI 4

Although the Book of Enoch is not part of the canon of Scripture, we feel it is appropriate to quote it at length, for it fits in with the other parts of Scripture which we have discussed so far. Also, it adds to what we know from both the Old and New Testament and fills in many of the blanks with details not found anywhere else.

Next is a section from Enoch XXVII 11 to XIX 3, in which he describes places of an other-worldly nature. In relation to *Tartarus* and a future destiny facing the wicked angels and their associates, he describes what he saw:

And I saw a deep abyss, with columns of heavenly fire.

I saw there seven stars like great burning mountains, and to me, when I inquired regarding them, the angel said: "This place is the end of Heaven and Earth: this has become a prison for the stars and the host of Heaven. And the stars which roll over the fire are they which have transgressed the commandment of the Lord in the beginning of their rising, because they did not come forth at their appointed times. And He was wroth with them, and bound them till the time when their guilt should be consummated (even) for ten thousand years."

And Uriel said to me: "Here shall stand the angels who have connected themselves with women, and their spirits, assuming many different forms, are defiling mankind, and shall lead them astray into sacrificing to demons till the day of the great judgment in which they shall be judged till they are made an end of. And the women also of the angels who went astray shall become sirens."

And I, Enoch, alone saw the vision, the ends of all things: and no man shall see as I have seen.

Book of Enoch XVIII 11 to XIX 3

Here we are told of women angels who went astray. In Egypt, *Isis* was a leading goddess, as were *Athena* and *Aphrodite* in Greece.

Enoch was, or rather is, a very enigmatic entity insofar as we are given very little information about him. He is only mentioned in a couple of verses in Genesis 5, telling us who his father was and that he "walked with God." We are also told that he was "translated" and did not experience death. That is, he was taken up by Yaweh and never died, as was Elijah (see *2 Kings 2:11*). The name Enoch means *"tuition, initiation or teaching,"* yet we find no tuition from him in the Scriptures. Many Biblical scholars might dismiss the Book of Enoch because it is not part of the canon. However, the fact that Jude, the half-brother of the Messiah, quotes directly from the Book of Enoch gives its author much credence. In his own writings, Enoch is referred to as a "scribe of righteousness."

The overriding fact that the apostles and disciples knew of Enoch's writings and quoted them gives gravitas to this book and suggests that we should be aware of its contents and take notice.

* * * * * *

The revelations of the Book of Enoch substantiate the evidence advanced in this hypothesis thus far. In discussing the pyramids and other ancient monuments, many profess to believe that aliens or extra-terrestrials came to Earth from afar and were responsible for these buildings. The theory advanced here would support this supposition. The only difference is that the Scriptures do not label these beings as "aliens" or "extra-terrestrials," but refer to them as "fallen angels," "sons of God" or the *"Nephilim."*

Enoch calls them "stars," "spiritual beings" and the "Watchers."

These beings left their spiritual abode in the heavens, came to Earth and materialised in the realm of the senses. Here they bred with humans and produced a hybrid of human and spirit people. These beings were great in size and, because of their genetic make-up, were wicked beyond redemption. During a period of several hundred years on the Earth, they spread their corruption and infected all of mankind save for eight souls. The mastermind behind this worldwide irruption of the *Nephilim* was Satan and his *raison d'être* was to totally destroy the entire human race so that the line of the Messiah would be broken and his birth aborted. In this way Satan hoped to nullify the prophecy of Yaweh, given in Genesis 3:15, which stated that the "seed of the woman" would crush the head of the serpent.

But his plan failed. Noah and his family were the only souls left on this Earth whose lineage was pure and uncontaminated by the *Nephilim* and their offspring. Yaweh destroyed the whole of the population because of their sinful state in a worldwide deluge and preserved Noah and his family. Thus the line of the Messiah was saved and the seed of the woman was perpetuated.

After the Flood, when men began to increase in number again in the Earth, there was a second irruption of these fallen angels and the *Nephilim* roamed once more. By the time Moses led the children of Israel out of the bondage of Egypt, the whole area of Canaan, the Promised Land, was filled with the *Nephilim* and their descendants. Satan again endeavoured to thwart the prophecy of Yaweh and prevent the Israelites from possessing the land by populating the region with giants. But his scheme failed when Joshua and his armies defeated these beings and destroyed the 60 "giant cities of Bashan" and their king, Og.

The fallen angels who were responsible for the first corruption of the Earth prior to the Flood are imprisoned in a place called *Tartarus*, there to await a future judgment. We are told that the Messiah went and heralded his triumph before these beings after his resurrection in much the same way as the Roman generals of old heralded their victorious conquests before the city of Rome on returning from some far-flung battlefield.

We have no knowledge of what happened to the fallen "sons of God" who caused the second contamination of the Earth after the Flood. Perhaps they are still wandering the Earth, hiding out in some dark, evil forest, wary of the advance and onslaught of man.

But what does all this mean and where is it leading us? In this next section we will discuss the significance of the pyramid shape and introduce a new concept: the *Pyramid of the Apocalypse*.

If the first part of this book seemed like a leisurely cruise down a lazy, meandering river which occasionally threw up interesting sites along the way, then get ready for the rapids. For in this next section the excitement and tension should increase and cause you to hang on to the sides of the boat with white knuckles. But, after the rapids, we will return to the calm of peaceful waters and the security of dry land, figuratively speaking.

The journey continues.

The next several chapters were already published in my second book, Apocalypse 2000. However, these chapters have been amended and updated and are now presented with much new information.

— THE AUTHOR.

BACK TO THE FUTURE

Before examining the predictions of the Book of Revelation, it is important first to understand how prophecy works. About one-third of all Biblical texts are prophetic. That is, they foretell future events before they occur. If the events forecast come to pass, the veracity of the prophecy is borne out. If the event fails to materialise, then the prediction is shown to be false.

This is never the case, however, in Biblical prophecy. For instance, there are 737 distinct prophecies throughout the entirety of the Scriptures.[63] Some of these prophecies are mentioned but once or twice. Others are repeated hundreds of times. Of these predictions, 594 have been fulfilled to date, with 100% accuracy every time. Put another way, over 80% of the prophecies have already been fulfilled down to the last letter. The remainder of the prophecies pertain to our future and it is at these that we shall be looking.

No other book ever written, either secular or religious, is as prophetic in its nature as is the Bible. No other books contain such prophecies concerning the future and, if they did, their non-fulfilment would have long since proved them wrong. There are 845 quotations from the Old Testament in the New Testament and 333 of these refer to the Messiah.

The Messiah literally fulfilled 109 prophecies relating to himself in his first coming. In the last 24 hours of his life, 25 specific prophecies came to pass, all of which were written into the Old Testament between 500 and 1,000 years before his birth.[64] According to the laws of probability, the chances of 25 specific predictions coming to pass in one 24-hour period of a particular person's lifetime must be billions to one.

We will now recount a few of these prophecies from the Old Testament which were fulfilled in the last 24 hours of the Messiah's life. It was prophesied that:

1. The Messiah would be betrayed for 30 pieces of silver
   (Zechariah 11:12)
2. He would be betrayed by a friend   *(Psalm 41:9)*
3. He would be forsaken by his disciples   *(Zechariah 13:7)*
4. He would be accused by false witnesses   *(Psalm 35:11)*
5. He would be dumb in the presence of his accusers   *(Isaiah 53:7)*

6. He would be scourged   *(Isaiah 50:6)*
7. He would have his garments parted   *(Psalm 22:18)*
8. He would be mocked by his enemies   *(Psalm 22:7,8)*
9. He would be given gall and vinegar to drink   *(Psalm 69:21)*
10. Not one bone in his body would be broken   *(Psalm 34:20)*
11. He would die in the presence of malefactors and thieves
                                                                 (Isaiah 53:12)
12. The 30 pieces of silver would be used to buy the potters' field
    (Zechariah 11:13)

During the course of his lifetime the Messiah prophesied many things himself. On one occasion he told his disciples how it would come to pass that he would have to go to Jerusalem, suffer many things at the hands of the chief priests and be killed. When Peter heard this, he rose up and said to the Messiah in essence: "No way is this going to happen as long as I am around. I will defend you." But the Messiah rebuked Peter and said: **"Before the cock crows twice, you will deny me three times."**

(Matthew 26: 69-75)

Subsequently, during the detention of the Messiah and his subjection to torture, various people accused Peter of being with him. After Peter's third denial, the sun began to rise and the cock crowed. Suddenly Peter remembered what the Messiah had said to him and he wept bitterly.

At another time, the Messiah sat down close to a well to rest. A Samaritan woman came and began to draw out water. The Jews normally would never speak to a Samaritan, as they were considered the lowest form of life, but the Messiah spoke to this woman. He said to her: *"Woman, have you no husband to draw out the water for you?"* She replied: *"Sir, I have no husband."* And he said to her: *"You had five husbands and the man you have now is not your husband."* At this she looked at him intently and replied: *"Sir, I perceive you are a prophet"* *(John 4:19)*. At yet another time, close to the end of his ministry, he walked with his disciples as they admired the magnificence of the Great Temple in Jerusalem. As they marvelled at it, he told them: *"Not one stone shall be left upon another."* Thus he prophesied the destruction of the Temple. Less than 40 years later this prophecy was fulfilled when a Roman general named Titus and his soldiers destroyed the Temple so completely that not one stone was left upon another.

In one study, a scholar named Grant R. Jeffrey (in his book *Armageddon: Appointment with Destiny*)[65] assessed the likelihood of some of these prophecies coming to pass by applying numerical probabilities to them. For instance, in *Micah 5:2* it is prophesied that the Messiah would be born in the village of Bethlehem. Now there were thousands of villages in Israel at that time. So the chances of him being born in Bethlehem, a tiny insignificant hamlet, were actually thousands to one. Jeffrey came up with a conservative estimate of 200 to 1. Then he took another prophecy: that the Messiah would make his entrance into Jerusalem on an ass *(Zechariah 9:9)*. Now kings do not ride around on an ass, so Jeffrey put the probability of this coming to pass at 50 to 1.

So the combined odds of both of these prophecies coming to pass regarding one man is 200 x 50 or 10,000 to 1. Jeffrey continued on with 11 other specific prophecies concerning the Messiah. Among the prophecies he tested are the following:

	PROBABILITY
1. **The Messiah would be born in Bethlehem** *(Prophesied in Micah 5:2)*	1 in 200
2. **He would enter Jerusalem on an ass** *(Prophesied in Zechariah 9:9)*	1 in 50
3. **He would be betrayed by a friend** *(Prophesied in Psalm 41:9)*	1 in 10
4. **Have his hands and feet pierced** *(Prophesied in Psalm 22:16)*	1 in 100
5. **Be sold for 30 pieces of silver** *(Prophesied in Zechariah 11:13)*	1 in 100
6. **Have his betrayal money thrown down in the Temple and exchanged for the potters' field** *(Prophesied in Zechariah 11:13)*	1 in 200
7. **Be crucified in the presence of thieves** *(Prophesied in Isaiah 53:12)*	1 in 100

He continued on in this manner, assigning probabilities to eleven different Old Testament prophecies relating to the Messiah. When he determined the probability of these predictions being fulfilled in the course of the lifetime of one man, the statistical chances worked out at one chance in 10 billion times a billion. Or one chance in 10,000,000,000,000,000,000.

He equated the possibility of these prophecies coming to pass with this simple analogy:

"Suppose you gave me a ring from your finger. I take this ring and go up in an aeroplane and fly over the seven oceans of the world. Somewhere over one of the oceans, I throw your ring out the window. Then I return to you and I give you a boat and a fishing rod. I tell you to sail over all the oceans of the world. When you feel lucky, you can stop the boat and let down your fishing line, and you have one chance to hook your ring and claim it back."

For when he calculated the probabilities, based on the numbers given, he deduced that it would be less than one-twentieth of a square inch of the total area of all the combined sea beds of all the oceans in the world. That represents about the size on one printed letter on this page.

Jeffrey took only eleven predictions into consideration. As I have already stated, the Messiah literally fulfilled 109 prophecies from the Old Testament, 25 specific ones in the last 24 hours of his life. Imagine what the statistical probabilities would be of those coming to pass!

Now I know that some people will argue that all these Gospels were written after the death of the Messiah. Others will claim that the authors of the Gospels contrived to deceive in their references to the prophecies of old. But this argument makes no sense.

These were ordinary men doing ordinary work. They were not scribes or priests or religious leaders. Mark was a shepherd, Matthew a reviled tax-collector. Luke was a physician, a doctor. Do you think that they would actually sit down together and try to hatch such a plot and carry it out? Could you persuade four of your friends to sit down and write four different accounts of an incident stretching over 89 chapters and many thousands of words? I think not. As you will discover, there is a lot more to this than meets the eye.

To give one example of how prophecy unfolds - which is very pertinent to our study and to the world we live in today - we need only look at Israel. In hundreds of prophecies throughout the Old Testament, it was prophesied that the Israelites would be driven out of Palestine and Jerusalem, that they would be scattered to the four corners of the world (wandering Jews), and that everywhere they would go, they would be persecuted, despised and hated.

In 70 AD this prophecy began to be fulfilled. After he sacked Jerusalem, Titus slaughtered about one million Jews. The rest were scattered to the four corners of the globe. They have been vilified and persecuted every-where they have gone. This persecution culminated in the gas chambers of the Nazis, where millions of them were murdered. So this particular prophecy, which appears hundreds of times, has literally been fulfilled in one ethnic group.

But wait. In dozens of other prophecies we are told that in the last days Yaweh would gather his people again and establish them in Palestine and in Jerusalem, where they would have their own homeland at last. This would be done to show the rest of the nations that we were living in the last days. Around the turn of the 20th century, a few Jews began resettling in Palestine. Then in May 1948 Israel became a nation once again almost 2,000 years after the dispersal of its people. When next you view images on TV concerning the Jewish people in Israel, you are watching prophecy being fulfilled. About $5^1/_2$ million Jews now live in Israel and world peace is contingent on what happens there. Even though the Jews possess only one-sixth of 1% of all Arab land, they are nonetheless hated by most Arabs. Why have the Jewish people suffered so much? Why is it that, wherever they have gone, they have been humiliated and persecuted?

With the Crucifixion of the Messiah, the sorrows of the Jewish race began, for when they rejected their Messiah they brought calamity upon their own heads. When they were baying for the blood of the Messiah, they shouted with one voice:

"His blood be on us and on our children."

Matthew 27:25

Ever since that day the sword has been upon the Jewish people, for Yaweh had promised them that His judgment would fall on them in the future tribulation. But Yaweh first promised to restore his people to Israel and Jerusalem and indicated that, by doing so, this would be a sign to other nations.

And He shall set up an ensign for the nations, and assemble the outcasts of Israel, and gather together the dispersed of Judah from the four corners of the Earth.

Isaiah 11: 11,12

Bear in mind that this was written about 650 years before Christ. Yet here we are, over 2,600 years later, and the Jews are celebrating their return to their homeland! This is only one of many Old Testament passages which foretell of the return of the nation of Israel after the worldwide scattering of its people.

So here we are in the 21st century. The Jewish people have been back in Israel for more than 50 years now. This is prophecy coming to pass before our very eyes. And we are also told that in the future this world will perish on the rock which is Jerusalem *(Zechariah 12: 2-4).*

Prophecy is history written in advance. Because the Scriptures have been ignored for so long by so many, we do not know or understand how to interpret them. It is clear from the character of the Bible that it is not the work of man, for man could not have written it.

As Clarence Larkin, in his book *Dispensational Truth,* says:

"It details with scathing and unsparing severity the sins of its greatest personages, men such as Abraham, Jacob, Moses, David and Solomon, charging them with falsehood, treachery, pride, adultery, cowardice, murder and gross licentiousness. And it presents the history of the Children of Israel as a humiliating record of ingratitude, idolatry, unbelief and rebellion. It is safe to say that, without specific guidance and direction to do so from the Holy Spirit, the Jews would never have chronicled the sinful history of their nation in this way."

The Book of Revelation is almost entirely prophetic. It deals with the last days of man's life on this Earth as we know it. This book has wrongly been called "The Revelation of St. John the Divine," for its correct title is given in chapter one, verse one: "The Revelation of Jesus Christ ..." The word "revelation" in the Greek is *"apokalupsis,"* which means *"unveiling,"* as in the taking away of a veil to reveal the face. In another sense it can mean to take away a veil in order to reveal future events in much the same way that curtains are drawn back to reveal a stage.

What we will be examining in this section is a summary of many of the prophecies contained in the Apocalypse, the Book of Revelation. We will endeavour to decode many of these predictions and put them into ordinary language. We shall also examine many of the signs we are told will precede these future events. We shall take both the prophecies and the signs and look at them in the light of many of the events which are happening around us in the world today.

Many of the incidents portrayed in the Apocalypse are quite frightening, so we will also be demonstrating how they may be avoided. For there is an alternative, there is an escape route, there is another path which leads away from the events portrayed in the prophecies of the Apocalypse. Right now, though, it's back to the future.

Parousia

Not long before his death, the Messiah spoke privately with some of His closest friends. This meeting took place on the Mount of Olives, which is a hill close to Jerusalem. They asked Him a most interesting question, recorded in Matthew 24:

> "Tell us," they asked, "when shall these things be and what will be the sign of your coming (*Parousia*) and of the end of this age?"

I will now reveal what His answer was. I will then elaborate on each point and tie these in with the prophecies of the *Book of Revelation*. These signs, foretold by the prophet Jesus Christ, are directly related to the Great Tribulation period, which is to last for seven years.

Verse 4
And Jesus answered: Watch out that no one deceives you. For many will come in my name, claiming "I am the Christ," and will deceive many.

Verse 6
You will hear of wars and rumours of wars, but see to it that you are not alarmed. Such things must happen, but the end is still to come.

Verse 7
Nation shall rise against nation and kingdom against kingdom. There will be famines and earthquakes in various places.

Verse 8
All these things are the beginning of birth pangs.

Verse 10
At that time many will turn away from the faith and will betray and hate each other, and many false prophets will appear and deceive many people.

Verse 12
Because of the increase of wickedness, the love of most will grow cold.

Verse 21
For then there will be great distress, unequalled from the beginning of the world until now, and never to be equalled again.

Verse 22
If those days had not been cut short, no one would survive, but, for the sake of the elect, those days will be shortened.

Verse 24
False christs and false prophets will appear and perform great signs and miracles to deceive even the elect, if that were possible.

Verse 25
See, I have told you ahead of time.

Verse 35
Heaven and Earth will pass away, but my words will never pass away.

In Luke 21, we have a parallel discourse in which the Messiah elaborates on this prophecy:

Verse 25
There will be signs in the sun, moon and the stars. On the Earth, nations will be in anguish and perplexity at the roaring and tossing of the sea.
Verse 26
Men will faint from terror, apprehensive of what is coming on the world.
Verse 28
When these things begin to take place, stand up and lift up yours heads, because your redemption is drawing near.
Luke 21:25,26,28

Note this last comment. The Messiah says that when we see these things we will know that our redemption is near. I would argue that all these things are happening right now. But let us take a closer look. The first sign the Messiah said to watch out for is:

1. False Christs, False Prophets and Deception

Have you noticed lately how many weird cults and sects appear in the news? Hundreds if not thousands of new groups are sprouting up all over the Western Hemisphere. Most of them have a leader who claims to have authority from God. All believe that they possess the truth.

There has also been a huge increase in the numbers of "false prophets." Every time you open a newspaper or magazine you are confronted with advertisements offering personal predictions about the future. You can phone in to radio stations with your personal problems and have a "professional" read the Tarot cards to tell you how you might deal with your situation. Three out of every four people who pick up a newspaper in the UK read their horoscopes. Everywhere, mystic and new age shops are opening. In these you can obtain books and information on all the occult arts and new age practices. Everything from Tarot cards to astrology charts to birthstones and crystals. Again, this is a manifestation of the prevalence of false prophets and deception which we were told we would see as we approach the last days. Nobody is teaching our children any alternative Christian doctrine. As a result, they are lapping up this deception to fill the spiritual void in their lives.

We are specifically forbidden to have anything to do with fortune-tellers, soothsayers, necromancers and other false prophets who are in opposition to the true God and His son. Time and time again we are warned of such people in the Bible, but because we do not know these truths we are easy prey for the agents of darkness. Suppose you wanted to know the future, and you were standing in a hall with two doors. On one door is the name Jesus Christ. On the other is the name Louis Cifer. Which door would you go through? Most people I know have no problem going to fortune-tellers, reading their horoscope or having their palms read. But when I try to tell them what the Messiah says about their future, they don't want to know. In fact, many get downright annoyed.

The first thing we are told to watch out for in the Tribulation period is people who claim to be true Christians and prophets of the true God. We are told that when we see these signs beginning to manifest themselves, we will know that the time is near. Open your eyes. Look around you. The writing is on the wall.

2. **You will hear of wars and rumours of wars ... nation shall rise against nation and kingdom against kingdom.**

The United States recently approved a huge increase in its military budget. North Korea and China have the capability to devastate American cities with nuclear warheads. India and Pakistan are now nuclear powers. Russia has almost twice as many nuclear weapons as the United States. Between them, these two countries have 35,000 nuclear weapons, strategic and tactical.

All over the globe, wars are breaking out, and rumours of wars abound in scores of other regions. Elsewhere, old adversaries are renewing their conflicts.

In verse 7 it is stated that "*kingdom shall rise against kingdom.*" The Greek word for kingdom is *ethnos,* from which we get our English word "ethnic." In other words, ethnic-cleansing, one tribe against another.

Wars and rebellions receive prominent coverage in our newspapers and on our TV screens on a daily basis. But these are mere portents of the last great war which will be fought at the end of the seven years of the Great Tribulation. We were told that when we see all these things coming to pass it will be like the beginning of labour pains. As the birth gets closer, the intensity of the pain increases. We will see more and more wars and potential for war between more nations. We will see more "ethnic-cleansing" between differing peoples. All these things must come to pass.

Look at the pages of history. They are filled, from the earliest days, with the accounts of battles and triumphs of one army over another. Ever since Cain slew his brother, Abel, man has continuously gone to war with his neighbour. They said that the first world war was the war to end all wars. How little they know. In verse 22 of Matthew 24 Jesus said that **"unless those days are shortened, no flesh would be saved."** It is only in these latter years that countries have come to possess weapons capable of destroying all living things on the face of the Earth. If we don't learn from history, we are bound to repeat it.

3. **There will be great earthquakes, famines and pestilence in various places.** *(Luke 21:11)*

Earthquakes have been increasing in frequency and intensity in every decade since records began in the late 1800s. Up to the 1950s, there was an average of two to four major earthquakes per decade. In the 1960s, there were 13 major earthquakes. In the 1970s, there were 51; in the 1980s, 86. And between 1990 and 1996 there were over 150 major earthquakes.[66]

Aside from earthquakes, we are told that people will be **"perplexed with the roaring and tossing of the seas."** I believe that the Messiah was referring here to an increased incidence of unpredictable weather. Global warming is blamed for the peculiar weather we are experiencing in every quarter of the world. Tornados and hurricanes rip through towns and villages, leaving havoc, devastation and death in their wake. Freak waves inundate low-lying lands and drown thousands. Floods on a scale never before witnessed have displaced millions of people. In every country in the world the weather patterns are changing. The polar ice caps have melted and receded by 150 miles in the past 10 years. The hole in the ozone layer is now as big as North America, including Canada. Even if we wanted to do something to reverse this trend, we could not.

When it comes to famines and pestilence, it is the same story. Famine is on the increase around the globe despite the fact that there is over-production of food in the developed world. One would think that, in these days of fibre-optics, cyberspace and the internet, we could have found a way to feed hungry people. At a time when famines are continuing to ravage the Third World, farmers elsewhere are being taken off the land at an alarming rate. And this pattern is being repeated world-wide. Is this a coincidence, or is something else occurring here? Jesus told us that there would be a huge increase in pestilence (disease) in the last days. It is hard to know where to start, for almost on a weekly basis we hear of new, stronger viruses and the discovery of new forms of lethal bacteria.

Despite medical advances, old diseases, once thought conquered, are making a comeback and are killing millions again. Cholera and malaria are examples of these: 3,000 children die each day from malaria. Tuberculosis is another disease we thought was under control. Now three million people per year are dying from TB. Heroin and crack-cocaine addiction are other forms of pestilence which stalk our cities, sucking life from our young people. And then there is AIDS.

It is the same story in every country in Africa. In some villages, only old men and women and young orphaned children are to be found. Over 25 million people are now HIV-positive in Africa and this figure is rising rapidly.

There is an urban legend circulating among the less-educated in Africa which is truly chilling. People believe that if you have AIDS and you have intercourse with an infant, your disease will be cured. Nine men were recently put on trial in South Africa for raping a 10-month-old baby girl. Sadly, this is happening all over the continent of Africa.

The population of the world is increasing at the rate of about 90 million per year and is set to double from six to 12 billion in 40 years. The Millennium Institute recently listed the following alarming environmental projections:

- Species are becoming extinct at the rate of 104 per day (that's almost 38,000 species of animals, fish, plants etc becoming extinct every year).

- In the next 10 years one-third of all species which exist at present will have disappeared.

- In less than five years, over half of the world's crude oil reserves will have been used up.

- In about 60 years from now the concentration of carbon dioxide in the Earth's atmosphere will have doubled.[67]

Next time your mind is filled with TV images of war, famine, pestilence, disease and natural disasters, remember that your redemption is close at hand.

"Stand up and lift your heads, because your redemption is drawing near."

Luke 21:28

TIME OF THE SIGNS

To say that the Western Hemisphere is mainly Christian is a misnomer. Any vestiges of Christianity are fast disappearing and are being replaced with neo-paganism. We are in a post-Christian era and our moral values have descended accordingly.

When describing the moral and spiritual state of the world of the last days, the Messiah compared it to two other distinct periods of history. Firstly, he said that it would be like the days of Noah, when all the people of the world were "eating, drinking, marrying and given in marriage." The other time he compared it to was that of Lot, when he lived in the cities of Sodom and Gomorrah. Let us take a closer look at these two scenarios and see if we notice anything unusual about them:

> "Just as it was in the days of Noah, so shall it be also in the days of the Son of Man. People were eating, drinking, marrying and being given in marriage up to the day Noah entered the Ark.
> Then the Flood came and destroyed them all.
> It was the same in the days of Lot. People were eating and drinking, buying and selling, planting and building.
> But the day Lot left Sodom, fire and sulphur rained down from Heaven and destroyed them all.
> It will be just like this on the day the Son of Man is revealed."
>
> *Luke 17: 26-30*

The background to the time of Noah is found in Genesis chapter six, which we have already looked at extensively. This tells us that in those days the number of people living on the Earth had increased greatly. But they had also increased in violence and immorality. We are told as well that they were *"eating, drinking, marrying and given in marriage."* The implication is that this was their main activity in life: to eat well and get drunk so that they could fulfil the lusts of the flesh.

From a study of these chapters in Genesis, we can see that, because of the influence of the *Nephilim*, people of the world at that time had descended almost to the level of animals. As part of their religious practice they used to burn their own children in sacrifice to their pagan gods. They had degenerated to the level of wild savages to such a degree that we are told:

> The Lord saw how great man's wickedness on the Earth had become, and that every inclination of the thoughts of his heart was only evil all the time.
>
> *Genesis 6:5*

This is why God's judgment fell on the world at that time. Only Noah and his wife, their three sons and their wives were saved from the destruction which ensued. God gave Noah the instruction to build the Ark and fill it with animals. He was building the Ark for a long time, maybe 70 years, before the Flood came. Throughout this time the people mocked Noah for building this huge vessel when nobody had ever seen rain before, let alone a flood. So they continued on in the same manner of life. But then one day, when they least expected it, the fountains of the deep were broken up and the floodgates of the heavens were opened and it began to pour.

Every person, animal and bird was drowned. The whole Earth was engulfed by this cataclysmic deluge. The floods continued for 150 days before the waters began to recede. It was almost a year later before Noah and his family landed and got off the Ark. We are told that "as it was, so shall it be." When the conditions which prevailed in the days of Noah are repeated, this will indicate the proximity of the Second Coming.

Likewise in the days of Lot, when he lived with his wife and two daughters in the city of Sodom. The conditions there bear a striking similarity to those of Noah's day. Let us take a look at the background to his situation:

> The two angels arrived at Sodom in the evening, and Lot was sitting in the gateway of the city. When he saw them he got up to meet them and bowed down with his face to the ground.
> "My Lords," he said, "please turn aside to your servants's house. You can wash your feet and spend the night and then go on your way early in the morning."
> Before they had gone to bed, all the men from every part of the city of Sodom, both young and old, surrounded the house.
> They called to Lot: "Where are the men who came to you tonight? Bring them out to us so that we can have intercourse with them."
>
> *Genesis 19:1,2,4,5*

The story goes on to show that, in order to stave off the men and boys of Sodom, Lot offered them his two daughters. But they were not interested in his daughters. They wanted the two men so that they could gang-rape them. So they threatened Lot. But the angels pulled Lot back into the house and struck the men with blindness. Then they told Lot to gather up his wife and two daughters and escape into the mountains because God was going to destroy the city and the other towns around it. They were instructed not to stop and not to look back. As they escaped, God rained down burning sulphur on Sodom and Gomorrah. But Lot's wife looked back and was turned into a pillar of salt.

So the conditions were the same in the life of Lot as they were at the time of Noah. And so shall it be in the latter days before the second advent of the Messiah.

> It was the same in the days of Lot. People were eating and drinking, buying and selling, planting and building.
>
> *Luke 17:28*

The inference from this was that they were good days economically. People lived to enjoy food and drink. There was plenty of profitable economic activity, which meant a lot of building and planting of food. People were well-off. This gave them ample time to enjoy the finer things of life, art, gourmet food and the best wines. And we are then told that "all of the men of Sodom, both young and old" came around to Lot's house because they wanted to rape the two men to whom he had given shelter.

Homosexuality in the Bible is a vile sin. And it was because of this rampant promiscuity that God destroyed Sodom and Gomorrah and the towns around them. We read that:

> The Lord said: "The outcry against Sodom and Gomorrah is so great and their sin so grievous ..."
>
> *Genesis 18:20*

The moral climate surrounding these two events, the deluge at the time of Noah and the destruction of Sodom and Gomorrah, are examples of the coming judgment upon the Earth as recorded in the Book of Revelation. Because of man's rejection of God and of His Messiah, the wrath of God will fall once again on mankind. But just as Noah and his family were taken out before the Flood and Lot and his family were removed before the burning sulphur fell on Sodom and Gomorrah, so too the people of God will be removed when the Messiah comes back briefly in the clouds to "Rapture" his own. Thus, those of us who believe in God and accept His son as Our Lord and Saviour will be saved from the wrath and the Great Tribulation which will fall suddenly on those who least expect it. Paul, speaking of these last days, says:

> For when they shall say "peace and safety," then sudden destruction will come upon them, as labour pains on a pregnant woman, and they will not escape.
>
> *I Thessalonians 5:3*

Is there not a striking similarity between the conditions which prevailed in the days of Noah and Lot and conditions in the world today? People were well-off. Business was flourishing. The building and construction industry was prospering and there was plenty to eat and drink. Consequently, people did not have to work too hard. There was also widespread violence. The pursuit of pleasure was the main objective and homosexual activity and immorality were rife.

Today, we are constantly bombarded by the liberal secular humanist agenda telling us that, if it feels good, we should do it. Films, magazines and TV are continually pushing the "free sex for all" agenda. Thus all the attendant ills which accompany these sins are prevalent. Divorce is on the increase everywhere. Sexually-transmitted diseases are rampant. It is the same within the gay community. And, for the most part, the majority of young people today accept homosexual practice as being normal.

But all sinners have the opportunity to turn from their vices and receive the free gift of grace and eternal life. In the New Testament, Paul, referring to homosexuality, writes:

> Because of this, God gave them over to shameful lusts. Even their women exchanged natural relations for unnatural ones.
> In the same way, the men also abandoned natural relations with women and were inflamed with lust for one another.
> Men committed indecent acts with other men, and received in themselves the due penalty for their perversion.
>
> *Romans 1:26,27*

This is Yaweh's view. I did not write the Bible. But, as a Christian, I am bound by my conscience to uphold what I believe. I would hope that people with opposing views would be tolerant of the Christian position. After all, we are constantly being asked to be tolerant of the gay community.

We are all sinners and we all fall short of the calling of God. I am a sinner, and no one knows that better than I. "God loves the sinner, but He hates the sin." The Messiah died for all mankind. Everyone can be saved if they so choose. Remember Mary Magdalene? She was caught in adultery, the penalty for which was death. Yet Jesus said: "Neither do I condemn thee. Go thy way and sin no more." He did not condemn her. In fact, she became one of his closest friends and was at the foot of the Cross with the other women when his disciples were absent.

"As it was then, so shall it be." This is what the Messiah told us to watch out for almost 2,000 years ago. When we see the same conditions prevailing in the world as those in the days of Noah and Lot, we are to know that the day is at hand.

Because of the immoral state of the people, God made a judgment against them. He did this as an example to us. In both instances he removed the righteous people before he destroyed the rest. The immorality and perversion of our world today is a mirror-image of the days of Noah and Lot. The Earth is ripening for judgment. The day is at hand. It is make-up-your-mind time. The choice is yours.

Money Talks

In the first and second epistles of Paul to Timothy we are given additional information as to the conditions pertaining to the "last days" or "latter days." The reference here is to the last days prior to the Rapture of the people of God and the subsequent beginning of the seven years of Great Tribulation. In 1 Timothy 4:1, Paul gives us an interesting insight:

> **The spirit clearly says that in the latter times some will abandon the faith and follow deceiving spirits and things taught by demons.**
> *1 Timothy 4:1*

The above verse tells us that people will be tricked by deceiving spirits and demons. Deception leads to another sign of the last days, apostasy.

This is a turning away from Yaweh and from Christian morality to a reliance on self. For hundreds of years the Western Hemisphere has prospered because it has relied on Christian principles and the laws originally given to Moses. But now many of these laws are being cast aside. On an almost universal scale we can see that man is living in total opposition to the precepts of Christianity.

> **But mark this: there will be terrible times in the last days.**
> **People will be lovers of themselves, lovers of money, boastful, proud, abusive, disobedient to their parents, ungrateful, unholy,**

without love, unforgiving, slanderous, without self-control, brutal, not lovers of the good, treacherous, rash, conceited lovers of pleasure rather than lovers of God.

2 Timothy 3:1-5

The Christian ideal is totally opposite to all of the above. But when we look around us at society today what we are witnessing is precisely what is stated in the above passage. Today, people love themselves. We are told in the Second Commandment that we should love our neighbour as ourselves. But people today love themselves in a selfish, egotistical manner. As a result, they are proud and boastful.

Lovers of money. Was there ever a time in recorded history in which money was so important? Today, for most people, money is god. Unless people have it, they cannot find contentment. Our whole life seems to revolve around the pursuit of money. And, once we have it, we become lovers of pleasure rather than lovers of God. And people who acquire money almost always succumb to pride. In fact, pride is perhaps the one sin we can readily see in other people but never in ourselves. And pride always comes before a fall.

In the last days, people will become *"abusive, disobedient to their parents, ungrateful, unholy."* We are becoming more and more insular. And more and more *"ungrateful."* We take things for granted and very seldom pause to say "thanks." For we have become *"unholy."* We have no regard for the "higher powers." Society is becoming more and more materialistic and less and less spiritual.

In the last days, Paul tells us that people will be *"without love,"* meaning that they will become more callous and objurate. Jesus said the same when speaking of the last days. **"Because lawlessness will increase, the love of many will grow cold"** (*Matthew 24:12*). Thus people will become *"unforgiving,"* for their hearts will turn to stone because of their propensity to sin. People will become *"slanderous."* The reference here is to lying and liars. This is especially evident in our political leaders today. In every country we have political leaders who are both liars and lovers of money.

"Not lovers of the good" refers to the many who will hate and despise those who believe in the Messiah and try to promote Christian morals and teachings. In the last days people will be *"lovers of pleasure rather that lovers of God."* Party, party, party. If it feels good, do it. All over the world, getting stoned and having sex is what is fashionable.

If ever a time in history was in keeping with Paul's description of the spiritual bereftness of the last days, it is now. But if we are aware of these things then we do not have to be deceived by them.

The day of the Lord will come like a thief in the night.
While people are saying "peace and safety," destruction will come on them suddenly, as labour pains on a pregnant woman, and they will not escape.
But you, brothers, are not in darkness so that this day should surprise you like a thief.
You are all sons of the light and sons of the day. We do not belong to night or to darkness.

1 Thessalonians 5:2-5

We are never told by Yaweh or by the Messiah that conditions in the world will improve prior to His return. We are told to expect that things will get progressively worse. Wars and rumours of wars, famines and earthquakes, child pornography, teenage pregnancies, abortion on demand, rampant child abuse, corruption in high places. The list is endless.

Violence and murder are an almost daily occurrence everywhere in the present time. This breakdown in respect for human life surely indicates that we are living in the generation which will witness the return of the Messiah. And this is our one and only hope, for without the certainty of His second coming, we are doomed. But the good news is that He will return to save us from the wrath to come. And after the wrath he will begin to put this world back in order. This is our certain hope.

THE COUNTERFEIT

Having examined many of the signs we are told will be evident in the events leading up to the Apocalypse, we are now almost ready to delve into the Book of Revelation and consider what it has to say. Later, we will discuss how we can avoid the period known as the Great Tribulation. But first I would like to examine the character of what Scripture calls the Antichrist. We are told that a powerful political leader will rise to prominence in a future seven-year period and that this individual will dominate world events. But, before he can assume power, all the Christians must be removed to make way for the seven years of Great Tribulation.

The Devil's Advocate

"Anti" means "instead of" and not "against," as most people think. So this man, who will be directly controlled by Satan, is "instead of" Christ. He will be the devil's messiah, as it were. He will have a brief but eventful reign in the Earth lasting for seven years from the beginning of the Great Tribulation. This man will rise very fast on the world's political stage and he will attain tremendous power and influence. He will be the head of a confederacy of ten extremely rich and powerful "kingdoms." He will be the most charismatic and eloquent of all leaders. The world will love him. He will talk peace but will wage war. Most, but not all, will be deceived into thinking that he is the one who can bring peace to the world. How is this man going to gain such power? We can only speculate on this. Historically, many dictators rose to power on the back of some disaster or other in their homeland. Hitler, for instance, came to prominence after the economic collapse of Germany in the 1920s. So the Antichrist may well emerge as the man to lead the world in prosperity and peace after some global catastrophe. This could be a financial crash or perhaps a largescale military confrontation which pushes the world to the brink of a nuclear holocaust.

One way or another, this man will gain unprecedented worldwide political and military power. Not only will he have wonderful presence and communications skills, he will have what seems like magical powers as well. With these he will deceive the whole world, except for the elect of God, who will see through his mask.

He will be the most powerful and charismatic political leader ever to take office. Clarence Larkin, in his book *Dispensational Truth,* says of this man:

> "He will be a composite man. One who embraces in his character the abilities of Nebuchadnezzar, Alexander the Great and Caesar Augustus. He will have the marvellous gift of attracting unregenerate men. The irresistible fascination of his personality, his versatile attainments, superhuman wisdom, great administrative and executive ability, along with his powers as a consummate flatterer, a brilliant diplomatist, a superb strategist, will make him the most conspicuous and prominent of men. All these gifts will be conferred on him by Satan, whose tool he will be."

This very powerful leader will have an ally. In Revelation, this accomplice is called the "False Prophet." He will be a religious man who will give support to the Antichrist. The "False Prophet" will head a worldwide religious movement which will look like the real thing, but it will be a sham. The "False Prophet" will deceive many with "lying signs and wonders." He will have extraordinary spiritual powers, which most people will believe come from God. But his source of power will be the devil himself.

In the first century, the disciples of the Messiah performed many "signs, miracles and wonders" in the name of Jesus. This man and his followers will likewise perform many miracles and wonders. But, according to the Word of God, these will be "lying signs and wonders."

The general public are being deluged at present with a plethora of movies, TV programmes and books which all promote and support "magic." *Buffy the Vampire Slayer, Lord of the Rings* and *Harry Potter* are examples of these. I believe that all of these are being used to "soften the ground" and prepare the people for this future leader and his accomplice, who will deceive the entire world with their "lying signs and wonders."

This new religious movement will have its basis in pagan worship, with an adherence to astrology and the study of the signs of the Zodiac as its foundation. Again, I believe that we can already see the burgeoning of this future religious sect with the emergence of the New Age movement all over the world. But it is not "new," because this religion is ancient: its foundations go back to Babylon in Old Testament times and to the activities of the *Nephilim.*

Sex will play a big part in this new religious worship, as also will the belief that we are all gods who have the power within us to make peace with and heal the planet.

Look around you. Already this Earth is filled with the disciples of New Age paganism. We see it everywhere and it is being propelled by the media, especially television.

This is similar to the situation in Sodom and Gomorrah prior to their destruction. Ezekiel 16:49 provides some insight into the conditions which prevailed:

> **Behold, this was the iniquity of thy sister Sodom: pride, fullness of bread and abundance of idleness was in her and in her daughters.**

So here we are given three sins of Sodom:
1. Pride
2. Fullness of Bread
3. Abundance of Idleness

This is an accurate description of many countries in the Western Hemisphere today. Because we are so well-off, we do not need Yaweh. We are self-sufficient with fullness of bread and, as a result, an abundance of idleness. It does not say here "abundance of unemployment." There is a difference. Many employers cannot find people to fill job vacancies today in spite of the fact that many millions are unemployed. This is because there is an "abundance of idleness."

These are the conditions which prevailed in Sodom and Gomorrah before their destruction. These are the conditions the Messiah told us to look for prior to His second coming.

In ancient times, the sun and the penis were worshipped as the givers of life. In many pagan countries, towers or obelisks representing the male organ were pointed towards the sun in recognition of the life-giving qualities of both. Egypt was a well-known centre for these phallic symbols. The obelisk which stands in St. Peter's Square in Rome is the same obelisk which once stood at the ancient temple of Heliopolis, which was the centre of Egyptian paganism. It was hauled to Rome at great expense by Caligula in 37-41 AD. Where these towers or obelisks were built, they represented the erect penis and were pagan symbols for the worship of sex.

There is a spiritual void in the world today and the religious are not filling it. Because of the recent scandals which have rocked the church, Roman Catholicism has lost its moral authority. Because we do not know the Bible and have little knowledge of the Word of Yaweh, good people are floundering in their faith. Because most priests have little knowledge of, or belief in, the Scriptures, they cannot feed their flocks. Empty religious rituals, based on the traditions of men and the doctrines of men, do not wash with the young people any more. So the spiritual void is being filled with music, drugs, alcohol and sex.

This spiritual bereftness that we are witnessing all across the world is the genesis for the New Age religion which will have as its leader a man described in Revelation as the "False Prophet."

Together with the Antichrist, these two will usher the world into an era of pseudo peace. According to the prophet Daniel, this leader will sign a peace deal with Israel guaranteeing military protection. The Jews will buy into this peace and the word of the Antichrist. But this era of peace and prosperity for the world will be short-lived, for it will lead to a war which will leave millions of Jews dead and end with the final great battle, which will be fought over Jerusalem.

With the fall of the Berlin Wall and the dissipation of communism, the new buzz-word is "democracy." Many of the ifluential politicial leaders and diplomats are working together to ensure peace and prosperity for all. The stage is being set for the revealing of a great political leader who will usher the world into a new era of peace. But this man will be the Antichrist, the son of Satan, and his goal will be total destruction. In the following passage, the Antichrist is called "*the man of lawlessness*" and the "*lawless one.*"

> Do not let anyone deceive you in any way, for that day will not come until the rebellion occurs and the man of lawlessness is revealed, the man doomed to destruction.
>
> He will oppose and will exalt himself over everything that is called God or is worshipped, so that he sets himself up in God's Temple, proclaiming himself to be God.
>
> And now you know what is holding him back, so that he may be revealed at the proper time.
>
> For the secret power of lawlessness is already at work. But the one who now holds it back will continue to do so until he is taken out of the way.
>
> And then the lawless one will be revealed, whom the Lord Jesus will overthrow with the breath of His mouth and destroy by the splendour of His coming.
>
> The coming of the lawless one will be in accordance with the work of Satan displayed in all kinds of counterfeit miracles, signs and wonders, and in every sort of evil that deceives those who are perishing.
>
> *II Thessalonians 2:3-4, 6-10*

We are now ready to examine the prophecies of the Messiah relating to the last days and the seven years of the Great Tribulation. Then, with the knowledge of the events which are to occur in these future times, we shall consider how it may be possible for us to avoid becoming victims of these apocalyptic predictions.

THE UNVEILING

> The Revelation of Jesus Christ, which God gave to him to show his servants what must soon take place.
>
> *The Book of Revelation 1:1*

Some people call this book "The Revelation of St. John the Divine." But this is incorrect. Its divine title is **"The Revelation of Jesus Christ."** The Greek word for revelation is *apokalupsis*, which means "unveiling." Thus Jesus Christ is unveiling the course of future events in the same way as you would draw curtains back so that you could view a stage. It can also mean the taking away of the veil so that we can see the face. Regarding this book, both descriptions are valid, for Jesus Christ is unveiling the events so that we may see what lies ahead. Also, in the future time, all will see the face of the Messiah. The Book of Revelation has for centuries been a closed book. Even students of the Bible have very little understanding of it. Many of the events pertaining to the last days of this world as we know it are stated in this book. Other prophetic passages from both the Old Testament and New Testament come to fruition in this book. The prophet Daniel received much information regarding these end days. When he had recorded it, God told him to **"seal up the words of this prophecy until the time of the end."** It is for this reason, I believe, that few have been able to decipher its secrets.

But now the Book of Revelation is beginning to unveil itself. And, although it contains descriptions of chaos and holocaust, we are assured by the Messiah himself that we are blessed if we read or hear these words.

> **Blessed is the one who reads the words of this prophecy, and blessed are those who hear it, and who take to heart what is written in it, because the time is near.**
>
> *Revelation 1:3*

Many ministers and religious teachers spend much of their time preaching the writings of the Gospels and Epistles and yet ignore the Book of Revelation. This is a paradox, since in this last book of the Bible we have Jesus himself speaking directly to us, for it is His revelation.

In this section, I will endeavour to summarise some of the events prophesied in Revelation. This is no easy job, as it is quite difficult to decode. However, I shall do my utmost to explain the parts which are understandable and tie these in with other parallel prophecies from the Scriptures.

Off the south-eastern coast of Turkey lies a small island named Patmos. The apostle John was incarcerated there because of his preaching of the resurrection of the Messiah. The Romans had a quarry on this island and John probably worked out his sentence there. He was an old man in his nineties at that stage. It was while he was on Patmos that he received the Revelation and was instructed to write down what he saw and heard. In verse one of chapter four it is stated:

> After this I looked and there before me was a door standing open in Heaven. And the voice I had first heard like a trumpet said: "Come up here and I will show you what must take place after this."

He then goes on to detail what he saw in this other place called "Heaven." What he describes is an amazing spectacle. He sees a throne and the One who is sitting on this throne is Yaweh. This throne is surrounded by 24 other thrones which, we are told, are occupied by 24 Elders. Who these Elders are, we do not know. But they bow down and worship Yaweh.

After this, John tells us, he sees in the right hand of Him who sits on the throne a scroll with writing on both sides. This scroll is sealed with seven seals. But who is worthy to open the seals and look inside? John weeps because no one could be found in Heaven or on Earth who could open the seals and look inside.

Then John sees a Lamb standing in the midst of the throne. The Lamb takes the scroll from the right hand of Him who sits upon the throne. Then all the Elders sing:

> "You are worthy to take the scroll and open its seals.
> Because you were slain and with your blood you purchased men for God."
>
> *Revelation 5:9*

Then the throne was encircled by 10,000 times 10,000 angels (which is 100 million of these spirit-men) and they began singing in praise of the One who sat on the throne and of the Lamb, who is Jesus.

In chapter six, John watched as the Lamb opened the first of the seven seals:

I looked and there before me was a white horse. Its rider held a bow, and he was given a crown, and he rode out as a conqueror bent on conquest.

The Lamb opened the second seal. Then another horse came out, a fiery red one. Its rider was given power to take peace from the Earth and make men slay each other. To him was given a large sword.

The Lamb opened the third seal, and there before me was a black horse. Its rider was holding a pair of scales in his hand.

Then I heard what sounded like a voice saying: "A quart of wheat for a day's wages, and three quarts of barley for a day's wages, and do not damage the oil and the wine."

The Lamb opened the fourth seal. I looked, and there before me was a pale horse. Its rider was named death, and Hades was following close behind him.

They were given power over a fourth of the Earth to kill by sword, famine and plague, and by the wild beasts of the Earth.

Revelation 6:1-8

These are sometimes referred to as the Four Horsemen of the Apocalypse. But what does all this mean? To find out, we go back to the parallel passage in Matthew, chapter 24.

The first things we are told to watch out for, according to the Messiah, are false prophets and false christs. Many will go out to deceive many, he said. He also told us to watch out for the one great false deceiver who would say "I am the Messiah" (Matthew 24:5). This is the Antichrist, who will emerge on the world political stage soon after the Rapture. He will put himself forward as the one who can bring peace to a world on the brink of war and turmoil. The people of the world will welcome this man with open arms. They will believe that they need to unite under a strong dictator who can deliver peace. This is why we see the first rider appearing on a white horse carrying a bow with no arrow, for this man will promise peace and reconciliation. It will be he who will broker a peace deal between Israel and the Arab nations guaranteeing them protection. This will mark the beginning of the seven years of Tribulation, according to the prophet Daniel (Daniel 7:27). A deceptive period of peace and stability will follow. Even the Jews will trust this powerful political leader. But although everyone will love this man and believe that they are entering a new era of world peace, his tenure will end in the greatest military holocaust ever witnessed on the Earth.

So the rider on the white horse is the Counterfeit Christ, also called the

Man of Sin, the Son of Perdition, the Antichrist.

We can see from the way things are developing in the world politically that the stage is being set for a single world government. Who would have thought just a few short years ago that the cold war would be over? Who could have envisaged the total collapse of communism in Russia and eastern Europe in such a short time? Almost overnight, the world's political landscape changed. Now democracy is sweeping the globe, promising freedom and prosperity for all. Democracy is the vehicle and money is the oil which promises to deliver this better future for mankind. This will be the promise of the rider on the white horse.

> **Then another horse came out, a fiery red one. Its rider was given power to take peace from the Earth and make men slay each other. To him was given a large sword.**

The second sign Jesus spoke of in *Matthew 24* was: **"Ye shall hear of wars and rumours of wars ... Nation shall rise against nation, and kingdom against kingdom."** This relates directly to the rider on the red horse, for in the Great Tribulation, after a pseudo peace which will last only a relatively short time, all hell will break loose.

The world at the present time is at a dangerous crossroads, with hundreds of conflicts going on and hundreds more bubbling under the surface, waiting to erupt. When the rider on the fiery red horse is let loose, all these tensions will be realised, with war and slaughter on a scale no one could even imagine.

> **The Lamb opened the third seal, and there before me was a black horse. Its rider was holding a pair of scales in his hand. Then I heard what sounded like a voice saying:**
> **"A quart of wheat for a day's wages, and three quarts of barley for a day's wages, and do not damage the oil and the wine."**

We can relate this to the third sign given by the Messiah when he foretold of those last days: **there will be famines.** The rider on the black horse delivers these famines. Black always denotes famine. And weighing-out of bread always denotes scarcity. Many famines have been foretold in the Bible. Take the story of Joseph and his multi-coloured coat. When Pharaoh had a dream, he could not find anyone in his court who could interpret his dream for him. He questioned all his soothsayers, mediums, fortune-tellers and astrologers. But they were bereft of useful information in those days, just as their counterparts are bereft of the truth in our day.

So Pharaoh called for Joseph. He asked Joseph if he could interpret the dream. Joseph replied that he could not, but said that God would give him the answer. Pharaoh recounted his dream to Joseph. In the dream, Pharaoh had been standing on the bank of the Nile. Seven fat and healthy cows came up out of the river. These were followed by seven lean cows who swallowed up the fat ones.

Then he saw seven ripe and healthy ears of corn growing on a single stalk. After them came seven other ears of corn, thin and scorched by the east wind. The seven thin ears swallowed up the seven healthy ones.

Joseph told him that the two dreams had the same meaning. Egypt was going to experience seven years of great abundance of food. But these would be followed by seven years of famine. This famine would ravage the land and the seven years of abundance would be forgotten because the famine would be so severe.

He suggested to Pharaoh that he choose a man to oversee the economy for the seven good years. This man would build warehouses and store one-fifth of the harvest during each of the seven years of plenty so that they would have enough food to sustain them through the seven years of famine.

Pharaoh listened to the interpretation and understood its significance. He also realised that it would make sense to follow Joseph's advice. So he gave Joseph the job. He elevated him so that only Pharaoh was above Joseph in the hierarchy of the Egyptian empire. From being the lowest of the low in the state jail, Joseph was elevated to the second-highest office in the land. And all because he trusted in Yaweh.

Later in the story we find that everything occurred just as Joseph had said it would. After the seven years of abundance there followed seven years of bitter famine. During this time all the countries around about implored Egypt to sell them food to sustain them through the famine. In these short seven years, Egypt amassed all the gold and treasures of these nations by selling them food. This is historical fact.

Now the rider on the black horse denotes a coming famine. You can scoff at this prospect or you can believe it. Pharaoh was wise enough to take the prophecy to heart and put measures in place to avert it.

I believe that this rider on the black horse is foretelling a great economic holocaust, a time in which a day's wages is worth a mere quart of wheat and three quarts of barley. One way or another, this is describing the collapse of the economic and monetary systems of the world. All around us today we can see signs of this impending financial collapse.

> **The Lamb opened the fourth seal. I looked, and there before me was a pale horse. Its rider was named Death, and Hades followed close behind him.**
> **They were given power over a fourth of the Earth to kill by sword, famine and plague, and by the wild beasts of the Earth.**
>
> *Revelation 6:8*

This is the fourth judgment mentioned by Jesus in Matthew 24:7. It is the judgment of "pestilence." The Greek word used here is *thanatos*, meaning death, in this instance caused by pestilence and disease. "Pestilence" is followed by the grave (*Hades*). These two words occur together because the latter results from the former. Hades follows in the train of death, because death ends in the grave. Wars, famines and the resulting pestilence are the means used by death and are always followed by a common outcome – committal to the grave.

We discussed earlier the huge problem at present with the spread of pestilence and disease. Yet what we are seeing now is nothing compared to the devastation which will be unleashed in the Great Tribulation, for we are told that half the population of the world will die as a result of the wars, famine, pestilence and disease which these Horsemen of Revelation represent. At today's figures, this means that approximately three billion people will die.

Again we are urged to heed the words of the Messiah when he said:

> **When you see all these things begin to come to pass, lift up your heads. Your redemption is near.**
>
> *Luke 21:28*

Is it not patently obvious that these prophecies, written almost 2,000 years ago, are unfolding before our very eyes? We were told that these events could be likened unto a woman in labour pains. The contractions become more frequent and more violent as the actual birth draws closer. So, too, we will see these convulsions become more frequent and more violent as we approach the seven years of Great Tribulation.

Thus this world must inevitably go through the anxiety, pain and bloodshed of the Great Tribulation before it can be reborn into the freedom of Paradise Regained.

As Jesus spoke it:

I tell you the truth, until Heaven and Earth disappear, not the smallest letter, nor the least stroke of a pen, will by any means disappear from the Law until everything is accomplished.

Matthew 5:18

The Seven Seals, the Seven Trumpets, the Seven Vials

The Fifth, Sixth and Seventh seals are then opened. I will give a brief summation:

The Fifth Seal

After the Rapture or "catching away" of the Christians, a huge population will be left to endure the seven years of wrath. Many of those who mock Christianity now and who refuse to heed the warnings will be isolated. People will turn to Yaweh and to the Messiah for salvation and help. It is going to be a dreadful seven years, but there is hope.

We are told that a large number of Jews will be converted to the teachings of the Messiah in this Tribulation. These will total 144,000 in all, 12,000 from each of the twelve tribes of Israel. Somehow, these 144,000 will be converted and will become powerful evangelists. As a result of their preaching, multitudes of people are going to believe and discover that the Messiah is their only hope. But there is a downside here, for many of these believers will die as a result of their faith.

We are told later on that the Antichrist will demand total allegiance. This will require everyone to display a mark or brand on their right hand or on their forehead. This mark will be a number. It is the mark of the Beast, whose number is 666. Anyone who refuses to display this mark will be unable to buy or sell or do business. And many who refuse because of their faith will be executed by the Antichrist and his one-world government forces. The inference from the Fifth Seal is that large numbers of Christians will die during the Tribulation period.

The Sixth Seal

This talks of an earthquake so massive that every mountain and every island will be removed from its place. The people of the world will be so terrified that they will call upon the rocks to fall on them.

Fall on us, and hide us from the face of Him who sits on the throne and from the wrath of the Lamb.
For the great day of their wrath has come, and who can stand?

Revelation 6:16,17

The Seventh Seal

The Seventh Seal introduces the seven Trumpet judgments. These are another series of woes which will fall upon the Earth in due course. After these Trumpet judgments, there will be another series of judgments, called the Vial judgments. There are seven of these also.

We do not know if all these judgments occur simultaneously or follow one another. However, I will submit a brief summary of these Trumpet and Vial judgments. Later, we will focus on particular aspects of them.

First Trumpet: *Revelation 8:7*

When the first angel sounds his trumpet, hail and fire, mixed with blood, is cast down upon the Earth. One-third of all the grass and one-third of all the trees will be burned up.

First Vial: *Revelation 16:2*

The first vial is poured out and causes horrible sores to appear on those who display the mark of the Beast. We are told that one-third of all the grass, trees and plants will be burned at the sounding of the first trumpet. Could it be that what is occurring right now with the ozone layer is a precursor to these woes? Already in many countries people are being scorched by the sun because of damage done to the ozone layer.

Scientists are saying that if the depletion of the ozone layer reaches 15%, millions will die from skin cancer. Once the thin ozone layer is damaged beyond a certain level, it cannot be repaired. The effect of this will be an increase in world temperatures and global warming. As a consequence, we can expect a decrease in available food and an increase in famine.

All these environmental hazards fit in exactly with the prophecies of the end times. They all seem to be occurring at the same time. And this is not just my opinion. It is scientific fact.

Second Trumpet: *Revelation 8:8,9*

When this second trumpet is sounded, something looking like a huge mountain, all ablaze, will be thrown into the sea. As a result, all life in one-third of the oceans will perish and one-third of all ships will be destroyed.

Second Vial: *Revelation 16:3*

The second vial foretells a similar catastrophe to that brought about by the sounding of the second trumpet: a huge burning object, resembling a star, will fall into the ocean and destroy all life and all ships in one-third of the seas.

This could be a huge meteor. Or, then again, John could be describing some type of nuclear holocaust. It could be another environmental disaster like that of Chernobyl. The Messiah told us in his discourse on the Mount of Olives that there would be an increase in earthquakes and volcanic eruptions in the last days. This is already occurring.

Third Trumpet: *Revelation 8:10,11*

This announces a huge star or meteor called "Wormwood." This star falls like a blazing torch on to all the freshwater rivers and lakes, polluting the water in one-third of the entire world. Many will die as a result of drinking the poisoned water.

Third Vial: *Revelation 16:4*

The third vial causes the springs and fountains of drinking water to be turned into "blood." This fits in with the prophecy of the third trumpet, which John described as a huge blazing star which fell upon the freshwater springs and polluted one-third of the world's water.

How many countries in the world have biological weapons of war? A great many, I would suggest. We know that such deadly weapons are already on the market. A small amount of one such poison, poured into a reservoir, could kill two million people. And there are radical fundamentalist Muslims who would love to inflict this "justice" on the West, particularly on the United States, which they detest.

Whether this "Wormwood" refers to biological warfare or to nuclear fall-out, we shall have to wait and see. But the potential for either is a stark reality in our precariously fickle world.

Fourth Trumpet: *Revelation 8:12*

As a consequence of the sounding of this trumpet, one-third of all light will disappear. The sun, moon and stars will lose one-third of their light. This will have catastrophic effects on the temperature of the Earth.

Fourth Vial: *Revelation 16: 8,9*

> The fourth angel poured out his bowl on the sun, and the sun was given power to scorch people with fire.
> They were seared by the intense heat and they cursed the name of God, who had control over these plagues, but they refused to repent and glorify Him.
>
> *Revelation: 16:8,9*

Fifth Trumpet: *Revelation 9:1-12*

As if things were not bad enough, we are here given a description of an eagle in flight proclaiming in a loud voice:

> Woe, woe to the inhabitants of the Earth because of the trumpet blasts about to be sounded by the other three angels.
>
> *Revelation 8:13*

This fifth trumpet introduces an evil scenario. We are told that a place called the Abyss is to be unlocked. Out of this pit will come hideous demonlike creatures which look like locusts. These creatures will have the power to torture with their sting, but not to kill.

They will not be able to touch those who are "sealed" by God, for these are protected. But everyone else will be prey to these scorpionlike creatures, who will inflict their torture for five months. Because of this agony, men will seek death, but they will not find it. They will long to die, but death will elude them.

Fifth Vial: *Revelation 16:10,11*

When the fifth vial is poured out there will be darkness over the "Kingdom of the Beast."

> Men gnawed their tongues in agony and cursed the God of heaven because of their pains and their sores, but they refused to repent of what they had done.
>
> *Revelation 16:10,11*

Sixth Trumpet: *Revelation 9:13*

The angel who blows the sixth trumpet will release mounted troops numbering 200 million. These 200 million troops will kill one-third of mankind as they sweep across the breadth of the Earth. Going on today's population figures, they will slay about two billion people.

Sixth Vial: *Revelation 16:12*

The sixth vial will be poured out on the River Euphrates, causing it to "dry up" and allow the "kings of the east" to march unhindered towards the Middle East for the final showdown at Armageddon. This fits in with the prophecy of the sixth trumpet, which described an army numbering 200 million which would come from the east and slaughter one-third of the world's population on its westward march.

The Euphrates has always been the ancient dividing line between Europe and the Orient. In the original Greek, "east" is literally translated as "*kings of the sun rising.*" This is an obvious reference to the people of Asia. This prophecy says that an army numbering 200 million will cross the Euphrates to engage with troops from the West. China is the only country in the world today which can muster an army of 200 million. Yet this prophecy was penned almost 2,000 years ago. Can you see how the jigsaw is fitting together?

There now go out "deceiving" spirits, and these motivate the "kings of the earth" to gather in preparation for combat. The prophecy of the sixth vial ends with all the hosts of the enemy lined up for battle.

Seventh Trumpet: *Revelation 11:15*

This introduces the vial judgments which are described in chapters 12-18. These events are more terrible than the ones already foretold. Although we are given these seal, trumpet and vial judgments in order, there is some evidence to suggest that they will occur simultaneously, for all these judgments culminate in the seventh judgment, which is common to all of those given previously: a huge earthquake.

> Then I heard a loud voice from the temple saying to the seven angels: "Go, pour out the seven bowls of God's wrath on the Earth."
>
> *Revelation 16:1*

Seventh Vial: *Revelation 16:18*

The pouring out of the seventh vial coincides with the prophecies of the seventh seal and the seventh trumpet. This describes a catastrophic earthquake which will destroy cities and cause islands to disappear.This earthquake will be followed by hailstones weighing about 100 pounds each falling from the sky on men. In each of the three final judgments it is stated that the great earthquake will be preceded by:

> ... **Flashes of lightning, rumblings, peals of thunder and a severe earthquake.**
>
> *Revelation 15:18*

We cannot know for sure what this means. But looking back at recent history and looking forward to the scenario which is unfolding, it sounds like a nuclear strike. Man today possesses the weaponry to wipe out all life on planet Earth many times over. The big powers are now gearing up for this day. Although the Valley of Megiddo is the focal point, the entire world will be involved in this conflagration.

World peace is contingent upon what happens in Israel. The Arab/Israeli conflict is what will draw these vast armies to this region. And the *raison d'être* for them being there is the oil in the Middle East. There is much prophecy about Jerusalem in these final days and how it will be a rock on which many nations will perish. We are told that the fighting in this area will be so fierce that the blood will reach up to the bridles of the horses to a distance of 200 miles.

Who would have thought that a small nation of about five million people occupying such a tiny area could be the fuse which ignites the world?

THE ABYSS

When the fifth angel sounds his trumpet in Revelation 9, we are confronted with a frightening picture. A "star" is given the key to the Abyss. A star is another name for an angel of God. This entity is the jailer of the Abyss. Out of the Abyss comes smoke and out of the smoke come locusts which have the power to torture but not to kill.

> And the agony they suffered was like that of the sting of the scorpion when it strikes a man.
> During those days men will seek death, but they will not find it; they will long to die, but death will elude them.
>
> *Revelation 9:5,6*

The king of the "locusts" who emerges from the Abyss is named *Apollyon*. We have already spoken of him at some length earlier in this book. Later, we shall return to add some further information regarding his activities during the Apocalypse.

I believe that the descriptions given in this section regarding these "locusts" serve a dual purpose. Firstly, they are telling of the spirit forces at work behind the scenes and, secondly, they are describing the physical realities of actual warfare as we shall experience it in the Earth.

But these evil spirits who will come out of the Abyss are real, actual demons. And when they are released during the Great Tribulation they will wreak havoc on the unbelieving people of the world. We are told in chapter 9 of Revelation of a huge army from the East numbering 200 million. This army will slaughter one-third of the world's population as it cuts its way westward towards the Middle East. John was shown a vision almost 2,000 years ago and he had to describe what he saw in terms of his own experience. Could it be that what he was describing is in fact a 21st century high-tech war?

> And this is how I saw in the vision the horses and those that sat on them: the riders had breastplates the colour of fire and dark blue and yellow as sulphur. The heads of the horses are like the heads of lions and out of their mouths came smoke, fire and sulphur.
> A third of mankind was killed by these three plagues, by the fire and the smoke and the brimstone that came out of their mouths.

> For the power of the horses is in their mouths and in their tails: for
> their tails were like snakes, having heads with which they inflict
> injury.
>
> *Revelation 9:17-19*

Is John describing real creatures or is he describing a nuclear war? It
sounds like modern warfare when he speaks of smoke, fire and sulphur.
Perhaps he is describing the firing of missiles, for such weapons could kill
one-third of mankind in a very short space of time. He talks of   h o r s e s
and those riding upon them. He says that their power was in their heads
and in their tails. This sounds like a description of missiles, for missiles
explode when their "heads" strike their target. The tails, he says, were like
snakes. This could be the trail a missile leaves behind as it snakes it way
through the air *en route* to its target. This applies to the earlier description
of the locusts from the Abyss.

> The locusts looked like horses prepared for battle. On their heads
> they wore something like crowns of gold, and their faces resembled
> human faces.
> Their hair was like a woman's hair, and their teeth were like lions'
> teeth.
> They had breastplates like breastplates of iron, and the sound of
> their wings was like the thundering of many horses and chariots
> rushing into battle.
> They had tails and stings like scorpions and in their tails they had
> power to torment people for five months.
>
> *Revelation 9:7-10*

When John talks of a head with a crown and a human face, could he be
describing the headgear of a fighter pilot? When a helicopter rotates its
blades, it resembles a woman's hair blowing in the wind. And the noise
from attack helicopters would resemble many horses and chariots rushing into battle. The stings in their tails could be their guns and missiles
and the sting they produce could be the effect of germ warfare. John said
that these locusts had wings which sounded like the thundering of many
horses. Well, locusts fly and swarm in great numbers. John has to be
describing warplanes and bombers and helicopters. I believe that he
called them locusts because he was seeing a vision of something in the
future which was totally alien to him. Remember, John was in his
nineties when he had this vision. So when he saw a "swarm" of aircraft
in flight, he could only describe them in terms of his own experience. He

said that they had teeth like lions' teeth. The missiles and rockets which fighter aircraft and helicopters carry could indeed be said to look like lions' teeth.

John had never experienced the roar from jet engines, so he says that they sounded like the thundering of many horses and chariots rushing into battle. What he is trying to describe is a huge aerial assault using the latest high-tech weaponry.

Should we therefore be afraid? No.

Almost everybody realises that the world is on a slippery slope. They can all see the dangers ahead, but they do not have any answers. The people who should be afraid are those who stick their heads in the sand and say: "Everything is going to be all right." We should try to encourage these people to take heed of the prophecies. Then perhaps they might have a chance of avoiding the chaos of the last days.

Two Witnesses

In chapter 11 of Revelation we are given an account of "Two Witnesses." These two men will be raised up and empowered by Yaweh. Nobody knows who these men will be. Some believe one will be Elijah, who was taken up and Raptured in the Old Testament (*see II Kings 2*). In the days of Ahab, Elijah shut up heaven so that no rain fell for $3^1/_2$ years (*I Kings 17:1*). This is what it says in Revelation regarding God's two witnesses:

> If anyone tries to harm them, fire comes from their mouths and devours their enemies.
> These men have the power to shut up the sky so that it will not rain during the time they are prophesying. And they have the power to turn the waters into blood and to strike the Earth with every kind of plague as often as they want.

Revelation 11:5-6

The second witness, some believe, will be Moses, for only he had the power to turn water into blood and cause plagues to come on the land, as he did when in captivity in Egypt (*Exodus 7:19, 19:15*). Also, on the Mount of the Transfiguration, it was Moses and Elijah who appeared talking to Jesus (*Matthew 17:1-11*). The powers to be assumed by these two men are those which were previously exercised by Moses and Elijah in Old Testament times. These two witnesses will prophesy for $3^1/_2$ years against those who rule the world. The Antichrist and his minions will hate them exceedingly, but will be powerless to kill them until the $3^1/_2$ years has elapsed. Then the "beast from the abyss" will attack them and kill them. Their two slain bodies will be left on the street for $3^1/_2$ days. We are told that the people of the Earth will gaze on their corpses and rejoice at their deaths because these two prophets had "tormented" them for so long. Then something amazing occurs:

> But after the three-and-a-half days the breath of life from God entered them and they stood on their feet, and terror struck those who saw them.
> And they went up to Heaven in a cloud while their enemies looked on.
>
> *Revelation 11:11,12*

The only way the people of the nations could view this scene in the present is on global television, for we are told that everybody in the world will see their dead bodies on the street. Of course, this does not sound surprising until you realise that the prophecy was written almost 2,000 years ago. The unbelievers will be celebrating the deaths of these two "fundamentalists" when suddenly they come back to life and stand before them. As the people who watch are seized by fear, the two prophets will be taken up to Heaven in a cloud, just as the Messiah was in *Acts 1:10,11*. Of course, many believe these predictions to be mere flights of fancy, that no such thing will ever happen. Let me tell you, the Bible is full of miracles and almost unbelievable feats. From the dividing of the Red Sea to the Messiah feeding 5,000 with a few loaves and fishes. From Yaweh creating the universe to the Messiah raising Lazarus from the dead. Revelation, likewise, is a book of signs, miracles and wonders.

The *Book of Revelation* is itself a phenomenal miracle. For right now you are reading history before it happens. And you can be assured that all these things will happen. Some day soon the people of the world will see these two prophets bearing witness for Yaweh. And that day may be closer than we think.

Cosmic Battle

Chapter 12 of *Revelation* describes a battle in heaven between Satan and his evil angels on the one hand and Michael and his angels on the other. Apparently Satan still has access to the heavenly realm, for we are told in *Job 1:6-12* that Satan entered the presence of God. And in this chapter of Revelation it says the same:

> For the accuser of our brothers, who accuses them before our God,
> day and night, has been hurled down.
>
> *Revelation 12:10*

However, a battle ensues, and Satan is defeated and cast down to Earth, and his angels with him.

> And there was war in Heaven. Michael and his angels fought
> against the dragon and his angels. But he was not strong enough,
> and they lost their place in Heaven.
> The great dragon was hurled down, that ancient serpent called the
> devil, or Satan, who leads the whole world astray.
> He was hurled to the Earth and his angels with him.
>
> *Revelation 12:7-9*

When the devil is cast out of Heaven, he is filled with wrath, for he knows that his time is short. So he goes after what is called "the woman," to kill her. This is a figure of speech referring to Israel. The devil now tries to kill all the remaining Jews. But Yaweh helps them to flee into the desert, where they are protected for $3\frac{1}{2}$ years. The devil then goes after those Christians who obey Yaweh's word.

It is during the second half of the seven years of Great Tribulation that all hell, literally, is going to break out. For the devil, having been expelled from Heaven, knows that he has but a short time left. It is interesting that in the above verse he is referred to as "he who leads the whole world astray."(Although Satan was expelled from Heaven long ago, apparently he still has some limited access to the heavenly realm. For we are told that he daily accuses the brethren there before God. *Revelation 12:10).*

We are left in no doubt as to who this entity is, for he is given five titles here: the **dragon**, the **ancient serpent**, the **devil** or **Satan**, the **accuser**. The Messiah referred to this future expulsion when he made a prophetic statement recorded in the *Gospel of Luke 10:18.*

"I saw Satan fall like lightning from Heaven."

It is after Satan is driven out of Heaven and down to Earth that he completely takes control of his chosen one, the Antichrist, and his man literally becomes the devil incarnate. He will now break the peace treaty he made with the Jews and will seek to destroy them. He will also at this time try to exterminate all who have turned to the Messiah by refusing to

151

accept the mark of the Beast. Many Christians will be martyred for their faith during this harsh time.

Brand of Hell

Two beasts are featured in chapter 13 of Revelation. The first beast is the Antichrist, who we know will be a political leader. He will appear on the world stage after the Rapture. We are told in this chapter that the first beast, the Antichrist, appears to receive a head wound which is fatal. But, miraculously, he is healed from this fatal wound and lives again. We can only surmise as to the details of this miracle. Perhaps this political leader is assassinated. Everybody knows that he is dead, but then he is raised from the dead by the power of the dragon (Satan) and, as a result, the whole world worships him and worships the dragon who gave the Antichrist his authority.

As we said before, the word "anti" does not mean "against" but "instead of." He will be instead of "Christ," and the world will embrace him, just as it rejected the true Messiah. This Antichrist will be raised from the dead just as Jesus was. When the unbelieving hoards witness this resurrection, they will pledge their allegiance to this son of Satan.

> **The whole world was astonished and followed the Beast (Antichrist).**
> **Men worshipped the dragon (Satan) because he had given authority to the Beast, and they also worshipped the Beast.**
> *Revelation 13:3,4*

The Beast is none other than "*Apollyon*," who has been released from the Abyss and who formerly roamed the Earth, causing destruction in the days of Noah. It is he who is now termed "Antichrist."

So this man will become the most notorious dictator the world has ever seen. He will openly slander Yaweh and the Messiah and he will hunt down those people who turn to God and kill many of them because of their faith. He will be assisted in this by a second beast, who is the False Prophet. As the Antichrist is a political leader, so the False Prophet will be a religious leader. He will be empowered by Satan to perform many deceitful signs and wonders so that he may deceive the inhabitants of the Earth. He will have such "magic" power that he will perform a miracle which will truly dazzle and amaze the populace.

> **He ordered them to set up an image to the Beast (Antichrist), who was wounded by the sword and yet lived.**

> **He was given power to give breath to the image of the first Beast, so that it could speak and cause all who refused to worship the image to be killed.**
>
> *Revelation 13:14,15*

Is it any wonder that the unbelieving people of the world will give their allegiance to this man? For this Scripture tells us that the False Prophet will have the power to make images of the Antichrist come to life and speak. Such images could be statues or pictures of the Antichrist. When we ponder how some of the huge blocks were cut and set in place within the pyramids and other massive ancient buildings, we receive our answer here in this example of the awesome power available to Satan and his host. Many of those believers in God who are not deceived will be put to death for refusing to bow down to the image of the Beast. Furthermore, this False Prophet, who will be working in tandem with his master, the Antichrist, will put in place a system designed to ostracise all those who refuse to accept his sovereignty.

> **He also forced everyone, small and great, rich and poor, free and slave, to receive a mark on his right hand or on his forehead, so that no one could buy or sell unless he had the mark, which is the name of the Beast or the number of his name.**
> **This calls for wisdom. If anyone has insight, let him calculate the number of the Beast, for it is a man's number. His number is 666.**
>
> *Revelation 13:16-18*

In other words, the Antichrist and his government are going to form a club. If you are not a member of this club, you will be boycotted. You will not be able to buy or sell or do business unless you join this club. In order to get into the club, you will have to display this mark of the Beast either on your right hand or on your forehead.

The above verse tells us that the system of accounting employed by the Antichrist will keep track of the buying and selling activities of everyone in the world. Is it not extraordinary that this was written almost 2,000 years ago, yet only in the last few years has the technology to do this become available? Surely it is a powerful sign that we are approaching the fulfilment of these very words when we see them become a reality before our eyes.

One possibility is that this brand or mark of the Beast will be a microchip inserted just beneath the skin. As I write, there are advertisements on TV encouraging people to use "laser" cards instead of cash.

Financial gurus tell us that we are destined for a "cashless society." Plastic is so much more sensible and does away with many cash transactions. But plastic cards can have disadvantages. You can lose them, you can break them, or they can be stolen. The thing which makes the card work is the tiny microchip within it. All the information is stored in this tiny chip: your date of birth, your credit rating. To overcome the problems associated with plastic cards, these chips could be inserted beneath the skin of the right hand. We cannot say for sure if this is how the "mark of the Beast" will be worn during the seven years of Great Tribulation. We are merely observing the way society is going and postulating that this may be the case. The people who will have to endure these times will know when they occur. But anybody who does accept this mark is inviting eternal damnation. For we are warned in no uncertain terms of the consequences of this choice:

> If anyone worships the Beast and his image and receives his mark on the forehead or on the hand, he too will drink of the wine of God's fury, which has been poured full-strength into the cup of his wrath.
> He will be tormented with burning sulphur in the presence of the holy angels and of the Lamb.
> And the smoke of their torment rises for ever and ever.
> There is no rest day or night for those who worship the Beast and his image, or for anyone who receives the mark of his name.
>
> *Revelation 14:9-11*

It is going to be a tough choice, for if you do not accept this mark, you will be denied the right to purchase the things you need. People in this situation will have to forage for themselves. They will have to grow their own food and provide for their own wellbeing and that of their families. They will have to learn self-sufficiency and survival very fast in order to have a chance of making it through the seven years. On top of having to survive without being able to buy or sell or do business, such people will have to contend with the wrath of Satan, for it is prophesied that he will hunt down and kill many of these good souls. But there is hope, for Yaweh has promised to help those who endure to the end.

You can accept the mark of the Beast and enjoy the benefits for a short season, or refuse the mark and risk losing your life. But you will ultimately reap the rewards of everlasting glory if you stick it out to the end. So there is really only one choice to make. Let that choice be eternal life. Whoever accepts this mark is pledging allegiance to the Antichrist, and to Satan, who gives him his power. Once you make this decision, there will be no going back.

The majority of the world's population will accept this mark whole-heartedly. Not only will these people openly worship the Antichrist, they will give themselves totally over to Satan and openly worship him as well.

When many of those who have pledged their allegiance to God are being murdered because of their refusal to accept this mark, the rest of the world will endorse and support the killings. But there is an opportunity for all of us to be spared these terrible times before they occur. All we have to do is put our trust in Yaweh and in His son.

Apollo Rules

When the Messiah foretold the time of the Apocalypse, he compared it to the conditions which prevailed during the days of Noah and in Sodom and Gomorrah: **"As it was, so shall it be."** We have seen that the same spiritual forces which were evident during the time of Noah will again be unleashed upon this Earth when the same fallen angels are released from *Tartarus* during the seven years of Great Tribulation. Thus the violence and destruction and immorality which prevailed before the Flood and in Sodom and Gomorrah, caused by the *Nephilim,* will once again be acted out on a worldwide scale during the Apocalypse.

The ruler over these demonic angels from the Abyss is *Apollyon,* or, in Hebrew, *Abaddon.* This being is named in Revelation as the Beast who is the political leader called the Antichrist. Whether *Apollyon* is an actual person or a spirit which possesses the man who becomes the Antichrist, we cannot say (as Satan entered Judas in *John 13:27*). However, this godlike man will be embraced and worshipped by the world in much the same way as the Apollo of Greek legend, who has always been the epitome of what the world considers the perfect man. For Byron, Apollo was *"the god of life, and poetry, and light, the sun in human limbs array'd."* For Swinburne, he was *"the word, the light, the life, the breath, the glory."* Apollo is the Western man's ideal of man. When Shakespeare's Hamlet extols his vision of man, he is extolling Apollo: *"What a piece of work is a man! How noble in reason! How infinite in faculty! In form, in moving, how express and admirable! In action, how like an angel! In apprehension, how like a god! The beauty of the world."* Reason, nobility, form, action, apprehension, beauty – these are Apollo's essential attributes.

We are told in Revelation that Apollyon will have an accomplice called the False Prophet. This man will possess magical powers which will enable him to delude the masses into following the Beast who is the Antichrist.

> And he performed great and miraculous signs, even causing fire to come down from Heaven to Earth in full view of men.
> Because of the signs he was given to do on behalf of the first Beast (Apollyon), he deceived the inhabitants of the Earth.
>
> *Revelation 13:13,14*

Here is further evidence of the powers available to these spirit beings, which they would have employed in their construction projects of the pre-Flood era. All this will come to pass during the seven years of the Great Tribulation. Since these are the same spiritual powers which were in evidence in the time of Noah, it is fair to assume that similar evil was perpetrated back then.

The two prophets who bear witness on behalf of Yaweh and cannot be touched by ordinary man are eventually slain by the Beast who comes up out of the Abyss, *Apollyon*. His name in both Hebrew and Greek means "destruction" or "destroyer" and his spirit power enables him to kill Yaweh's two prophets when nobody else could.

In Revelation 17 we are given some curious information regarding the Antichrist:

> The Beast which you saw once was, now is not, and will come up out of the Abyss and go to his destruction.
> And the inhabitants of the Earth, whose names have not been written in the Book of Life from the creation of the world, will be astonished when they see the Beast, because he once was, now is not, and yet will come again.
>
> *Revelation 17:8,9*

This statement has bamboozled most commentators. I have read many interpretations of it, yet none seemed to make any sense. However, if our etymological assumptions are correct, and *Apollyon* of the Apocalypse is indeed *Apollo* of the Ancient World, then this prophecy has a clear meaning. For Apollo **once was**, in the 1,000 years or so from Jared to Noah before the Flood. He now **is not**, because he has been incarcerated in *Tartarus* as a consequence of his involvement in the contagion which afflicted all humankind, bringing about the Flood. And **yet will come again** means that he will rise up out of the Abyss in the near-future Apocalypse and will manifest himself in the person of the Antichrist.

Furthermore, we are told, when he does materialise, **he will go to his destruction**. Most commentators believe that this means *he will be destroyed*. But his name means "destruction." And we know that the

Antichrist will create havoc, culminating in half of the world's population being obliterated. Therefore this *Apollo*, the Destroyer, will proceed to fulfil his mission, which is the destruction of mankind. Obviously, this is precisely what he did in the pre-Flood era, when violence filled the Earth and blood flowed freely.

Thus we have a clear connection between the antediluvian avatars and builder-gods of the early days of Greece, Rome and Egypt, and the gods of the Apocalypse to come, the Beast or Antichrist and the False Prophet, both of whom receive their power from the dragon, who is Satan.

Other players will be on the stage in this time also, but the leading roles in the Apocalypse are reserved for Satan and his accomplices.

FINAL COUNTDOWN

In the mid-1930s, Hitler set about building up an arsenal bigger than any ever seen. He built fighter planes and bombers. His panzer tanks were more powerful and faster than anything previously built. In a very short time he had a military force capable of conquering most of the world. Many who watched as he built up his military machine demanded action. They argued that if they did not arm themselves, their security could be endangered. Of course, liberal elements warned against such reaction. They argued that if they began to build up arms, this would only increase the chances of war. So they took no action.

As soon as he was ready, Hitler overran Poland, barely having to fire a shot. He continued to invade and conquer with ease, breaking all his peace treaties in so doing. By the time all the rest of the world got involved and he was finally stopped, up to 70 million people were dead.

The latter half of the seven years of the Great Tribulation will make the first and second world wars look like a minor side show. All the main protagonists are arming themselves to the teeth in preparation for this final conflict. The stage is set. It is only a matter of time.

We are told in Ezekiel 38 and 39 that a "**great power from the north**" will attack Jerusalem. If you study a map, you will see that the "great power" north of Palestine is Russia. Many scholars believe that Russia and an alliance of Moslem nations will combine to make this assault. This will happen sometime during the middle years of the Great Tribulation. It will come as a complete surprise to Israel, which will be dwelling in peace at this point. For we are told that the Antichrist will broker a peace agreement between Israel and her Arab neighbours, guaranteeing Israel protection (*Daniel 7:27*). This will mark the beginning of the seven years of Tribulation.

Because Israel will not be expecting an invasion, there will be a sort of pseudo peace during the initial stages of the seven years. But at some point the "**great power from the north**," together with the "**king of the south**," will launch a surprise attack. In so doing, they will catch everyone unawares and their incursion will succeed. However, according to Ezekiel, God will destroy these armies in the hills north of Jerusalem. But not before they have plundered Jerusalem, slaughtering two-thirds of the city's inhabitants. The remaining one-third will escape into the desert. But when these armies retreat to the hills north of Jerusalem, they will be utterly routed (probably by the Antichrist and his Western alliance). The peace treaty which was brokered by the Antichrist will have been broken. At this stage, the Antichrist will have been raised from the dead and totally empowered by Satan. The Russian and Moslem armies having been defeated, the Antichrist, with the military might of the West behind him, will move to fill the power vacuum which exists in the Middle East. He will set up camp in Jerusalem, where the temple will have been rebuilt, as has been prophesied. The Antichrist will then fulfil another prophecy by entering the temple and setting himself up as the true Messiah, demanding worship of himself and uttering blasphemies against the God of Heaven.

> He shall speak great words against the Most High, and shall wear out the saints of the Most High, and think to change times and laws.
>
> *Daniel 7:25*

> He shall do according to his will and shall exalt himself above every God, and shall speak marvellous things against the God of Gods.
>
> *Daniel 11:36*

In the New Testament, we have Paul's corroboration of Daniel's words:

> He will oppose and will exalt himself over everything that is called God or is worshipped, so that he sets himself up in God's Temple, proclaiming himself to be God.
> The coming of the lawless one will be in accordance with the work of Satan, displayed in all kinds of counterfeit miracles, signs and wonders.
>
> *II Thessalonians 2:4,9*

While this is going on, the "Kings of the East" will decide to make their move. This is the first reference in the Bible to the people of Asia and the Far East, yet we are told that an army numbering 200 million will massacre one-third of the population of the world as it cuts a swathe westward.

Never before has the Bible referred to any great powers either from the north or the Far East until these end-time scenarios. It is only in recent years that China and Russia have become superpowers with nuclear weapons and arsenals capable of mass destruction. Again we marvel at the accuracy of prophecy as we see these players align themselves to fulfil their destiny.

The River Euphrates has always been the dividing line between the Middle East and China and the Far East. We are told that this great river will be dried up to make way for this 200 million-strong army. The Euphrates is 1,700 miles long. This huge army will continue to move south-west, with Palestine as its destination. Conflict with the Antichrist and his Western powers will be inevitable.

The Antichrist is to receive his authority from a confederation of ten nations. Most scholars of "end-times" prophecy believe that this confederacy will be made up of the remnants of the revived Roman Empire. Since the United States is largely made up of European people who are descended from the old Roman Empire, it is feasible and probable that it would be part of a military alliance with Europe and other Western nations.

The EU is fast becoming the strongest financial power block in the world. For the EU, the United States and every other world power, oil is essential to keeping the wheels of industry turning. Anything which might interfere with or threaten this oil supply would have to be dealt with.

It is for this reason that the Americans, along with all the other allied nations, moved so quickly into the1991 Gulf War. As one pundit put it: "If they were growing carrots in Kuwait, the Iraqis would still be there."

The world is aligning itself into four main power blocs. On one side you have the Russian people, who are politically close to another main power bloc, the Arabs. Both have one thing in common: they dislike and distrust the West and especially America. Anytime there is an international incident, the Russians almost always side with the Arab nations, and vice versa.

It is also economically and politically expedient for Russia to ally itself with its Moslem neighbours, who are rich in oil dollars, since its own economy is not healthy. In exchange for cash and oil, the Russians supply military hardware and know-how.

Both the Americans and the Russians have large fleets of nuclear submarines, each armed with about 200 nuclear warheads, capable of destroying thousands of cities and millions of lives. And these missiles can reach their targets in a matter of minutes.

China has the capability now of hitting targets in the West. India and Pakistan have recently become nuclear powers and have been rattling their sabres at each other. India now has a population in excess of one billion. China, with a population estimated at 1,200 million people, has been cultivating closer links with its other Asian neighbours. The threat from the "Kings of the East" may be a confederacy of these nations, with the oil of the Middle East becoming their primary focus. This is the third major power bloc, Russia and the Arab nations being the other two.

Then there is the West: the United States and its allies. After the Unites States, Europe ranks second in world terms as an economic and military power.

These then are the four main power blocs.

We are told that God will gather all the armies of the world to battle in this area of the Middle East. The Valley of Megiddo in northern Israel forms a land bridge between three continents. During the final $3^1/_2$ years of this time of trouble, many will die as a result of other conflicts, of disease and because of the general breakdown which will occur in society. But it is in Armageddon that the final button will be pushed to plunge the world into the throes of destruction.

It is reasonable to assume that a huge military force will gather in the Middle East to confront the threat posed by the 200 million-strong army arriving from the East. There can be only one outcome to this stand-off: all-out war.

In 1410 BC, Zechariah, writing of this day, prophesied:

Behold the day of the Lord comes when I will gather all nations against Jerusalem to battle ... then shall the Lord go forth and fight against those nations.

Zechariah 14:1-3

Earlier, I quoted some of the descriptions used by John to attempt to convey an understanding of the visions he both saw and heard. He spoke of a vision which might have been describing military aircraft. These had "*breastplates of iron and the sound of their wings was like the sound of many horses and chariots rushing into battle ... out of their mouths came fire, smoke and sulphur, and one-third of mankind was killed by the three plagues of fire, smoke and sulphur ...*" We also referred to the "Wormwood" which will fall into one-third of the world's drinking water, polluting it and bringing death to all who drink it. Could this be biological warfare? Or could it be the result of nuclear fall-out?

In the above quotation we are told that one-third of the population of the world will be killed by what John calls three plagues of fire, brimstone and sulphur. I am convinced that he is describing three nuclear strikes. The first strike will be when the Russians, along with their Moslem comrades, are destroyed in the mountains north of Israel by the Antichrist and his powerful Western alliance.

The second will result from the nuclear warheads used by the vast army of the East as it slaughters all before it in its drive towards the Middle East. The third and final nuclear strike will be the seventh and last of the Seal, Trumpet and Vial judgments.

At the end of the seven years of Great Tribulation, the vast army from the East will have arrived at the Valley of Megiddo. Here it will be confronted by the powerful military alliance from the West, led by the Antichrist. There will be a stand-off.

John describes what will happen:

> **Then they gathered the kings together in the place that in Hebrew is called Armageddon.**
> **Then there came flashes of lightning, rumblings, peals of thunder and a severe earthquake. No earthquake has ever occurred since man has been on Earth, so tremendous was the quake.**
> **The great city split into three parts, and the cities of the nations collapsed.**
>
> *Revelation 16:16,18,19*

After these vast armies have gathered, there will be a stand-off, then someone will push the button to release the first nuclear missile. With that, an unstoppable chain-reaction will occur. All the submarines on both sides will launch their deadly weapons. Land-based missiles from all parts of the world will be automatically fired. Hundreds and thousands of missiles will pass each other in the air. This is why John describes it as:

Flashes of lightning ... just like the images we see on television as we witness missiles and shells being fired into the blackness of the night;

Rumblings ... the sound of distant explosions as the bombs strike their targets;

Peals of thunder ... caused by the initial firing of the weapons and their impact when they hit;

And a severe earthquake like no other ... The words "nuclear strike" or "explosion" were not in John's vocabulary. So when he saw all the missiles hit their targets, he could only describe this as a "tremendous earthquake."

And the cities of the nations collapsed ... just as Hiroshima and Nagasaki collapsed over 50 years ago. There is only one thing which can cause all the cities of the nations to collapse at the same time. John is describing a nuclear strike. The history of the world is the history of war.

It is said in the Bible that all wars and famine and death and sickness are caused by the devil and Satan (*Hebrews 2:14*). It is the agency of evil spirits working through people and through physical catastrophes which brings about death and destruction. Even though it appears that man is the cause and the maker of war, the real power lies with the invisible spiritual influences which are manipulating situations and pulling the strings in the background.

A further description of this holocaust, which I believe is a nuclear strike, is given to us in chapter 16 of Revelation:

> **From the sky huge hailstones of about a hundred pounds each fell upon men. And they cursed Yaweh on account of the plague of hail, because the plague was so terrible.**
>
> *Revelation 16:21*

There have been instances in history of very large showers of hail, but I do not believe that this is what John saw. Firstly, these "hailstones" were described as each weighing more than 100 pounds. Next, the hailstones fell upon "all" men, the inference being that they fell on all the people around the globe at the same time. Ordinary hailstones would not fall all over the world simultaneously. But missiles could. Especially when one side pushes the button and automatically forces the other side to do likewise. Thirdly, it says that men cursed Yaweh because the plague was so terrible. Well, I cannot envisage mankind cursing God over a shower of hailstones, no matter how severe. But here it describes the effect of this shower as being a "plague." This accords with another passage already mentioned:

> **"One-third of mankind was killed by these three plagues, by the fire and smoke and the brimstone ..."**
>
> *Revelation 9:18*

I believe that John saw all these missiles and nuclear warheads falling out of the sky and exploding. Thus, all the cities of the nations collapsed, and men cursed Yaweh because of this fiery plague. John could only use words which were familiar to him, so he speaks of seeing large objects falling from the sky and causing a plague. He calls them "hailstones." But I believe that what he was actually seeing was a shower of missiles and nuclear warheads. This is the third and final plague of fire, smoke and brimstone. This is Armageddon.

The prophet Zechariah provides us with a chilling prophecy relating to this battle and the nations involved in it:

> This is the plague with which the Lord will strike all the nations that fought against Jerusalem: Their flesh will rot while they are still standing on their feet, their eyes will rot in their sockets, and their tongues will rot in their mouths.
>
> *Zechariah 14:12*

When the atom bombs fell on Hiroshima and Nagasaki in 1945, the force of the explosions was such that the fire spread over an area of 30 miles in milli-seconds. People within that radius were burned to a crisp, vaporised, before they could move a muscle. This is what occurs with a nuclear explosion. This is why the above prophecy, written over 400 years before the birth of the Messiah, states that "their flesh will rot while they are still standing on their feet, their eyes will rot in their sockets and their tongues will rot in their mouths." Further evidence that the final battle of Armageddon is going to be a worldwide nuclear holocaust.

The Messiah is coming back to finish the battle and establish His reign on this Earth for 1,000 years.

He will not be entering Jerusalem on the back of a donkey this time, but on a white horse as a military leader, and he is going to exact revenge on his enemies and on the enemies of God:

> I saw Heaven standing open, and there before me was a white horse, whose rider is called faithful and true. With justice, he judges and makes war.
> The armies of Heaven were following him, riding on white horses and dressed in fine linen, white and clean.
> On his robe and on his thigh he has this name written:
> King of Kings and Lord of Lords.
>
> *Revelation 19:11-16*

The Messiah will go forth to do battle against the Beast and the False Prophet. These two will be captured and thrown alive into the lake of burning sulphur. All the flesh-eating birds will then be summoned to devour those who have been killed, and the birds will gorge themselves on their flesh. Next, the dragon, the ancient serpent, who is the devil, or Satan, will be bound and cast into the Abyss for 1,000 years. At the end of this 1,000-year period, Satan must be set free for a short time.

When the Messiah lands on the Mount of Olives, the mountain will split in two. Half will move towards the north and half towards the south. Fresh water will gush forth from beneath the mountain and will flow half to the eastern sea and half to the western *(Zechariah 14:4,8)*. Then Jesus will begin to establish His kingdom. Thus will we see the fulfilment of the prophetic prayer which has come to be known as "The Lord's Prayer":

Thy kingdom come, Thy will be done on Earth, as it is in Heaven.

Those who will be martyred because of their faith during the Great Tribulation will be resurrected to reign with Christ for 1,000 years. It will take seven months to burn the weapons which are left over after the final holocaust, but there will then begin a reign of peace, a time of Paradise Regained.

SECRET GARDEN

Have you ever wondered what it might be like to live in a hassle-free world? No more having to compete in the workplace, no more worries about bills, violence, murder, rape. Not having to put up with bad weather and bad news.A world in which you do not have to be concerned about the safety of your children or their future. A place where everyone loves everyone else and there is an abundance of food and long life. No more wars, no more starvation, no more inequality and injustice. Well, you've come to the right place.

When the Messiah returns to establish His kingdom, the world will enter a period of wondrous blessings for 1,000 years. It will be Paradise Regained. The Hebrew word for *"Eden"* in the Book of Genesis means *"garden of delights."* Paradise is only mentioned three times in the Bible and it is always a place on the Earth. It has nothing to do with Heaven. When the Messiah comes back to reign, we will be entering Paradise.This future kingdom will be ruled by the Messiah, and He will rule with real justice.

When Jesus was dying on the Cross, we are told that three of the four men who were being crucified at the same time railed against Him and said: *"If you are the Son of God, then why do you not save yourself?"* And they cursed Him. But the fourth man told them to be quiet and said to Jesus: **"Remember me when you come into Your kingdom"** (*Mark 23: 40-42*). Then Jesus told this man that he would be with him in Paradise. (Please note that four men were crucified with Jesus, not two, but that's another story).

Those of us who are saved will be with Jesus in this Paradise kingdom alongside believers (saints) who did not succumb to the mark of the Beast and thus survived the Great Tribulation. The believers who are killed by the Antichrist during the seven years will be resurrected and will reign with the Messiah for 1,000 years. Furthermore, Jewish saints from the Old Testament will be resurrected and will be present in this millennial kingdom. It will be our task to put the Earth back in order after the devastation caused by the holocaust. We are given much information about this period in the Old Testament. For instance, there will be no more war in this glorious time, for men will **"beat their swords into ploughshares and their spears into pruning hooks. Nation will not take up sword against nation, nor will they train for war anymore"** (*Isaiah 2:4*).

Look at all the billions of dollars which are currently being spent on arms and on maintaining defence forces. This will be no more, for in this future time we will be using our energies to cultivate food for everyone – a great abundance of food:

> "The days are coming," declared the Lord,
> "when the reaper will be overtaken by the ploughman and the planter by the one treading grapes. New wine will drip from the mountains and flow from all the hills."
>
> *Amos 9:13*

In other words, there will be so much food, year in, year out, that when one man is still gathering the crops, another man will be preparing to start ploughing again. So we will have no need to worry about where our next meal is coming from. Famine and starvation will be no more. There will be a renewal of the Earth's atmosphere and of the soil and the animal and plant kingdoms. Isaiah tells us of this future *"Garden of Delights"*:

> The wolf will live with the lamb, the leopard will lie down with the goat.
> The calf and the lion and the yearling together; and a little child will lead them.
> The cow will feed the bear, their young will lie down together, and the lion will eat straw like the ox.
> The infant will play near the hole of the cobra, and the young child put his hand into the viper's nest.
> They will neither harm nor destroy on all my Holy Mountain, for the Earth will be full of the knowledge of the Lord as the waters cover the sea.
>
> *Isaiah 11:6-9*

Sounds like a nice place to be! We are told that our lifespan will be a lot longer than at present. Indeed, to die at the age of 100 will be regarded as dying young. All is not going to be total perfection, however, for we are informed that Jesus will rule with a "rod of iron." This would imply that some people will step out of line on occasion. However, the overall picture is one of a blessed existence of peace and prosperity, with the Messiah overseeing everything from his seat of governance in Jerusalem. When He returns to Earth to live and reign for 1,000 years, then those promises He made during his first coming will be realised.

Blessed are the pure in spirit, for theirs is the Kingdom of Heaven.
Blessed are those who mourn, for they will be comforted.
Blessed are the meek, for they will inherit the Earth.
Blessed are those who hunger and thirst for righteousness, for they will be filled.
Blessed are the merciful, for they will be shown mercy.
Blessed are the pure in heart, for they will see God.
Blessed are the peacemakers, for they will be called the Sons of God.
Blessed are those who are persecuted because of righteousness, for theirs is the Kingdom of Heaven.

Matthew 5:3-10

Interestingly, further on in this same chapter Jesus makes an informative statement:

For I tell you that unless your righteousness surpasses that of the Pharisees and the teachers of the Law, you will certainly not enter the Kingdom of Heaven.

Matthew 5:20

We were always taught that when a person dies they either go to heaven or to hell. But this is not true. When the Lord comes back to take with Him the believers at the time of the Rapture, then we who are alive will be brought to this place called Heaven for the duration of the seven years of the Great Tribulation. All those Christians who passed through the portal of death since the day of Pentecost will be raised and will be there, too. But the future for us and for the rest of mankind is here on Earth, first in the 1,000-year Kingdom of Christ and later in the New Heaven and New Earth. So He is coming back to reign. And our future is to be with Him on this planet called Earth, but in an infinitely improved state.

Eye has not seen nor ear heard, neither has it entered into the heart of man, the things that God has prepared for those that love him.

I Corinthians 2:9

During this 1,000-year period, Satan will be bound and no longer free to deceive the nations. Over time, the population will grow exceedingly. Then, at the end of the 1,000 years, Satan will be set free for a short time. After his release, Satan will corrupt large numbers of those living on the

Earth and deceive them into mounting an attack against the people of God. We are given very little information about this period, so we cannot comment much upon it. However, is it not amazing that, after living in veritable Paradise for 1,000 years of bliss under the rule of the Son of God, man could once again rebel and choose to reject God and His Messiah? This illustrates the utter depravity and evil of the human heart. But we should not be totally surprised at this, for Adam and Eve lived in a perfect world, yet they made a free-will decision to disobey Yaweh. Also, before Lucifer fell he was the *"anointed cherub"* (*Ezekiel 28:14*) and he *"walked in the Garden of God and was perfect"* (*Ezekiel 28:13*), yet by his free will he chose to rebel against the Most High God. So people during this 1,000 years will live in a near-perfect Paradise, but they will still have free will and therefore will be responsible for their actions and decisions. When these followers of Satan launch their attack, they will be consumed by fire from Heaven. Then the devil, who deceived them, will be thrown into the lake of burning sulphur where the Beast and the False Prophet had been thrown 1,000 years earlier (*Revelation 20:7-10*).

After this there will come what are called the "Great White Throne" judgments. All the dead will be judged here. Whosoever's name is not found written in the Book of Life will be thrown into the lake of fire.

The last two chapters of Revelation describe a New Heaven and a New Earth. God Himself, our Father, is coming to live with Jesus, His Son, and with us in this new Eternal Kingdom. All of past history is but a mere preface to that day in the future when Yaweh will be joined with His family. Then He will be with His sons and daughters who chose to love Him by their own free will. He will have then what every father wants: children to share His love with.

> Then I saw a new Heaven and a new Earth, for the first Heaven and the first Earth had passed away, and there was no longer any sea.
> I saw the Holy City, the New Jerusalem, coming down out of Heaven from God, prepared as a bride beautifully dressed for her husband.
> And I heard a loud voice from the throne saying: "Now the dwelling of God is with men, and He will live with them. They will be His people, and God himself will be with them and be their God. He will wipe every tear from their eyes. There will be no more death or mourning or crying or pain, for the old order of things has passed away."
>
> *Revelation 21:1-4*

169

Oh what a glorious day that will be! All the pain and all the tears and heartache and suffering of this life will be forgotten when this future dawns:

> For I reckon that the sufferings of this present time are not worthy to be compared with the glory which shall be revealed in us.
>
> *Romans 8:18*

This is the good news. This is what we have to look forward to. This is why the Messiah suffered and died and rose again. So that you and I might live. What fun and joy lies ahead for those of us who believe and await His return with patience. But only those whose names are written in the Book of Life will enjoy this future Paradise:

> The desert and the parched land will be glad; the wilderness will rejoice and blossom. Like the crocus, it will burst into bloom; it will rejoice greatly and shout for joy. The glory of Lebanon will be given to it, the splendour of Carmel and Sharon; they will see the glory of the Lord, the splendour of our God. Strengthen the feeble hands, steady the knees that give way; say to those with fearful hearts: "Be strong, do not fear, your God will come. He will come with vengeance. With divine retribution, He will come to save you."
> Then will the eyes of the blind be opened and the ears of the deaf unstopped. Then will the lame leap like a deer, and the mute tongue shout for joy. Water will gush forth in the wilderness and there will be streams in the desert. The burning sand will become a pool, the thirsty ground bubbling springs. In the haunts where jackals once lay, grass and reeds and papyrus will grow. And a highway will be there; it will be called the Way of Holiness. The unclean will not journey on it; it will be for those who walk in that Way; wicked fools will not go about on it. No lion will be there, nor any ferocious beast get up on it; they will not be found there. But only the redeemed will walk there, and the ransomed of the Lord will return. They will enter Zion with singing, everlasting joy will overtake them, and sorrow and sighing will flee away.
>
> *Isaiah 35:1-10*

But how may each of us gain access to this Garden of Delights and be spared a dreadful demise during the Apocalypse? To do this we must be part of the Great Escape.

THE GREAT ESCAPE

The point has been made previously that the Bible is a prophetic book. We already pointed out that the Messiah literally fulfilled 109 predictions from the Old Testament in his sojourn in the Earth as Jesus. We spoke of how 25 of these prophecies were fulfilled in this one man in one 24-hour period. The odds against something such as this happening are billions to one. Yet the Messiah fulfilled all the prophecies relating to Himself down to the last "jot and tittle." There are 845 quotations from the Old Testament in the New Testament and, of these, 333 refer to the Messiah.

The Messiah's life was attested to by no fewer than 22 different historians of his day, such as Tacitus, Suetonious, Serapian, Phlegon, Lucien, Josephus. Many of these historians were antagonistic towards him, yet they recorded his lifetime in some detail. Josephus was a famous general in the Asmonean army and a noted historian of this era. He not only recorded the life of Jesus but actually wrote of the resurrection. And Josephus was not a Christian. Such was the impact of the life, death and resurrection of Christ that even secular historians of the day testified to his works.

So it is an established historical fact that the Messiah existed. Our present-day calendar even begins with his birth. Bearing in mind that this man walked the Earth and fulfilled all the predictions relating to his life, what is next up on the prophetic schedule? Well, if the first coming of the Messiah was an important subject of Old Testament prophecy, then his second coming is even more important. For there are **20 times more** prophecies in the Old Testament pertaining to his second coming than there are regarding his first. In fact, his return is the second most-mentioned subject in all Biblical prophecy.[68] Paul, in his Epistles, mentions the second coming 50 times, yet he speaks of baptism only 13 times. Let us go first to the Book of Acts and examine the departure from the Earth of the Messiah when he dwelt among us as the man called Jesus:

> **And when He had spoken these things, while they beheld, He was taken up: and a cloud received Him out of their sight.**
>
> *Book of Acts 1:9*

This happened on the Mount of Olives, not far from Jerusalem. The Messiah had just finished giving instructions to his Apostles when he began to ascend from the mountain in a cloud. The Book of Acts describes what occurred next:

> And while they looked steadfastly towards Heaven as He went up, behold two men stood by them in white apparel.
> Which also said: "Ye men of Galilee, why stand you gazing up into Heaven? This same Jesus, which is taken up from you into Heaven, shall so come in like manner as you have seen Him go into Heaven."
>
> *Book of Acts 1:10-11*

The two men who delivered this message were probably Michael and Gabriel, the messengers or spirit-men of whom we spoke in earlier chapters. But one thing they omitted to divulge was precisely when he would be coming back. The early Christians believed that his return was imminent. That is why many of them in those early days used to go up on the flat roofs of their houses to wait and watch out for him. It was the promise of his second coming which kept these early Christians so motivated.

Yet, here we are, almost 2,000 years further on, and he still has not returned. Over time, our understanding of the significance of the second coming has been largely lost in a plethora of religious dogma.

There are two parts to the second coming. The first is known to many Christians as the "Rapture." This refers to a time when Jesus will return to the Earth briefly to "rescue" those who are true believers. The Bible teaches that one day every Christian who is still alive will "vanish" to meet Christ. The people who remain on Earth will have to endure the holocaust of terrible events predicted in the Book of Revelation. But let us begin by taking a look at the Rapture. Jesus himself first spoke of it in *John 14:1-3*.

> Let not your hearts be troubled; ye believe in God, believe also in me.
> In my Father's house are many mansions; I go to prepare a place for you.
> And if I go to prepare a place for you, I will come again and receive you unto myself: that where I am, there ye may be also.

So we have this promise from the Lord himself that He will be coming back to take us out of this evil world to a place prepared by Him.

As noted earlier, historians of the time recorded the existence of Jesus. And even Josephus mentions the resurrection of the Messiah. The resurrection is the cornerstone of the Christian faith. Instead of gazing at a defeated, tortured dead Christ hanging from the Cross, what should be on the altar is an open tomb with the stone rolled away and a notice emblazoned in large capital letters: "HE IS RISEN." Our victory is in the resurrection of the Messiah and what He accomplished by His death.

Many passages in the Gospels relate to the risen Christ. Doubting Thomas, after hearing of the resurrection, said that until such time as he could touch the actual wounds on the body of the Master he would not believe. Jesus subsequently appeared to Thomas and invited him to touch His body, saying:

> Touch me and see; For a spirit has not flesh and bones as you see me to have.
>
> *Luke 24:39*

In John chapter 21 we are told of the appearance of the risen Christ to Peter and some of the disciples after they had decided to return to fishing. When they encountered Him on the shore, in his risen body, He was already cooking breakfast, so they all gathered around and ate fish with Him. He had previously told them that He would not drink wine again until all were in Paradise, where they would drink new wine with Him. I especially like this particular passage in the New Testament, as I enjoy good wine and love to catch and eat fish.

Saul of Tarsus was the one Yaweh chose to spread the good news of the resurrection among the peoples of the Gentile nations. He had been travelling to Damascus to arrest the Messiah's disciples when a light from heaven shone on him and he was blinded. After three days, his sight was restored, and he preached of having seen the Messiah. From that time onwards, he became known as Paul, author of the various epistles. Here is his eyewitness account of the resurrection of the Messiah:

> Christ died for our sins, according to the scriptures; that He was buried, that He was raised on the third day, according to the scriptures; and that He appeared to Peter, and then to the twelve. After that, He appeared to more than five hundred of the brothers at the same time, most of whom are still living.
> Then He appeared to James, then to all the Apostles, and last of all He appeared to me also.
>
> *I Corinthians 15:3-8*

If you are an eyewitness to an accident or a crime, you are a primary witness. According to Paul, there were more than 500 primary witnesses to the Messiah's resurrection. When the time arrives for His return, this is what we are told will occur:

> For the Lord Himself will come down from Heaven with a loud command, with the voice of the Archangel and with the trumpet call of God, and the dead in Christ will rise first.
> After that, we who are still alive and are left will be caught up together with them in the clouds to meet the Lord in the air. And so will we be with the Lord forever.
>
> *I Thessalonians 4:16,17*

I know that it must seem almost impossible to accept that perhaps as many as several hundred million Christians living today all over the world could suddenly vanish in the twinkling of an eye. Yet this is precisely what we are told will occur when the Lord returns in majesty from the skies. Let us examine a parallel account of this event in *I Corinthians 15:52*.

> Listen, I tell you a mystery; we will not all sleep (die), but we will all be changed – in a flash, in the twinkling of an eye – at the last trumpet.
> For the trumpet will sound, the dead will be raised imperishable, and we will be changed.

How fast can you blink your eye? That's how quickly we are going to vanish off this Earth. Then the time called the Great Tribulation will begin. But the good news is that we will not have to endure this period of chaos, for we will have been removed beforehand.

When I say "We will be removed," I am referring to those who believe in the Messiah. This is the simple message and promise which He himself delivered while on this Earth. That is, whosoever believes in Him will be saved from the wrath to come. But if you do not believe, then you will remain on Earth to go through the Great Tribulation as recorded in the Apocalypse.

Probably the best-known verse of Scripture is *John 3:16*. Occasionally, on TV, you may see a person in a crowd at a sporting event holding aloft or waving a sign that reads: *John 3:16*. This is a simple message which contains a great truth. It states:

> For God so loved the world that He gave His only begotten Son, that whosoever believes in Him shall not perish but have eternal life.

There is only one man who paid for our sins and only one man Yaweh ever raised from the dead. That man is the Messiah, and it is only through Him that we have any hope. Only through believing in Jesus Christ can any of us escape the judgments and wrath which are about to fall on mankind and on the entire world.

> Since we have now been justified by His blood, how much more shall we be saved from God's wrath through Him.
>
> *Romans 5:9*

This assurance that we are to be saved from the wrath to come is repeated in other passages of Scripture. There are some Christians who will say that everyone must pass through the horrific events of the Apocalypse. But if that is true, then the above verse is a lie, and Paul did not know what he was talking about. Look again at the concluding part of the above verse. It tells us that **"we shall be saved from God's wrath through Him."**

In his Epistle to the Thessalonians, Paul repeats this promise ... **"and to wait for His Son from Heaven, whom He raised from the dead – even Jesus, who rescues us from the coming wrath."**

Could this be any clearer? We are either saved from the wrath to come, meaning the Apocalypse, or we are not, and the simple and direct promise is that those who believe in the Messiah will be saved, just as Noah and his family were saved from the Flood. For the Flood and Sodom and Gomorrah are archetypes or symbols for the coming judgments. And just as Noah and his kin were saved at the time of the Flood, so also did Lot and his family have to be removed before the judgments could fall on Sodom and Gomorrah.

In the same manner, the righteous who believe in the Messiah must be taken out of the way and removed from this Earth before the events prophesied in the Book of Revelation can take place. Of course, the "Rapture" is not a unique concept in the Bible. Enoch was "taken" by God and apparently did not die. Likewise, Elijah was taken up to Heaven "by chariots" so that he did not see death (*II Kings 2:11*).

Chapter eight of the Book of Acts tells the story of Philip and the Ethiopian. This man was an important official in charge of the treasury or finance department of Candace, Queen of the Ethiopians. After Philip had told him the good news of the coming of the Messiah, he baptised him.

Then we are told that the Spirit of the Lord suddenly took Philip away and he appeared at a place called Azotus, many miles from where the two had been. So the idea of being "snatched away" from one place to another is not an isolated one in the Bible.

There are no indications as to when the Rapture may occur, yet there are many signs and portents relating to the coming Tribulation. However, while we can see many signs suggesting that the terrible events of the Apocalypse are imminent, we also know that we must be "raptured" before the Tribulation can begin. So it is feasible to surmise that the Rapture is also close at hand. In fact, it could happen at any time.

All we can do is watch and pray and wait for the Son from Heaven who has saved us from the wrath to come.

CATCH A FALLEN STAR

I would now like to return once more to the Book of Enoch to bring to your attention a most intriguing passage in which the metaphors which are used refer to humans and to angels. In terms of the deluge, Noah and the violence and corruption which filled the Earth prior to the Flood, this commentary is extremely significant.

> And again I saw with mine eyes as I slept, and I saw the Heaven above, and behold a star fell from Heaven, and it arose and ate and pastured amongst those oxen.
>
> After that I saw the large and the black oxen, and behold they all changed their stalls and pastures and their cattle, and began to live with each other.
>
> And again I saw in the vision, and looked towards the Heaven, and behold I saw many stars descend and cast themselves down from Heaven to that first star, and they became bulls amongst those cattle and pastured with them (amongst them).
>
> And I looked at them and saw, and behold they all let out their privy members, like horses, and began to cover the cows of the oxen, and they all became pregnant and bare elephants, camels and asses.
>
> And all the oxen feared them and were affrighted at them, and began to bite with their teeth and to devour, and to gore with their horns.
>
> And they began moreover to devour those oxen; and behold, all the children of the Earth began to tremble and quake before them and to flee from them.

Book of Enoch LXXXVI 1-6

In the chapter previous to this in the Book of Enoch we are given an account of the historical period from the time of Adam up to the time of Noah. But the story is told in terms of bulls and cows, meaning men and women. Adam and Noah are referred to as white bulls and Eve is referred to as a heifer (female cow) and as a cow. Cain is referred to as a black bull who went off and fathered many other bulls and oxen.

177

In the passage reproduced here, we are told that the oxen and cattle began to change their pastures and stalls and to live with each other. That is, the descendants of Cain and Adam and Eve intermarried. While this was going on, a "star" fell from heaven, and it arose and ate among the oxen. This is a reference to a fallen angel mingling with the inhabitants of the Earth. Then this fallen star (angel) was joined by many other stars. These in turn became bulls and ate and pastured among the other cattle (people).

The "privy members" of these entities are described as being as big as those of horses. There is an intriguing likeness here to the satyrs and certain Egyptian and Greek deities, which also had rather large privy members (i.e. penises). There are many ancient Egyptian pictures, preserved in stone from the earliest of times, portraying men with large penises. Could these be representations of those fallen men who descended on Mount Hermon in the days of Jared (circa 3500 BC) and were described by Enoch as having "privy members like horses"? They covered, or had intercourse with, the females, who in turn became pregnant. Now here is the interesting part. It is stated that they bore elephants, camels and asses. In other words, they did not bring forth after their kind, but instead produced mutants.

"Elephants," "camels" and "asses" are metaphors for the descendants of these stars which fell from heaven, the *Nephilim*. All of the ordinary inhabitants of the Earth were fearful of these cross-bred creatures. And we are told that the elephants, camels and asses began to devour the oxen (people), who in turn attempted to flee from them.

This is a detailed account of the first procreational engagement of spirit beings with the daughters of men prior to the Flood. It is told in figures of speech by Enoch, who is describing a dream he had to his son, Methuselah. The story then moves on to tell of the appearance of seven other space travellers:

> And again I saw how they began to gore each other and to devour each other, and the Earth began to cry aloud.
> And I raised mine eyes again to Heaven, and I saw in the vision, and behold there came forth from Heaven beings who were like white men: and four went forth from that place and three with them.
> And those three that had last come forth grasped me by my hand and took me up, away from the generations of the Earth, and raised me up to a lofty place, and showed me a tower raised high above the Earth, and all the hills were lower.

And one said unto me: "Remain here till thou seest everything that befalls those elephants, camels and asses, and the stars and the oxen, and all of them."

Book of Enoch LXXXVII 1-4

Enoch was a seventh-generation direct descendant of Adam. We are told that he walked with God and apparently did not die, but was "translated." The Book of Hebrews informs us:

By faith, Enoch was taken from this life, so that he did not experience death. He could not be found, because God had taken him away.

Book of Hebrews 11:5

The previously-quoted passage from the Book of Enoch appears to be describing this "translation." The seven archangels seen coming forth from the heavens are named by Enoch in another chapter. Their coming to Earth is in response to the violence and the cry which goes up from the people of the Earth. Three of the seven took Enoch by the hand and removed him to another dimension:

And I saw one of those four who had come forth first, and he seized that first star which had fallen from the heavens, and bound it hand and foot and cast it into an abyss: now that abyss was narrow and deep, and horrible and dark.
And one of them drew a sword, and gave it to those elephants and camels and asses: then they began to smite each other, and the whole Earth quaked because of them.
And as I was beholding in the vision, lo, one of the four who had come forth stoned (them) from Heaven, and gathered and took all the great stars whose privy members were like those of horses, and bound them all hand and foot, and cast them in an abyss of the Earth.

Book of Enoch LXXXVIII 1-3

This is a description of the imprisoning of the fallen angels, the *Nephilim*, whose orgy of evil and violence precipitated the Flood. These fallen angels are then bound and cast into the Abyss. We are told in the Book of Revelation how, in the future, during the events of the Great Tribulation, the pit of the Abyss will be opened and fearsome-looking locusts – an infernal cherubim – will be released. The ruler over this evil horde is named in the Greek as Apollyon, clearly identifiable as Apollo, who must have been one of these original *Nephilim*. The Abyss is probably *Tartarus*, where the risen Messiah went to reveal himself to these imprisoned angels.

Azazel is named in the Book of Enoch as being a leader of the fallen angels. Could Apollo of Greece and Apollyon of the Apocalypse be none other than Azazel, the first of the *Nephilim* to fall? The name Azazel crops up in Leviticus 16:8, 10 and 26. This name is translated as "scapegoat," but in the Hebrew it is Azazel, a proper name, and the appendage of the leader of the fallen angels.

Enoch describes the Abyss as being narrow, deep, horrible and dark. This matches the description of *Tartarus* in Peter as well as Jude: "gloomy dungeons" and "a place of darkness" (*Jude 6, 11; Peter 2:4*). We are also told by Enoch that this Abyss is an "abyss of the Earth." This fits in with Scripture as well as with the underworld or *Tartarus* of Greek mythology and with the abode of the dead described in Egyptian literature. All of these historical accounts seemingly refer to one and the same place.

Enoch also describes how the descendants of the *Nephilim*, the Titans and gods of Rome and Greece, the heroes of old, began to fight and smite each other. Such was the violence, we are told, that the whole Earth quaked. Again this mirrors the information proffered in Genesis chapter six, where we are told that the entire Earth was filled with violence and the "thoughts of men's hearts were only evil all the time" (*Genesis 6:5*). It is this unbridled evil and violence which prompted Yaweh to destroy all flesh by means of the great Flood. This worldwide deluge is featured in many ancient writings, such as the Epic of Gilgamesh, and it ties in also with the Sumerian flood story.[69]

Marriages between humans and gods are a well-known feature of Ugaritic, Hurrian and Mesopotamian mythology as well as of Greek, Roman and Egyptian historical record. Indeed, the heroic figure of Gilgamesh was held to be derived from just such a divine union, which gave him great physical strength, but not immortality.[70]

It is worth mentioning that, in Ugaritic literature, the term "sons of God" is used to describe members of the divine pantheon. And the earliest Christian writers, such as Justin, Irenaeus, Clement of Alexandria, Tertullian, Origen, as well as Josephus (Ant 1:31), believed that the "sons of God" were indeed angels.[71]

So the Book of Enoch is emphatic in its testimony of the union between fallen, evil spirit beings and women of the human variety. It also bears out the accounts elsewhere in the Bible of the ensuing immorality and violence perpetrated on the Earth by the offspring of this diabolic union. That this union was wrong is clear from the Old Testament law, which emphatically condemned cross-breeding of species. Similar treatment of crops was also prohibited (*Leviticus 19:19*), as was copulating with animals, which was a capital offence.

In other profane literature and traditions, unions between divine gods and humans is common, and the *Gigantes* of Greek mythology were thought to be the product of marriages between divine and earthly beings. In both the Book of Wisdom and the Book of Baruch, which are not commonly held to be part of the canon of Scripture, we find mention of the giants and heroes of the pre-Flood epoch.

> **And from the beginning also, when the proud giants perished, the hope of the world fleeing to a vessel, which was governed by Thy hand, left to the world seed of generation.**
>
> *Book of Wisdom 14:6*

The above verse refers to the destruction of the "giants," to the hope held out of escape from cataclysm via a vessel (the Ark) and to the preservation of the seed of the woman (*Genesis 3:15*), here called "seed of generation."

> **There were the giants, those renowned men who were from the beginning, of great stature, expert in war. The Lord chose them not, nether did they find the way of knowledge, therefore did they perish.**
>
> *Baruch 3:26,27*

After Enoch has recounted the story of the Flood and the exploits of the *Nephilim,* he then goes on to make a number of prophecies about Israel. He also describes visions of, and journeys to, places and events in future time. Many of these are apocalyptic in nature and they corroborate information found in the Book of Revelation and elsewhere in Scripture. Enoch was born in the year 3382 BC, so the Book of Enoch, written over 5,000 years ago, is one of the most ancient manuscripts to have survived to the present day. Is it not truly extraordinary that these ancient texts, written so long ago, pertain to events which have yet to occur?

The next major event in the schedule of prophecy – one which promises to shake this world to its very foundation – is the appearance of the Messiah, who will save us from the wrath to come.

THE PARALLAX VIEW

Is there intelligent life on other planets? This is a question which arouses much debate and speculation. Because there are billions of stars and planets scattered like dust across the vast plain of infinity, surely the laws of probability suggest that there has to be another world out there with some type of life on it. What sort of life could it be? Are there aliens or weird-looking extraterrestrials out there watching us and waiting for the opportunity to invade our planet and wipe out us humans? Or are we the unwitting guinea pigs of some sort of cosmic experiment carried out by a higher intelligence which is studying us in much the same way as we would watch a goldfish in a bowl?

The answer to the first question is yes, there is indeed intelligent life out there. But it is not of the alien or ET type. There is a sort of parallel universe in existence which is spoken of in Scripture, and I shall attempt to sketch a description of it in this chapter. Many people think of God and heaven in an obscure, ethereal, intangible way. They have no concept of who or what Yaweh is or where He is located. But if we examine the available information carefully, our perspective on this becomes much clearer.

Shortly before his suffering and death, the Messiah endeavoured to comfort his disciples by reassuring them that they would be reunited in the future. At this point in time, his apostles and disciples knew precious little, and understood less, of what he spoke. It was only later on, after the events they experienced at Pentecost, that they put the pieces of the jigsaw together and figured out what was going on. In John 14, the Messiah tells them that he is going to his Father:

> In my Father's house are many rooms: if it were not so, I would have told you. I am going there to prepare a place for you.
> And if I go and prepare a place for you, I will come back and take you to be with me, that you also may be where I am.
>
> *John 14:2,3*

The Messiah clearly states that he is going to his Father's house, where, he says, he will be preparing a place for them, i.e. his apostles and disciples and all who trust in him and follow him. He assures them that this house has many rooms in it to facilitate all the guests who will be arriving there one day. For he says that not only is he going to this house, but that he will return in a future time and take them with him: **"That where I am, there may you be also."** (King James Version).

If we take these verses at face value, they clearly state that the Messiah was returning to his Father's house, there to prepare a place for his people, for whom he would in due course return to Earth. This fits in with the "Rapture" of *I Thessalonians 4:15-18,* which describes the "catching away" of the believers to be with the Messiah while the events of the Apocalypse are being played out.

So where did the Messiah go? And where is he now? We know that in his new resurrected spiritual body he could accomplish feats which transcended the physical boundaries of flesh and blood. For instance, he could suddenly appear in the midst of his apostles when they were in a locked room. He walked on the road to Emmaus with two of the disciples for eight miles and they did not know him until he sat and broke bread with them. Then, when they knew who he was, he vanished out of their sight. In another passage, in John 21, he appeared on the shore while Peter and some of the other disciples were fishing. After toiling all night, they had caught nothing. But Jesus called to them to let their nets out again and so great was the weight of the fish they caught that they were unable to pull the nets back into the boat.

When they reached the shore, the Messiah already had some fish cooking (he must have had his rod with him), and he asked for a few more fish from their catch. Then he prepared the food and they ate breakfast together. When Doubting Thomas heard that some of the others had met the Messiah, he said that he would not believe until he had put his fingers into the wounds in his hands and his side. Jesus subsequently came to Thomas and invited him to touch him, saying: **"Look at my hands and my feet. It is I myself. Touch me and see; a ghost (***pneuma: spirit***) does not have flesh and bones, as you see I have."** *(Luke 24:39)*

So although the Messiah was the same man after the resurrection as he was before, his body had taken on a new spiritual dimension, enabling him to do greater things. We also have been promised such a body in the future. The point is, Jesus was a man. He ate, he drank and he had flesh and bones. And he departed from the Earth physically, through the heavens, to be with his Father.

Abraham, in Old Testament times, also looked forward to a place where he would abide in the future:

> For he (Abraham) was looking forward to the city with founda-
> tions, whose architect and builder is God.
>
> *Hebrews 11:10*

All the prophets and men of God mentioned in the Scriptures told of their hope of a better life in the future. The verse quoted above from Hebrews speaks of a future city with foundations whose designer or architect is Yaweh himself.

Similarly, there is a passage in II Corinthians which tells of a heavenly abode:

> Now we know that if the earthly tent we live in is destroyed, we
> have a building from God, an eternal house in heaven, not built by
> human hands.
>
> *II Corinthians 5:1*

The term "building" here is *oikodome* in the Greek, which means an edifice. So both these verses describe a city with foundations and a house in heaven which was not built by human hands, meaning that it was built by God. But where is heaven and where are these edifices located? Technically speaking, anywhere above the Earth is heaven. Also, the expanse which we refer to as space, which houses all the celestial bodies, is heaven. When the Messiah ascended from the Mount of Olives, it is said that he was taken up into heaven:

> They were looking intently up into the sky as he was going, when
> suddenly two men dressed in white stood beside them.
> "Men of Galilee," they said, "why do you stand here looking into
> the sky? This same Jesus, who has been taken from you into
> heaven, will come back in the same way you have seen him go into
> heaven."
>
> *Book of Acts 1:10,11*

This is corroborated in the Book of Hebrews, where it is stated that he has gone through the "heavens" (plural).

> Therefore, since we have a great high priest, who has gone through
> the heavens, Jesus the Son of God, let us hold firmly to the faith we
> profess.
>
> *Hebrews 4:14*

As was the case with the original "sons of God" who traversed space to fall to Earth in the early days of Jared, Enoch and Noah, the Messiah made a return journey to the celestial city and house of his Father. How could he do this with a body which was composed of both flesh and bone, as he demonstrated to the doubting Thomas? We cannot be expected to be able to comprehend this, since it has not been fully explained to us. But spirit beings are outside the ordinary physical constraints of flesh and blood. And while the first fallen spirit beings left their original abode and came into physical manifestation on this Earth, as told in Genesis 6, the Messiah surpassed their feat by returning to this heavenly city.

We mentioned earlier that the Scriptures seem to indicate the location of this city containing the House of Yaweh. The first hint is given in the account of the fall of Lucifer in Isaiah 14, where he [Lucifer] is quoted as saying: **"I will exalt my throne above the stars of Yaweh ... in the sides of the North"** (*Isaiah 14:13*). We are provided with further information as to the dwelling place of Yaweh and His Son in Psalm 75:6:

For promotion cometh neither from the East, nor from the West, nor from the South.

Therefore it comes from the **North**, the celestial approach to Yaweh's house or mansion, the place to which Satan aspires.[72] So it is safe to assume that the direction in which the Messiah departed when he left this wordly sphere was northward. The North Star is the only star in the sky which remains constant and unmoving. So the next time you look up at the starry sky, cast your eyes northward and know that it will be from this direction that the Messiah will once again traverse space and time to initiate the Rapture.

Right now, as you read this, the Messiah is residing in this heavenly mansion, seated at the right hand of the Most High, Yaweh. Earlier in this book, we recounted how Yaweh made man in His own image. The Messiah at one time said that anyone who had seen him had seen his Father. So if you can envisage the Messiah seated at the right hand of the throne of Yaweh, then perhaps you can imagine the fatherly figure, too. John describes what he saw of this heavenly abode in chapter 4 of the Apocalypse:

> ... there before me was a throne in heaven with someone sitting on it ...
> Surrounding the throne were twenty-four other thrones, and seated on them were twenty-four Elders. They were dressed in white and had crowns of gold on their heads.
>
> *Book of Revelation 4:2,4*

Who the 24 Elders are we do not know, so we will not speculate. These Elders are mentioned several times in the Apocalypse. Besides this grouping of Elders and the Messiah and Yaweh, we are told that an innumerable complement of angels, messengers or spirit-men inhabit and minister in this place called "heaven." This is the picture which is painted for us regarding the City of God and the house where the Messiah has gone to prepare a place for us. It has to be a vast place, for not only does it house these millions of spirit beings and their Lords, it also has to be big enough to take in all those who will be gathered together at the Rapture. This will be a lot of people considering all the millions who have put their trust and faith in the Messiah down through the last 2,000 years.

At present, there are estimated to be about 70 million Christians in the United States alone, and their numbers are all the time increasing in China, Africa, South America and other parts of the world. So there will be quite an amount of people vanishing off this Earth **"in the twinkling of an eye"** *(I Corinthians 15:52)* when the Messiah returns briefly to take those who believe in him to this place he is preparing for us. We will be there for only a relatively short period of time. The Great Tribulation is set to last for seven years, beginning when the Antichrist signs a peace deal with Israel, and ending with the Battle of Armageddon. There may be an interval between the Rapture and the start of the seven years of Tribulation. We do not know. But, at the end of the seven years, we will be returning with the Messiah to this Earth for the beginning of the millennial reign. During this 1,000 years, Israel will be apportioned the Promised Land, which will be divided up between the 12 tribes. At the end of the 1,000 years, there will be another, final rebellion, when Satan is released for a brief sojourn. After this rebellion is quashed, the Earth will be totally destroyed by fire. This is recorded in II Peter:

> By the same word, the present heavens and earth are reserved for fire, being kept for the day of judgment and destruction of ungodly men ...
> But the day of the Lord will come like a thief. The heavens will disappear with a roar.
> The elements will be destroyed by fire, and the earth and everything in it will be laid bare.
>
> *I Peter 3:7,10*

After this purging by fire, there will be a new heaven and a new earth. Satan and all those who believe not, and whose names are not written in the Book of Life, will be cast into the "lake of fire" and will experience the "second death." After all this cleansing has occurred, a new regime will be established. All the sin and death and sickness will be things of the past in this new heaven and new earth. Then the holy city, the New Jerusalem, will descend to the new earth:

> **Then I saw a new heaven and a new earth, for the first heaven and the first earth had passed away, and there was no longer any sea.**
> **I saw the Holy City, the new Jerusalem, coming down out of heaven from God, prepared as a bride beautifully dressed for her husband.**
> **And I heard a loud voice from the throne saying: "Now the dwelling of God is with men, and He will live with them. They will be His people, and God Himself will be with them and be their God. He will wipe every tear from their eyes. There will be no more death or mourning or crying or pain, for the old order of things has passed away."**
>
> *Revelation 21:1-4*

This is the future hope of all those who believe in Yaweh and in the Messiah. All of history is but a preface to this future Paradise Regained. This is when Yaweh finally comes to the New Earth to be with and dwell among his children. It is said: "**Now the dwelling of God is with men, and He will live with them.**" He will wipe away every tear from their eyes. There will be no more death, or mourning, or crying, or pain, for the old order of things will have passed away.

But look again at the first two verses of the above quotation. It says that John saw the Holy City, called the New Jerusalem, coming down from heaven, literally, to land on this new earth. This concept is so fantastical that one needs to consider its implications for a moment. This city is the city Abraham looked forward to, whose builder and architect is God. This is the heavenly house, or at least it contains the house that Paul spoke of in II Corinthians 5:1. This is what the Messiah was referring to when he told his disciples: "**In my Father's house are many rooms ... I go to prepare a place for you ...**" (*John 14:12*)

In the future, this Holy City, in which Yaweh and the Messiah and the 24 Elders and the millions of angels now abide, will literally and physically descend from the heavens and come to rest on this new earth. What a sight to behold! The record goes on to describe this city and those who will be privileged enough to reside in it:

> He said to me: "It is done. I am the Alpha and the Omega, the
> Beginning and the End. To him who is thirsty, I will give to drink
> without cost from the spring of the water of life. He who over-
> comes will inherit all this, and I will be his God and he will be My
> son. But the cowardly, the unbelieving, the vile, the murderers, the
> sexually immoral, those who practise magic arts, the idolaters and
> all liars – their place will be in the fiery lake of burning sulphur.
> This is the second death."
>
> *Revelation 21:6-8*

Here is both a blessing and a warning. To those who believe in the Messiah
and put their trust in him, Yaweh will give freely, and without cost, of the
water of life. But to those who do not believe, the second death awaits.

Then John is given a further opportunity to view this Holy City.

> And He carried me away in the spirit to a mountain great and
> high, and showed me the Holy City, Jerusalem, coming down out of
> heaven from God.
> It shone with the glory of God, and its brilliance was like that of a
> very precious jewel, like a jasper, clear as crystal.
> It had a great, high wall with twelve gates, and with twelve angels
> at the gates. On the gates were written the names of the twelve
> tribes of Israel.
> There were three gates on the east, three on the north, three on the
> south, and three on the west.
> The wall of the city had twelve foundations, and on them were the
> names of the twelve Apostles of the Lamb.
>
> *Revelation 21:10-14*

Note once again that the record tells us that the city comes down from
God out of Heaven to rest on the Earth. The number 12 runs through the
pattern of the design, as 12 denotes government in Biblical terminology,
i.e. twelve months in the year, twelve tribes of Israel, twelve signs of the
Zodiac, twelve Apostles etc. The passage continues:

> He measured its wall and it was 144 cubits thick, by man's
> measurement, which the angel was using.
> The wall was made of jasper, and the city of pure gold, as pure as
> glass.The foundations of the city walls were decorated with every
> kind of precious stone. The first foundation was jasper *(dark green
> and transparent with red veins)*, the second sapphire *(azure blue,*

almost transparent), the third chalcedony (*a kind of agate or onyx, bluish white*), the fourth emerald (*a vivid green*), the fifth sardonyx (*a mixture of chalcedony and carnelian, a flesh colour*), the sixth carnelian (*probably the carnelian, the red being vivid*), the seventh chrysolite (*yellow or gold in colour and transparent*), the eighth beryl (*a sea-green colour*), the ninth topaz (*today a yellow, but in ancient times pale green*), the tenth chrysoprase (*pale yellow and green*), the eleventh jacinth (*a deep flame-red or violet colour*) and the twelfth amethyst (*a violet colour*).

The twelve gates were twelve pearls, each gate made of a single pearl. The great street of the city was of pure gold, like transparent glass.
I did not see a temple in the city, because the Lord God Almighty and the Lamb is its temple.
The city does not need the sun or the moon to shine on it, for the glory of God gives it light, and the Lamb is its lamp.
The nations will walk by its light, and the kings of the earth will bring their splendour into it.
On no day will its gates ever be shut, for there will be no night there.
The glory and honour of the nations will be brought into it.
Nothing impure will ever enter it, nor will anyone who does what is shameful or deceitful, but only those whose names are written in the Lamb's Book of Life.

Revelation 21:17-21

(source: E.W. Bullinger, *Commentary on Revelation*, Kregal Publications, p.663).

The detail in this description is truly astonishing. We are told that there is no need for a temple in this city because Yaweh and the Messiah are its temple. Neither is there any need for light, because the glory of God is its light and the Lamb, Jesus, is its lamp. The gates of the cities of old had to be shut to protect their inhabitants from enemies and from the perils of the night. But in this future city the gates will remain open at all times, for there will be no night, and neither will there be any danger to those whose names are written in the Lamb's Book of Life. The narrative continues with a description of the River of Life:

Then the angel showed me the river of the water of life, as clear as crystal, flowing from the Throne of God and of the Lamb down the middle of the great street of the city. On each side of the river stood the tree of life, bearing twelve crops of fruit, yielding its fruit every month. And the leaves of the tree are for the healing of the nations. No longer will there be any curse. The Throne of God and of the Lamb will be in the city, and His servants will serve Him.

They will see His face and His name will be on their foreheads. There will be no more night. They will not need the light of a lamp or the light of the sun, for the Lord God will give them light. And they will reign for ever and ever.

The angel said to me: "These words are trustworthy and true. The Lord, the God of the spirits of the prophets, sent His angel to show His servants the things that must soon take place."

Revelation 22:1-6

"These words are trustworthy and true." We have the word of both the Messiah and his Father, the Most High Yaweh, that these things shall absolutely come to pass. Those who believe will have access to both the Water of Life and the Tree of Life. All one has to do to ensure that their name is included in the Book of Life is to personally accept Jesus Christ as Lord in their life and believe that God raised him from the dead (*Romans 10:9,10*). When an individual makes this very personal decision and truly believes, then they pass from death to life. In doing so, they will become eligible to participate in the next major event on the prophetic calendar – the Rapture – and also in the future millennial reign of the Messiah and the New Heaven and New Earth. And they will be admitted to the New Jerusalem, the Holy City, which will come down from Heaven to Earth.

But wait. In this commentary I have omitted a number of crucial verses from Revelation. These, I believe, give us the answer to the riddle as to why the Great Pyramid of Giza (and all the other pyramids of Egypt, Mexico and Guatemala) is shaped as it is. But before we look at what we are told in Revelation 21, I must return to some assertions I have already made.

These concern Satan, who is the Devil and the Adversary, also known as Lucifer, the Ancient Serpent, the Prince of the Power of the Air. One of Satan's primary endeavours is to attempt to duplicate what the True God has created. In the Garden of Eden, he appeared as a glorious angel of light in order to deceive Eve. Then we are told that his ministers masquerade as ministers of light. So the angel of light in Eden was a copy of a true messenger of Yaweh. Throughout the history of mankind from Old Testament times to the days when Jesus walked upon the Earth and for the past 2,000 years, the Devil has deceived the masses with his counterfeit religion. In the coming Apocalypse, the Antichrist will die from a head wound and will then be raised from death by the power of Satan. This will be a blatant imitation of the resurrection of the Messiah. By his very nature, Satan is constantly engaged in acts of deception and always attempts to duplicate, copy, ape and imitate what Yaweh does.

The Pyramid of the Apocalypse

I have become convinced that the pyramidal shape is a demonic exercise in counterfeit design, for I believe that the pyramid is a paradigm of the City of God which is at present in the heavens and which was seen and described by John in chapter 21 of the Apocalypse. In the midst of the earlier description of the New Jerusalem, we are presented with the following details:

> The angel who talked with me had a measuring rod of gold to measure the city, its gates and its walls.
> The city was laid out like a square, as long as it was wide. He measured the city with the rod and found it to be 12,000 stadia in length, and as wide and high as it is long.
> He measured its wall and it was 144 cubits thick, by man's measurement, which the angel was using.
>
> *Revelation 21:15-17*

The Greek text puts the dimensions of the city at 12,000 stadia. And the length and the width and the height are the same. A stadia is about 606 feet, which makes the city roughly 1,400 miles long on each side and 1,400 miles high. Some Biblical scholars have suggested that this city has been created in the shape of a cube. I believe that it is in the form of a pyramid and I believe also that the reason the Pyramid of Giza and the other ancient pyramids were built was to copy the heavenly city of Yaweh, the Holy City which is right now in the heavens. This is what I mean by the term "**Pyramid of the Apocalypse**."

Consider this for a moment. Lucifer was the most exalted celestial spirit being ever created by Yaweh. So powerful and wise was he that he became corrupted by his own beauty and thought to overthrow the Most High. As a result, he was banished from the presence of Yaweh, and those who rebelled with him fell to Earth. Because it is the nature of Lucifer to imitate Yaweh, he decided to construct a magnificent edifice for himself on this Earth. This building was to be a monument to his own pride and ego. So by way of his minions, the *Nephilim,* and the awesome spiritual power at his disposal, he designed and constructed this massive pyramid at Giza, using all his celestial prowess and astronomical knowledge to align it with the various star signs and constellations. In Ezekiel 28, it is said of Satan:

Thou sealest up the sum, full of wisdom and perfect in beauty.
Ezekiel 28:12

"Thou sealest up the sum" means "you are the finished pattern." Only an exalted celestial being could have masterminded the pyramids of that ancient epoch. Only a being or beings with such knowledge of the stars could have accomplished such things. Their original abode was among the celestial bodies in the City of God and they were present at the laying of the foundations of the Earth. Speaking to Job, Yaweh says:

Where wast thou when I laid the foundations of the earth? Declare, if thou hast understanding.
Who hath laid the measures thereof, if thou knowest? Or who hath stretched the line upon it?
Whereupon are the foundations thereof fastened? Or who laid the cornerstone thereof;
When the morning stars sang together and all the sons of God shouted for joy?
Job 38:4-8

This was in the distant past, prior to the corruption of Lucifer and his subsequent rebellion and fall.

In Graham Hancock's book *Heaven's Mirror* (page 66), he quotes from the Edfu Texts, which repeatedly state that the monuments of Egypt were built by the gods to represent "buildings in the sky" and were erected according to plans "which fell from heaven." He goes on to say that when the gods built them, they were modelled upon a place "that was believed to have existed before the world was created." This is further evidence to support our theory that the pyramids are earthly representations of a celestial dwelling.

Some Christian scholars have suggested that the Great Pyramid was built by Job or by some other Patriarch and believe that it is an altar designed by Yaweh himself which contains prophetic information relating to what the future holds for Christian believers. I cannot accept this to be the case, since all the information we require regarding our redemption and our future is provided in the pages between Genesis and Revelation. Furthermore, a "star shaft" leading from the King's Chamber in the Great Pyramid is associated with Draco. We have already concluded that Draco is the Dragon, who is the Devil and Satan, the Ancient Serpent (*Revelation 12:9*). Also, two of the other "star shafts" have been identified with Osiris (Orion) and Isis (Sirius), two of the main deities of ancient Egypt. All these clues would indicate that the architect of the monument was scribbling his identity all over the design in the same way that people like to see their own names appearing in lights. And the name which echoes from this building is that of Draco. It is his name and those of his associates which are writ large in the blueprint of the pyramid and in the light of the stars it points to.

Consider also what the depiction of the pyramid has come to represent. It is chiefly associated with masonic symbology and has links as well with other secretive organisations which have their foundations in the occult. It was the influence of the masons which led to the pyramid with the "all-seeing eye" being displayed on the back of the American one-dollar bill. This eye is referred to in some Eastern religions as the "third eye." It is said to represent a higher level of psychic consciousness which initiates must attain in order to arrive at a deeper understanding of the secrets of the occult.

An inscription in Latin is printed on the dollar bill: "Novus Ordo Seclorum" (see **Figure 17**). Briefly, this is the aspiration of those clandestine organisations which believe that the only way to achieve world peace is through "One World Government." Thus you will often hear powerful politicians speak of a "New World Order."[70] But the Latin word *seclorum* is the root for our English word secular. So the goal of these organisations is a one-world, secular, godless government which will eliminate world wars and ensure peace and safety for all.

In relatively recent times, Adolf Hitler and the Nazi leadership were known to be heavily involved in the occult and in Satan-worship, and this same symbol depicting the all-seeing eye was found above the entrance door of the bunker in which Hitler committed suicide. The origin of this powerful symbol can be traced back to the Egyptian deity Horus. One of the main gods of the Egyptian pantheon, Horus was probably an original *Nephilim* or a direct descendant. Thus the Eye of Horus appears to be linked to Lucifer and has an obvious association with the occult. This lends more weight to the argument that the symbol of the pyramid with the all-seeing eye, and indeed the pyramids themselves, are Satanic in origin. (Many refer to this eye on the back of the dollar bill as the "eye of Lucifer").

Also, if Yaweh did indeed build the Great Pyramid, he would have been breaking his own First Commandment, which states:

> **You shall not make for yourself an idol in the form of anything in heaven above or on the earth beneath ...**
>
> *Deuteronomy 5:8*

Here it is specifically stated that we must not make any images of anything in heaven above. If the Great Pyramid is an image of the heavenly city, then Yaweh would appear to be disregarding His own precepts, which I do not deign to think He would do. And, compared to the description of the New Jerusalem given by John in Revelation 21, the Great Pyramid is a poor copy indeed. It seems much more probable that all of the pyramids are counterfeit imitations constructed by Satan and his *Nephilim* comrades as altars to their own pride, an earthly reflection of a heavenly reality.

Figure 17
A detail of the Great Seal of the United States of America featuring the pyramid surmounted by the "all-seeing eye." This symbol is inscribed on the reverse side of the American one-dollar bill.

This would explain the vast amounts of innocent blood which have been spilt on these altars, especially in Central America, to assuage the anger and salve the bloodthirsty lust of these same gods of death.

The Great Pyramid had an outer casing of polished white limestone, making its exterior smooth and iridescent. Some believe that its capstone was made of gold. It must have been a glorious sight when first constructed, gleaming in the light as though it had been let down from heaven.

Now compare this with the New Jerusalem. This city is made of pure gold. Pure as crystal. It is not unreasonable to equate the Great Pyramid of Giza, in its original glory, with the New Jerusalem, as described by John in chapter 21 of the Book of Revelation. Thus I believe these ancient pyramids are copies of the City of God which in the future is to come down out of heaven: the **Pyramid of the Apocalypse**.

> **"Behold, I am coming soon. Blessed is he who keeps the words of the prophecy in this book."**
>
> *Revelation 22:7*

Only when the Messiah comes will we fully understand these mysteries, for now we see through a glass darkly. But when he returns, all shall be revealed.

I want to state here that the conclusions I have come to in this volume are based on piecing together in a logical manner the truths given to us in Scripture. I have been mindful throughout that to add to the prophecies of Scripture, or to take away from them, is a great sin. It is therefore with a humble heart that I submit this thesis, and I beg forgiveness of Yaweh and of His Son, my brother, the Messiah, if I have made any errors or misrepresented these truths. This is not my intent.

Where the Scripture is plain and simple, I can stake my life on its veracity. Where I have speculated, based on my research and insight, I have stated this to be so. But I believe many of the conclusions I have reached are accurate.

Conclusion

There is a parallel universe in existence which is peopled by intelligent life-forms. These beings look like us and have personalities and bodies similar to ours. But they are not flesh-and-blood humans as we are. Rather their nature is spirit. After the Messiah rose from the dead, by means of this spirit power, he travelled through space to reside in his Father's house. Scripture also tells us of a city, whose architect and builder is Yaweh, and this city is located high in the heavens. It is in this place that the Messiah sits at the right hand of the Father, awaiting the hour when he shall return to gather his people together.

The Father's throne is surrounded by 24 other thrones on which are seated 24 Elders. We know little of these beings. Countless millions of spirit men, angels, also reside in this heavenly habitation to serve Yaweh. These messengers are mostly invisible to us humans, but they are constantly at work on behalf of those of us who shall be the heirs to the promises of God.

At the culmination of the events predicted in the Book of Revelation, after the Great Tribulation and after the 1,000-year millennial reign of the Messiah, there will be a New Heaven and a New Earth. The curse and all death and sin will be abolished forever. The Paradise of God will be the new habitation of man. On to this new earth there will descend from heaven a holy city, the New Jerusalem. The length and breadth and height of this city will be equal in dimension, leading us to believe that this future metropolis will be pyramidal in shape. This is the **Pyramid of the Apocalypse.**

One of Satan's aliases is "the deceiver." By his nature, he is compelled to imitate and attempt to duplicate everything the True God does. But whereas Yaweh is the God of Truth, Satan is the father of lies. Therefore his version of truth always has fear and bondage as its end result. In the seven years of the Great Tribulation, the world will embrace the false messiah, the man sent by Satan in the guise of the Christ.

Because Lucifer and his fallen band of evil angels had their original abode with Yaweh, among the heavenly bodies, they are familiar with these surroundings. Having been the most highly exalted of all the created spirit beings, it is feasible to assume that the Great Pyramid was designed and constructed by Lucifer and his minions, the *Nephilim,* as a mirror-image of the celestial city and as a monument to their own arrogance.

Although the Messiah ascended to the house of the Father to prepare a place for us, and although those who believe in Him will be "spirited" away to this abode at the time of the Rapture, it is important to remember that this is not our ultimate destination. For we will be going to heaven with the Messiah for only a short time, seven years or thereabouts, while the horrific events of the Apocalypse are played out here on Earth. After Armageddon, we will return to Earth to serve the Messiah during his reign of 1,000 years. Thereafter, the Earth and all the elements will be consumed with fire and a new earth and new heaven will be established. This earth, not heaven, will be our final resting place. In this Paradise of God, we will enjoy eternal life with the Messiah, and Yaweh will come among us to dwell with His family. Then He will be our God and we will be His children, and there will be no more death or pain or mourning or crying, for the former things will have passed away (*Revelation 21:3,4*).

THE GREATEST STORY EVER TOLD

We have considered the spiritual dimensions of both Yaweh and His angelic host on the one hand and Satan and his entourage on the other. This spiritual realm is, for the most part, hidden to the ordinary person. In the Gospels, the accounts of the words and works of the Messiah are recorded in minute detail. But these words are largely ignored and little studied by the world today. Much of the Gospel of John is concerned more with the thoughts and ideas of the Messiah than with where he went at a given time and what he did there. I would like to highlight some of these utterances and reflect on their profound implications, bearing in mind that this was no ordinary man, but an emissary sent by Yaweh.

The opening of the Gospel of John is a beautiful and poetic piece of literary work.

> In the beginning was the Word, and the Word was with God and the Word was God.
> The same was in the beginning with God.
> All things were made by Him; and without Him was not anything made that was made.
> In Him was life; and the life was the light of men.
> And the light shineth in darkness; and the darkness comprehended it not.
> There was a man sent from God whose name was John.
> The same came for a witness to bear witness to the Light that all men through him might believe.
> He was not that Light, but was sent to bear witness to that Light.
> That was the true Light, which lighteth every man that cometh into the world.
> He was in the world, and the world was made by Him, and the world knew Him not.
> He came unto his own, and His own received Him not.
> But as many as received Him, to them gave He power to become the sons of God, even to them that believe in His name.
> Which were born not of blood, nor of the will of the flesh, nor of

the will of man, but of God.
And the Word was made flesh, and dwelt among us, and we beheld His glory and the glory as of the only begotten of the Father, full of grace and truth.

Gospel of John 1:1-14

It is by the way of this Word that Yaweh is made known to men, and it was His Son, the Messiah, who revealed Him by way of His words and His works.

John the Baptist is mentioned in this passage. He was a first cousin of the Messiah. In a parallel discourse in Luke 3, he makes a statement which has relevance to our study of the end-of-time prophecies.

> John answered, saying unto them: "I indeed baptise you with water, but one mightier than I cometh, the latchet of whose shoes I am not worthy to unloose. He shall baptise you with the Holy Spirit and with fire."

Luke 3:16

There are two baptisms here. One with water, the other with fire – the Holy Spirit. Many Christian churches put great emphasis on the former. In the Church of Rome, water baptism is essential if the infant is to escape the eternal fires of hell should it die prematurely. In some evangelical Christian churches, baptism by full immersion is carried out when adults or teenagers accept Jesus as their Lord. But many of the mainstream churches ignore the baptism of fire spoken of by John the Baptist. This is a spiritual baptism which only became known after the Messiah had risen from the dead and ascended to the Father. On the day of Pentecost, the Holy Spirit descended on the twelve Apostles. Tongues of fire sat on them and they spoke in tongues for the first time ever as they were infilled with spirit.

In the third chapter of John, the Messiah instructs one of the rulers of the Jews in this spiritual baptism. This man had to come to the Messiah under cover of darkness, for had it been discovered that he was collaborating with Jesus, he would have been cast out by the remainder of the ruling Jewish hierarchy.

> Now there was a man of the Pharisees named Nicodemus, a member of the Jewish ruling council.
> He came to Jesus at night, and said: "Rabbi, we know you are a teacher who has come from God. For no one could perform the miraculous signs you are doing if God were not with him."

In reply, Jesus declared: "I tell you the truth. No one can see the kingdom of God unless he is born again."

"How can a man be born when he is old?" Nicodemus asked. "Surely he cannot enter a second time into his mother's womb to be born."

Jesus answered: "I tell you the truth. No one can enter the kingdom of God unless he is born of water and the spirit.

Flesh gives birth to flesh, but the spirit gives birth to spirit.

You should not be surprised at my saying 'you must be born again.' The wind blows wherever it pleases. You hear its sound, but you cannot tell where it comes from or where it is going. So it is with everyone born of the spirit."

John 3:1-8

The Greek word translated as "born again" here is *anothen,* which literally means "*born from above.*" This refers to spiritual rebirth, which equates to baptism by fire. This baptism of fire supersedes baptism by water, for pouring water over someone's head does not necessarily produce a change in that person's heart. Later on in this same chapter, the Messiah sets out what we need to do to bring about this spiritual rebirth and gain access to the kingdom of God. This next verse is probably the best known in the entire Bible:

For God so loved the world that He gave His one and only Son, that whoever believes in Him shall not perish but have eternal life.

John 3:16

This simple promise is reiterated many times by the Messiah.

I tell you the truth. Whoever hears my word and believes Him who sent me has eternal life and will not be condemned; he has crossed over from death to life.

John 5:24

It matters not what a person did in the past or whether that person belongs to any particular creed or to none. This promise is to any who wish to avail of it and it is unconditional. For those who accept and believe the word of the Messiah, all the future blessings of Yaweh are theirs and they will have their place in the future Holy City, the New Jerusalem. But for those who do not accept His Word and refuse His offer of eternal life, a bleak future lies in store. At the end of the Gospel of Mark, a conversation the Messiah had with eleven of the Apostles is recorded. This took place after his death and resurrection but before his ascension.

> Later, Jesus appeared to the eleven as they were eating; he rebuked them for their lack of faith and their stubborn refusal to believe those who had seen him after he had risen.
> He said to them: "Go into all the world and preach the good news to all creation.
> Whoever believes and is baptised will be saved, but whoever does not believe will be condemned."
>
> *Gospel of Mark 16:14-16*

In the King James Version of the Bible, the word condemned is translated as "damned." This exhortation from the Messiah could not be clearer. If you believe, you are saved. If you do not believe, you will be condemned.

It is probably fair to say that many people in the world have yet to be convinced that the Messiah is right. I suggest that they would be well advised to read the Scriptures, beginning with the Gospel of Matthew. Just read what is written and listen to the words. Begin at chapter one and continue through to the end of the New Testament. You will be amazed at what you will learn and at how much you did not know. For many of us have had little or no instruction in this, the greatest of all literary works. It is no wonder that people are despondent, for it is written in Proverbs 29:28:

> "Where there is no vision, the people perish."

In this next passage, the Messiah speaks of himself as being the "bread of life."

> When they found him on the other side of the lake, they asked him: "Rabbi, when did you get here?"
> Jesus answered: "I tell you the truth. You are looking for me not because you saw miraculous signs, but because you ate the loaves and had your fill.
> Do not work for food that spoils, but for food that endures to eternal life, which the Son of Man will give you. On him God the Father has placed his seal of approval."
> Then they asked Him: "What must we do to do the works God requires?"

Jesus answered: "The work of God is this: to believe in the one He has sent."

So they asked him: "What miraculous sign then will you give that we may see it and believe you? What will you do? Our forefathers ate the manna in the desert; as it is written: 'He gave them bread from heaven to eat'."

Jesus said to them: "I tell you the truth. It is not Moses who has given you the bread from heaven, but it is my Father who gives you the true bread from heaven. For the bread of God is he who comes down from heaven and gives life to the world."

"Sir," they said, "from now on give us this bread."

Then Jesus declared: "I am the bread of life. He who comes to me will never go hungry, and he who believes in me will never be thirsty.

But, as I told you, you have seen me and still you do not believe.

All that the Father gives me will come to me, and whoever comes to me I will never drive away.

For I have come down from heaven not to do my will, but to do the will of Him who sent me.

And this is the will of Him who sent me, that I shall lose none of all that He has given me, but raise them up at the last day.

For my Father's will is that everyone who looks to the Son and believes in Him shall have eternal life, and I will raise him up at the last day."

John 6:25-40

All that is required to partake of this Bread of Life is to believe. And all that is required to avail of the River of Life is to believe. The work of God is to believe in the Messiah whom He sent. So often in religious orthodoxy, rules and regulations and traditions and doctrines and dogmas of men have to be observed in the cause of salvation. But with the Messiah, all is simple: Believe and thou shalt receive the gift of eternal life. This promise has been held out to us for all of 2,000 years, but the majority of our religious leaders have led us in the opposite direction: away from the light and into the darkness.

At that time Jesus, full of joy through the Holy Spirit, said: "I praise you, Father, Lord of Heaven and Earth, because you have hidden these things from the wise and learned and revealed them to little children.

Yes, Father, for this was your good pleasure.

All things have been committed to me by my Father. No one knows who the Son is except the Father, and no one knows who the Father is except the Son, and those to whom the Son chooses to reveal Him."

Then he turned to his disciples and said privately: "Blessed are the eyes that see what you see. For I tell you that many prophets and kings wanted to see what you see, but did not see it, and to hear what you hear, but did not hear it."

Luke 10:21-24

Those who believe in the Messiah will be included in the Rapture, the next major happening, which will usher in the seven years of the Great Tribulation. Many of those known to each of us – family members, friends, acquaintances – will have to remain on the Earth to endure the turmoil in the period leading up to the Battle of Armageddon. During this time of Tribulation, many will turn to the Messiah and put their trust in Him. The Antichrist, meanwhile, will demand total allegiance, and those who resist his authority and refuse to accept his mark will be hunted down and killed. In this way, many who believe will die in these times.

But, for now, we can look forward to the gathering together or Rapture of the saints; those of us who believe in the Messiah:

"My sheep hear my voice and I know them and they follow me and I give unto them eternal life, and they shall never perish; neither shall any man pluck them out of my hand. My Father, who gave them to me, is greater than all; and no one is able to snatch them out of my Father's hand."

The Messiah, as quoted in John 10:27-29

We are approaching the final chapters of the Greatest Story Ever Told. The prophecies pertaining to the "last days" or "end times" are beginning to be fulfilled. This planet is being driven towards the edge of the abyss. The world will be cast into a terrible turmoil before it is is reborn into Paradise Regained. It is a time-bomb whose fuse has long since been lit. The hoof-beats of the Four Horsemen of the Apocalypse are clearly to be heard by all who have ears to hear. In the meantime, those of us who choose to put our trust in the Messiah can comfort one another in the sure knowledge that we will be gathered up from this sphere before the holocaust begins. In this, we are truly blessed.

Blessed is the one who reads the words of this prophecy, and

blessed are those who hear it and take to heart what is written in it, because the time is near.

The Apocalypse 1:3

In closing, I would like to present a poem. This poem will take you on a journey through the prophecies in the Book of Revelation. It will provide you with a chilling reminder of the wrath to come, but it will tell you also of the riches of the grace available to you if you choose to accept it. I wrote this poem after finishing my first book, *Apocalypse Soon*. I am not a poet. However, after putting the first verse on paper, the rest simply seemed to flow. The poem is, to the best of my knowledge, Biblically accurate. Notes have been included at the end for reference purposes. Because these events are still in the future, I suppose this is a prophetic poem. May God be with you – The Author.

The Apocalypse

I

Upon the Isle of Patmos [1]
In prayer on the Lord's Day [2]
The Spirit took me speedily [3]
To an era far away.

II

He showed me things in visions [4]
Which no man can see
Of days to come in future [5]
Which verily shall be. [6]

III

This day is nigh upon us [7]
I feel convinced to say
Be ready or be warned [8]
Man's Sin the Earth shall pay. [9]

IV

The raptured church shall usher in [10]
A time before unknown [11]
The man of sin shall take control [12]
The world shall follow him. [13]

V

With subtle words [14]
And sleight of hand
And lies that shall deceive [15]
Upon their heads the mark to take [16]
That brings them to the grave. [17]

VI

The saints shall stand [18]
Upon that day
His Word to uphold [19]
Their blood will spill [20]
She'll drink her fill [21]
But in the end be told.

VII

For they shall be rewarded [22]
Who bend but do not break
To kiss the ring of Satan's son [23]
But trust in God's namesake. [24]

VIII

Blood and fire and famine [25]
Clouds black and noisome too [26]
Death will stalk the living [27]
The plague will prey on you. [28]

IX

The Antichrist will rule the world [29]
His will to bow the knee [30]
His priest who sits upon the hills
Will blind their eyes to see. [31]

X

The multitudes who throng the globe [32]
In tumult e'er shall be [33]
The seas shall roar [34]
The Beast will soar [35]
Devouring bond and free. [36]

XI

Black smoke of torment [37]
Ne'er shall cease
For those who take the mark [38]
The worm of death
Shall gnaw away
In death's bile grave so bleak. [39]

XII

Eternally to gnash and wail [40]
Because they chose the lie [41]
And heeded not the Master's Son [42]
Who gave His soul to die. [43]

XIII

That we should be forgiven [44]
Who trusted in the Word [45]
Chosen from the beginning [46]
To be our God's reward. [47]

XIV

His first fruits from the dead are we [48]
Who listened to his call [49]
His voice our ear remembered [50]
Predestined far beyond the Fall [51]
To walk in peace by waters still [52]
In Paradise our hearts to fill [53]
With pleasures glorious and thrill [54]
Which eyes have never seen or heard [55]
With Jesus Christ, Our Lord's Shepherd. [56]

XV

Some martyrs in that day shall fall [57]
The saints with patience must endure [58]
Who wrestle with the deathly pall [59]
Of Satan's minions, stink, vile, impure [60]
Who hunt them down and kill the free [61]
Refuse the mark, don't bend the knee [62]
For in the end you'll see the light [63]
Of God's abundant love and grace [64]
And riches reap and know delight [65]
And see your Saviour face to face. [66]

XVI

The time is near [67]
The angels wait
To put the sickle to the test [68]
To reap the harvest of our God [69]
To take the good [70]
And leave the rest [71]
To burn upon life's shallow grave [72]
In terrible and fervent heat
The remnant of Devil's chaff [73]
The evidence of sin's defeat. [74]

XVII

Beware you scornful and be warned [75]
For soon the Rapture will befall [76]
To catch away the faithful few [77]
Who heard His voice, who got reborn [78]
Who'll miss the wrath of the fearful day [79]
Who'll live forever. Wait and pray. [80]
Even so, come quickly, Lord Jesus. [81]

Patrick C. Heron

References

1   Revelation 1:9
2   Rev. 1:10
3   Rev. 4:2
4   Rev. 1:1,19
5   Mark 13:23
6   Rev. 4:1
7   Rev. 1:3
8   Matthew 24:44
9   Ephesians 5:6; Colossians 3:6
10 I Thessalonians4;17
11 Matthew 24:21
12 II Thessalonians 2:3,4
13 Rev. 13:3,4
14 Rev. 13:14
15 II Thessalonians 2:9-11
16 Rev. 13:16-18
17 Rev. 14:9-11
18 Rev. 13:10
19 Rev. 12:17
20 Rev. 13:7
21 Rev. 17:6 22 Rev.
22: 12; Matthew 10:41,42
23 Rev. 13:4
24 II Corinthians 1:9,10
25 Rev. 8:7
26 Rev. 8:12; 9:2,18
27 Rev. 6:7,8
28 Rev. 16:2

29 Rev. 13:3,4
30 Rev. 13:15
31 Rev. 17:9; 13:14
32 Rev. 14:6
33 Rev. 16:10
34 Luke 21:25,26
35 Daniel 7:7
36 Daniel 7:19
37 Rev. 14:11
38 Rev. 13:16
39 Rev. 6:8; Isaiah 14:11
40 Matthew 25:30
41 Rev. 9:20,21
42 Rev. 16:9
43 John 3:16
44 Ephesians 4:32; Colossians 2:13
45 I Thessalonians 2:13
46 Ephesians 1:4
47 I Corinthians 3:8; Colossians 3:24
48 Ephesians 2:4,5; James 1:18
49 Ephesians 4:1,4; Romans 8:28
50 Matthew 13:9
51 Romans 8:30
52 Psalm 23:2
53 Rev. 2:7
54 Romans 8:18

55 I Corinthians 2:9
56 Rev. 20:4
57 Rev. 20:4
58 Romans 5:3,4; Rev. 14:12
59 Ephesians 6:12
60 Rev. 18:2; 21:8
61 Rev. 12:17
62 Rev. 13:15
63 John 12:46; 8:12
64 Ephesians 1:6,7; 2:4
65 Ephesians 2:7; 3:8
66 I Corinthians 13:12:I John 3:2
67 Rev. 22:7; 14:14
68 Rev. 14:15
69 Rev. 14:16
70 Matthew 24:31
71 Matthew 25:32
72 Rev. 16:9
73 II Peter 3:10-12
74 I Corinthians 15:54
75 II Peter 3:3
76 I Thessalonians4:16,17
77 I Corinthians 15.-51,52
78 John 3:1-9
79 Romans 2:5
80 John 5:24; I Thessalonians 1:10
81 Rev. 22:20

EPILOGUE

In bygone days, miners used to carry canaries with them when they were working in deep shafts. If any toxic, odourless gases were present, the canaries would exhibit signs of distress and the miners would receive a timely warning to return to the surface before being fatally overcome.

Between the time I finished writing this book and its publication, a number of dramatic events have occurred, chief among them being the attacks on New York and Washington on September 11th 2001. In the aftermath of these acts of terrorism, the world was on a knife-edge, and a large-scale military campaign was mounted in Afghanistan by the United States and its allies to root out those believed to have been responsible for planning these outrages.

The conflict between the Israelis and the Palestinians has also intensified alarmingly in recent times and the Middle East is now closer to all-out war than for many years. The military action to topple the regime of Saddam Hussein in Iraq has added to the precarious situation in the region.

Someone once observed that on occasion you do not choose a book – it chooses you! My prayer is that the information contained in this volume will change your life for the better. But with knowledge comes responsibility. You may be able to help others by passing on what you learn. Many will have no interest in such matters and it is likely that these same people will be left behind to go through the time of tribulation known to us as the Apocalypse.

This book can be a legacy for those who find themselves caught up in the events which shall unfold in the dark days ahead.

Canaries are dropping dead before our eyes, but the world at large is not paying any attention.

> "Remember the former things of old; for I am God and there is none like me, declaring the end from the beginning, and from ancient times the things that are not yet done, saying: 'My counsel shall stand'."
>
> *Book of Isaiah 46: 9,10*

NOTES

1. Graham Hancock & Santha Faiia, *Heaven's Mirror*, Penguin Books.1998.
2. Ibid.
3. *Life in the Land of the Pharaohs*, published by Reader's Digest Association, London.1995.
4. E.W. Bullinger, *The Companion Bible*, Samuel Bagster and Sons, London.See App. 25.
5. *Life in the Land of the Pharaohs*, Reader's Digest Association, page 136.
6. Clarence Larkin, *Dispensational Truth*, published by Clarence Larkin Estate, PO Box 334, Glenside, Pa 19038, USA.1918.(Used with permission of the Rev. Clarence Larkin Estate).
7. The exact length of the Hebrew Cubit is still in dispute. Most scholars agree that it is somewhere between 21 and 25 inches in length.
8. These calculations are based on the assumption that, over time, some erosion may have occurred, leaving the present measurements less than they were at the time of actual construction.
9. I.D.E. Thomas, *The Omega Conspiracy*, Hearthstone Publishing, Oklahoma City U.S.A. 1986.
10. Ibid.
11. Alan and Sally Lansburg, *In Search of Ancient Mysteries*, Bantam Books, New York. 1974.
12. E.A.E. Redmond, *The Mythical Origin of the Egyptian Temple*, Manchester University Press, 1969.
13. Graham Hancock & Santha Faiia, *Heaven's Mirror*, Penguin Books.
14. Erich Von Daniken, *Arrival of the Gods*, Element Books, 1998.
15. Michael Drosnin, *The Bible Code*, Weidenfeld and Nicolson, London, 1997.
16. Chuck Missler, *Cup of Trembling* (video), Bethel Communications, PO Box 459, Edinburgh. Scotland, 1997.
17. Ibid.
18. Dr. Allen Roberts, *Cup of Trembling*.
19. Hal Lindsey, *Planet Earth – 2000 AD*, Western Front, Palos Verdes,

California, USA, 1994.

20. David Atkinson, *The Message of Genesis I – II*, Inter Varsity Press, Leicester, England, 1990, page 130.

21. The following are the eight places in the Old Testament where the expression "Sons of God" occurs; in each case the context will show them to refer to "Angels."
    Genesis 6: 2; 4;
    Job 1:6; 2:1; 38:7;
    Psalms 29:1; 89:6;
    Daniel 3:25.

22. E. W. Bullinger, *The Companion Bible*, Samuel Bagster and Sons, London. See App. 25.

23. Ibid. See notes on Genesis 14:15 and Deuteronomy 2:10,20.

24. Robert Young, A*nalytical Concordance to the Bible*, Lutterworth Press, London, 1879, p. 491.

25. Ibid. Pages 1086 and 1090.

26. According to a book entitled *Giant Cities of Bashan and Syria's Holy Places*, written by Dr. Josias Leslie Porter (London, 1865), many of these cities can still be seen and counted today.

27. Robert Young, *Analytical Concordance to the Bible*, Lutterworth Press, page 297.

28. Five denotes Divine Grace. It is 4 + 1. It is God adding His gifts and blessing to the works of His hands. The Hebrew *Ha'aretz* (the earth) by "Gematria" (i.e. the addition of the numerical value of the letters together) is a multiple of five. The Gematria of *Charis*, the Greek for Grace, is also a multiple of five. It is the leading factor in the Tabernacle measurements. Six denotes the *human number*. Man was created on the sixth day; and this first occurrence of the number makes it (and all multiples of it) the hallmark of everything connected with man. Man works six days; the hours of his day are a multiple of six. Athaliah usurped the throne of Judah for six years. Those of note who have stood out in defiance of God (Goliath and Nebuchadnezzar and the Antichrist) are all emphatically marked by this number. (Source: E.W. Bullinger, *The Companion Bible*, Samuel Bagster and Sons). App. 10.

29. A more complete list of the Scriptures which mention the *Nephilim* or their associates, the *Rephaim,* are listed on the next page:

Genesis	6:4	Deuteronomy	2:11	II Samuel	21:16
	12:6		2:20		21:18

13:7	3:11		21:20		
14:5	3:13		21:22		
15:20	9:2				
		15:21			
Numbers 13:23	Joshua	12:14	I Chronicles	20:4	
		13:12		20:6	
	15:8		20:8		
		15:14			
		17:15			
		18:16			

In the following instances, *Rephaim* has been incorrectly translated as "Dead"; it should be rendered "the *Rephaim*", as this is a proper name.

Job	26:5	Proverbs	2:18	Isaiah	14:9
			9:18		26:19
Psalm	88:10		21:16		

30. E.W. Bullinger, *The Companion Bible*, Samuel Bagster and Sons. See App. 44 viii.
31. Ibid. See App. 26.
32. Ibid. See note on Genesis 18:1 and App. 32.
33. Ibid. See App. 4.
34. Ibid. See note on Isa, 14:2, page 949.
35. Ibid. See App. 19.
36. Ibid. See note on Genesis 3:1.
37. *The Glory of Ancient Egypt*, published by De Agostini (UK) Ltd, Hammersmith Road, London.2001.
38. E.W. Bullinger, *The Witness of the Stars*, Kregal Publications, Grand Rapids, Michigan, USA.1893.
39. Ibid.
40. Joseph A. Seiss, *The Gospel in the Stars*, Kregal Publications, Grand Rapids, Michigan (1972), and Clyde L. Ferguson, *The Stars and the Bible*, Exposition Press, Hicksville, NY (1978).
41. V.P.Wierwille,*Jesus Christ Our Promised Seed*, American Christian Press, New Knoxville, Ohio.1982.
42. The scientists of Babylon were divided into three classes: writers of (1) charms to be placed on afflicted persons or houses; (2) formulae of the incantations; (3) records of observations which mixed up astronomy with astrology and resulted, in the case of any two

successive or concurrent events, in the conclusion that one was the cause of the other. Further conclusions were reached by reasoning from the "particular" to the "general". (Source: E.W. Bullinger, *The Companion Bible,* Samuel Bagster and Sons).

43. Keep on, then, with your magic spells
    And with your many sorceries,
    Which you have laboured at since childhood.
    Perhaps you will succeed,
    Perhaps you will cause terror.
    All the counsel you have received has only worn you out!
    Let you astrologers come forward.
    Those stargazers who make predictions month by month.
    Let them save you from what is coming upon you.
    Surely they are like stubble; the fire will burn them up.
    They cannot even save themselves from the power of the flame.

    Book of Isaiah 47:12-14

44. Ernest L. Martin, *The Birth of Christ Recalculated*, Pasadena Foundation for Biblical Research, 1980.
45. E.W. Bullinger, *The Companion Bible.* See App. 12.
46. Gordon J. Wenham, *Word Biblical Commentary,* Word Books, Waco, Texas. 1987. page 140.
47. J. Karst Eusebus-Werke, Vol 5, *Die Chronik*, Leipzig.1911.
48. E.W. Bullinger, *The Companion Bible.* See App. 124.
49. *Universal Dictionary,* Reader's Digest Association, London.1987.
50. Graham Hancock & Santha Faiia, *Heaven's Mirror,* Penguin Books.
51. Ron Wyatt, *Cup of Trembling* (video), Bethel Communications, PO Box 459, Edinburgh, Scotland.1997.
52. Graham Hancock & Santha Faiia, *Heaven's Mirror,* Penguin Books.
53. Sources: Givonna Magi, *All of Egypt,* Casa Editrice Bonechi, Florence, Italy.1996; *Life in the Land of the Pharaohs,* Reader's Digest, London.1995; Jo Forty, *Mythology: A Visual Encyclopedia,* Parkgate Books, London.1999.
54. E.W. Bullinger, *Witness of the Stars,* Kregal Publications, Grand Rapids, Michigan, USA.
55. Graham Hancock & Santha Faiia, *Heaven's Mirror.*
56. Ibid.
57. Ibid.
58. *Life among the Incas,* Reader's Digest, London.1995.
59. Graham Hancock & Santha Faiia, *Heaven's Mirror.*

60. Ibid

61. These quotes are taken from *The Book of Enoch*, translated by R.A. Charles. First published in 1917, SPCK, London.

62. E.W. Bullinger, *The Companion Bible*. See note on Genesis 5:29.

63. David Pawson, *When Jesus Returns*, Hodder and Stoughton, London.1995.

64. Clarence Larkin, *Dispensational Truth*.

65. Grant R. Jeffrey, *Armageddon: Appointment with Destiny*, Bantam Books, New York.1988.

66. Hal Lindsey, *Planet Earth – 2000 AD*, Western Front, Palos Verdes, California.1994.

67. Barney, Blewett and Barney, *Global 2000 Revisited: What Shall We Do?* Millennium Institute, New York.1993.

68. Clarence Larkin, *Dispensational Truth*.

69. Arthur Cotterell, Rachel Storm, *The Ultimate Encyclopedia of Mythology*, Lorenz Books, London, 1999.

70. Gordon J. Wenhem, *Word Biblical Commentary*. Word Books, Waco, Texas.1987.

71. Ibid.

72. E.W. Bullinger, *The Companion Bible*. See note on Psalm 75:6.

73. Barry Smith, *The Eye in the Triangle* (video), International Support Ministries, Marlborough, New Zealand.

APPENDIX

SUMMARY OF PRINCIPAL EVENTS
Based on the Chronology of Archbishop Usher
Source: *Companion Bible*: E.W. Bullinger

B.C.

4004	Adam created
3874	Seth b. "Adam begat a son in his own likeness" (Gen.5.3).
3769	Enos born.
3679	Cainan b.
3609	Mahaleel b.
3544	Jared b.
3382	Enoch b. "seventh from Adam" (Jude 14).
3317	Methuselah b.
3194	Adam's "day of grace" begins when he is 810 (Genesis. 6.3).
3130	Lamech b.
3074	Adam d. (930)
3017	Enoch translated, 57 years after the death of Adam.
2962	Seth d. (912).
2948	Noah b.
2864	Enos d. (905).
2769	Cainan d. (910).
2714	Mahalaleel d. (895).
2582	Jared d. (962).
2448	Japheth b.
2447	Ham b.
2446	Shem b. (Noah 502.
2353	Lamech d. (777).
2348	Methusaleh d. (969) in the first month of the Flood year.
2348 }	Flood year (600th year of Noah's life; see Gen.
2347 }	7.6, 11).

B.C.

2346	Arphaxad b. "two years after the Flood".
2311	Salah b.
2281	Eber b.
2247	Peleg b. "In his days the Earth was divided" (Gen. 10.26).
2217	Reu b.
2185	Serug b.
2155	Nahor b.
2126	Terah b.
2056	Terah's "generations" begin with birth of Haran.
2057	Peleg d. (239).
2007	Nahor d. (148).
1998	Noah d. (950).
1996	Abraham b. (1,992 years from the Nativity).
1978	Reu d. (239).
1955	Serug d. (230).
1946	Abraham's frst "call", in Ur of the Chaldees (Acts 7. 2-4).
1921	Terah d. (205). Abraham's second "call" (Haran). The 430 years of the sojourning begin (See note on Genesis 12.1 and App. 50 iii).
1920 } to } 1912 }	Abraham goes down into Egypt. Attempted destruction of the Seed (See note on Gen. 12. 10 & App. 23).

1911	Abraham (85) marries Hagar (Gen. 16.3).	1846	Shem (Melchizedek) d. (600); Abraham (150) marries Keturah.
1910	Ishmael b. (Abraham 86).		
1897	Covenant of Circumcision (Abraham 99).	1836	Jacob b. (Isaac 60).
		1821	Abraham d. (Isaac 75, Jacob 15).
1896	Isaac b. (Abraham 100).		
1891	Isaac becomes the "Seed" (Gen. 21, 10; 12.7); Ishmael is "cast out". The 400 years of Acts 7.6 begin.	1817	Eber d. (464); he outlives Abraham by four years.
		1812	The Famine of Genesis 26.1. The cause of sale of birthright?
1878	Salah d. (433).		
1863	Isaac (33) offered up.	1796	Esau (40) marries Hittite wives.
1859	Sarah d. (127). She is the only woman whose age appears in the Scriptures. For the significance of this cp. Galatians 4. In Sarah's age we have, allegorically, the period of duration of the Old Covenant.	1773	Ishmael d. 137 (Jacob 15).
		1759	Jacob (77) flees to Padan-aram.
		1758	His "servitude" begins.
		1752	His marriages.
		1751	Reuben b.
		1750	The chronology continues with the birth of Moses.
1856	Isaac (40) marries Rebekah.		

Summary of Principal Events (continued from 1571 BC)

1571	Moses b.	990	David b.
1544	Joshua b. (Moses 27).	974	David's first anointing (16).
1529	Caleb b.	960	David's second anointing came at 30.
1491	The Exodus.		
1490	The Tabernacle set up.	961	David's third anointing.
1452	Miriam, Aaron and Moses d.	962	Solomon reaches 40 years.
1451	Entry into the Promised Land.	917	The Temple is begun, 573 years after the Exodus (cp. Acts 13. 20-23).
1444	The "Wars of the Lord".		
1444	First Sabbatic Year. BC	910	The Temple is completed.
1000	The Kingdom. Saul, 40 years.		

About the Author

Patrick Heron was born in Dublin in 1952. When he was 24, he had a "Saul on the road to Damascus" type of epiphany while reading the Bible. Thus began his christian walk. He became interested in bible prophecy concerning the "end times" around 1996. He had an earnest desire to make this known to the general public. In 1997, his first book *Apocalypse Soon* was published and became a bestseller in Ireland.

Patrick has a B.Sc. and M.A. in Business Studies from Trinity College, Dublin and a Bachelor of Theology degree from The College of Biblical Research, Rome City, Indiana.

Patrick owns and runs his own business in Dublin where he lives with his wife Catherine and his daughters, Emily Leah and Klara. He is not associated with any particular church or denomination.

Printed in the United States
32173LVS00006B/70-141

9 781594 678943